Autobiography of Samuel S. Hildebrand

The Civil War in the West

Series Editor: Daniel E. Sutherland

Autobiography of Samuel S. Hildebrand

THE RENOWNED MISSOURI BUSHWHACKER

Edited by Kirby Ross

1870 edition

ROB ROY OF AMERICA

edited by

James W. Evans and A. Wendell Keith, M.D.

THE UNIVERSITY OF ARKANSAS PRESS

FAYETTEVILLE

2005

Manufactured in the United States of America

09 08 07 06 05 5 4 3 2 1

Designed by Ellen Beeler

♾ The paper used in this publication meets the minimum requirements of the American National Standard for Permanence of Paper for Printed Library Materials Z39.48-1984.

Library of Congress Cataloging-in-Publication Data

Hildebrand, Samuel S., 1836–1872.

Autobiography of Samuel S. Hildebrand : the renowned Missouri bushwhacker / edited by Kirby Ross.

p. cm.

"1870 edition edited by James W. Evans and A. Wendell Keith."

Includes bibliographical references and index.

ISBN 1-55728-799-6 (alk. paper)

1. Hildebrand, Samuel S., 1836–1872. 2. Missouri—History—Civil War, 1861–1865—Underground movements. 3. United States—History—Civil War, 1861–1865—Underground movements. 4. Guerrillas—Confederate States of America—Biography. 5. Guerrillas—Missouri—Saint Francois County—Biography. 6. Missouri—History—Civil War, 1861–1865—Personal narratives. 7. United States—History—Civil War, 1861–1865—Personal narratives. 8. Hildebrand family. 9. Saint Francois County (Mo.)—History, Military—19th century. 10. Saint Francois County (Mo.)—Biography. I. Ross, Kirby. II. Evans, James W. III. Keith, A. Wendell (Abraham Wendell), 1835–1897. IV. Title.

E517.H65 2005

973.7'478'092—dc22

2005017799

The University of Arkansas Press wishes to thank the Arkansas Archeological Survey and Jane Kellett for their assistance in the production of the map that appears in this volume.

Like Scott's Robb Roy McGregor, he possesses boldness, sagacity and prudence, qualities highly necessary in war, which become vices when misdirected.

—*St. Louis Republican*, 15 June 1869

"Some men are born great, some achieve greatness, and others have it thrust upon them." Sam Hilderbrand is of the latter class. He has been advertised and hunted till he has developed a capacity of eluding pursuit, and a bravery in defending himself, that make him a character with few parallels in history. The case of Rob Roy is not to be named with Hilderbrand's, while Sawny Bean, a countryman of Rob, gives the only similar instance of defiance of law, for he was hid in the cliffs and mountains of Scotland for years, made predatory incursion on the surrounding country for supplies, and was all the while eagerly sought for by officers of the government. Such a character is Sam Hilderbrand.

—*St. Louis Republican*, 16 July 1869

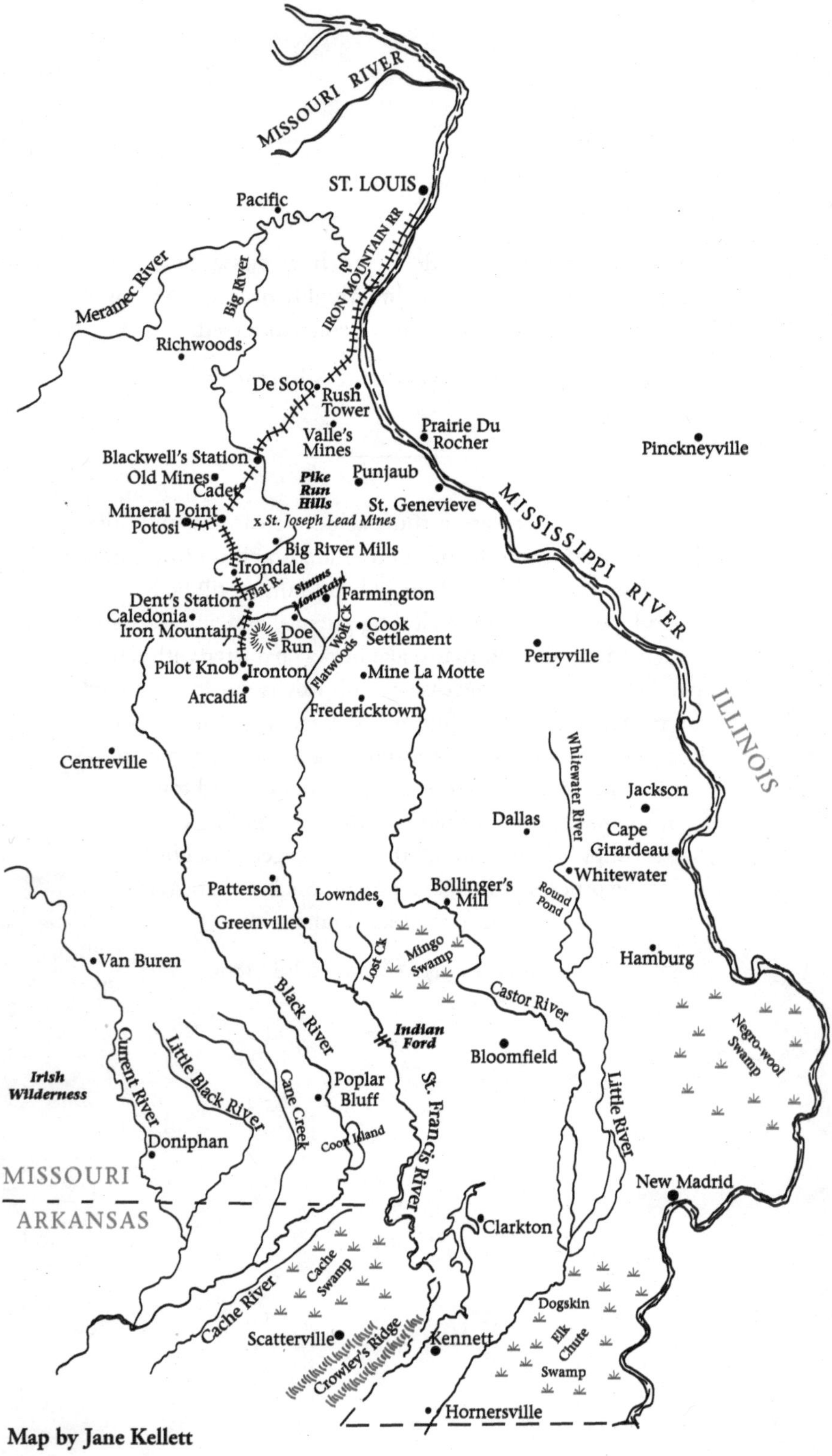

Map by Jane Kellett

Contents

CONTENTS

Series Editor's Preface

The Civil War in the West series has a single goal: to promote historical writing about the war in the western states and territories. It focuses most particularly on the Trans-Mississippi theater, which consisted of Missouri, Arkansas, Texas, most of Louisiana (west of the Mississippi River), Indian Territory (modern-day Oklahoma), and Arizona Territory (two-fifths of modern-day Arizona and New Mexico), but it also encompasses adjacent states, such as Kansas, Tennessee, and Mississippi, that directly influenced the Trans-Mississippi war. It is a wide swath, to be sure, but one too often ignored by historians and, consequently, too little understood and appreciated.

Topically, the series embraces all aspects of the wartime story. Military history in its many guises, from the strategies of generals to the daily lives of common soldiers, forms an important part of that story, but so, too, do the numerous and complex political, economic, social, and diplomatic dimensions of the war. The series also provides a variety of perspectives on these topics. Most importantly, it offers the best in modern scholarship, with thoughtful, challenging monographs. Secondly, it presents new editions of important books that have gone out of print. And thirdly, it premieres expertly edited correspondence, diaries, reminiscences, and other writings by witnesses to the war.

It is a formidable challenge, but by focusing on some of the least-familiar dimensions of the conflict, The Civil War in the West significantly broadens understanding of the nation's most dramatic story.

Samuel S. Hildebrand was a Confederate guerrilla, as well known during his lifetime as men like William C. Quantrill and Bloody Bill Anderson. While it may be hard to define the typical Civil War guerrilla, Sam Hildebrand's exploits make him a prime example of the bushwhacking rebel that gave the Union army fits and kept much of the Trans-Mississippi—especially Missouri—roiling in the 1860s. He killed dozens of men—soldiers and civilians, whites and blacks—during and after the war. Yet, Hildebrand was far from typical in one important way: he wrote his memoirs. While this act does not make him unique among Civil War guerrillas, it certainly places him in an exclusive group. It has also earned him the thanks of students of the war, because while Hildebrand wrote his book largely to justify his own bloody deeds, he provides, nonetheless, a valuable account of guerrilla life.

First published in 1870, Hildebrand's autobiography has long been out of print. There was no demand for it during most of the succeeding decades, when the reading public and scholars alike discounted the importance of the guerrilla conflict. Not until the 1970s did historians begin to appreciate the hidden depths of Hildebrand's shadow war. Now, in the early twenty-first century, we have come to understand that the guerrilla conflict shaped the entire Civil War in significant ways. The purposes, perspectives, and actions of men like Hildebrand now seem crucial for comprehending many of the war's complex military, political, and social dimensions. Consequently, while a Confederate autobiography like this one would have been dismissed until quite recently as mere Lost Cause nostalgia or propaganda, we now value it for its own sake.

Further enhancing the innate value of Hildebrand's recollections is the superb editorial work of Kirby Ross. An authority on the war in Missouri, Ross has separated fact from fiction in Hildebrand's account by checking every claim made by the author. He points out where Hildebrand exaggerated or flat-out lied, identifies people, places, and events in the story not fully explained by Hildebrand, and provides valuable historical context for the guerrilla's wartime and postwar worlds. Somewhat surprisingly, Ross discovered that Hildebrand's version of events holds up quite well against the historical record. Thus Ross has not only restored an important piece of literature to the field, he has also made Sam Hildebrand—the subject of dime novels during his lifetime and of amateur websites in our own—an important interpreter of a turbulent time.

Daniel E. Sutherland
Series Editor

Acknowledgments

First and foremost, the archival repositories in Missouri must be acknowledged and thanked. For all the research I have conducted on the Civil War in the last decade, I have found that Missouri has very few equals in regard to the broad array of historical materials that have been catalogued and preserved. Including the Missouri Historical Society in St. Louis, the Missouri State Archives in Jefferson City, the State Historical Society of Missouri in Columbia, and the Western Historical Manuscript Collection, with branches in Kansas City, St. Louis, Columbia, and Rolla, the sheer volume of available research materials borders upon breathtaking. Special note must be made regarding the recent efforts of the Missouri State Archives and the Office of the Missouri Secretary of State, on the watch of Matt Blunt; to digitize and place online individual service records of the tens of thousands of men who served both the Union and the Confederacy. Hopefully such efforts will continue with other documents. A word to historians also must be made concerning the Cyrus A. Peterson Papers housed at the Missouri Historical Society: there are books and articles waiting to be written that will rely upon the primary source materials gathering dust in this collection.

Mention should also be made of the specific individuals whose assistance and input helped to make my work on Hildebrand possible. Included are James E. McGhee, Bruce Nichols, Gene Murdock, Bettye Warner, Audruain Cato, Jack Hale Jr., Sean Haile, Darryl Lawson, and Alice Rae Warner. The unwavering support of my family was also critical, with special thanks going to Everett Smith and Dave Hill.

Last but not least, the historical work and vigilance of Cletis Ellinghouse and Raymond Burson in southeast Missouri must be noted. This region was a primary battleground in the Missouri guerrilla war during the Rebellion, but has been all but ignored by mainstream historians for the past 140 years. Arising in this vacuum, a dysfunctional system of historiography has taken root, with written works being disseminated that expressly mock the need to document sources and whose adherents personally attack those individuals who deign to ask that sources be produced. Into this breach both Ellinghouse and Burson have stepped, with both men being dedicated to holding writers to accepted, basic standards of accuracy and documentation when making representations of fact.

No matter how compelling the story might sound, to outside historians who come across unsourced work concerning this region, I would urge extreme caution. As for sourced work relating to the region, I would suggest use of the old Ronald Reagan maxim of "trust but verify," with great emphasis being placed on the word "verify"—that is, that the source can be found, and it says what it is alleged to say.

Kirby Ross
2005

Introduction

"It is alleged he was famous during the war as a daring bushwhacker, and his name became as notorious as those of Quantrel and Bill Anderson." So said Missouri's most prominent nineteenth-century newspaper, the *St. Louis Republican,* in speaking of Samuel S. Hildebrand after the end of the Civil War.

Since historical writers of the guerrilla conflict in Missouri have unceasingly focused for decades on western Missouri at the expense of the rest of the state, Sam Hildebrand has tended to be not as well-known in modern times as William Clarke Quantrill and Bloody Bill Anderson. When compared to these two men for his wartime deeds, what separates Hildebrand is the fact that he left behind a personal memoir of his exploits—in fact, Hildebrand is the most prominent Missouri guerrilla to have left behind such a memoir. Just as important, it is the best written and most detailed of any memoir written by a Missouri irregular. In the writing of it, two very literate biographers aided the illiterate Hildebrand, who, by his own account, attended but one day of school. It went through one printing in 1870, shortly after which Hildebrand was killed. Afterward, as interest in Hildebrand waned, so too did interest in the book. Over the years it has become quite rare, being found primarily in the special-collections departments of relatively few libraries and surfacing in personal collections only infrequently.

In reporting on Sam Hildebrand during his life, the *St. Louis Republican* sometimes offered diametrically opposing tones, ranging from quite critical to fairly sympathetic. In 1869 at least two articles referred to him as "Rob Roy," a moniker that Hildebrand's biographers adopted for their own use in publishing his memoir the following year. Historian Michael Fellman, who in 1989 published a preeminent analytical study of the war in Missouri, entitled *Inside War: The Guerrilla Conflict in Missouri during the American Civil War,* pays special notice to their choice to adopt the Rob Roy persona for their subject and, in doing so, to "[work] out of a popular literary tradition of the noble outlaw." According to Fellman, "Missouri guerrillas certainly believed in the noble outlaw—the better to convince themselves that though called lawbreakers, they were indeed serving nature's law."

Delving into the motives behind the proliferation of postwar memoirs by ex-guerrillas, Fellman writes:

> Doubtless, Hildebrand believed the guerrilla code that he or his editors articulated five years after the war. The code had served many as a psychological screen during the war, blocking out the conflict's brutality with webs of proclaimed social justification. After the war, the code became even more meaningful, providing a mold for the recasting of memories, so that the harsh parts of past experience were downplayed and the noble intentions highlighted. Using a legendary heroic literary form could accelerate this process of cultural and self-expurgation. In their memoirs, ex-guerrillas cleansed their histories in this manner. They insisted that they had always acted exclusively in self-defense, that they had avenged personal wrongs personally.

Likewise, Hildebrand defended his seven-year string of killings as being either the product of self-defense or deserved by the victims as a result of their own misdeeds. Consequently, he rationalizes killings of not only men involved in the murders of his brothers but also dozens of other persons, including a slave with whom he casually crossed paths, as well as an adulterous woman.

By 1870 Hildebrand was an outcast, living under an assumed name and having to make a meager living for his wife and six children by chopping wood. With the reshaping of his image through a sympathetic memoir, he might reclaim a place in society and at the same time provide a cloak of legal protection and moral justification for the deeds to which he was admitting and others of which he was accused. Apparently wishing to placate the one man who could help him most in such an undertaking, he was complimentary, even deferential, in his memoir toward the sitting Radical Republican governor, Joseph McClurg, who was certainly no friend of ex-Confederates in general or Sam Hildebrand in particular. Hildebrand was accused of many heinous acts, some extremely so, and by being as detailed as he was in his memoir, he could possibly preempt accusations of any crimes his detractors might raise and at the same time cast himself in a favorable public light. In this vein, Michael Fellman succinctly states, "Clearly, the two journalists who compiled this autobiography helped Hildebrand construct his defense."

In any event, Sam Hildebrand ran out of time. After his wife died the year following the publication of his memoir, Hildebrand proceeded to reemerge from his self-imposed anonymity in another, much more dramatic fashion. Entering a saloon just ninety-one days after her passing, Hildebrand spent the afternoon drinking. A barroom brawl ensued, followed by an arrest and a bloody encounter with a law-enforcement officer that concluded with a bullet being shot into Hildebrand's head, killing him instantly.

As a writer and historian specializing in the Civil War in southeast Missouri, over the years I have become quite familiar with Hildebrand's memoir. Historians who know of it are generally divided, either dismissing it outright as being nothing but fabrications or taking it unquestioningly at face value—even utilizing it to laud Hildebrand as a hero and an adherent of chivalric southern principles. My own opinion is that it fits somewhere in between these two extremes: while it is self-serving throughout and quite exaggerated in places, it can be quite useful as a historical resource. Certainly it cannot be dismissed out of hand, as my annotations attempt to show. For all of Hildebrand's musings, many of his stories can be corroborated by independent accounts from opposing and neutral sources. In some cases I have been able to obtain very obscure independent accounts that bear out much of what Hildebrand relates or at a minimum confirm his account's basic framework. In one case, for example, Hildebrand speaks of taking on a squad of Federals in a shed, and I have found an account by a Federal enlisted man who was in that shed. In another case he speaks of a squad of Federals pursuing him down a creek, and I have found an account by a Federal involved in that pursuit. These are but two examples, but there are literally dozens of others.

Hildebrand's memoir is complicated by the fact that more than once he or his biographers have merged two separate occurrences into single events. In some instances this was probably an intentional literary device, and in others it was probably the result of a merging of memories over the years. For all that has been written on the guerrilla war in Missouri (notwithstanding historians' obsessions with west-central Missouri), rare is the book that offers a look at how Federal counterinsurgency operations were conducted. The Hildebrand book, with its new annotations, offers a comprehensive primer in this regard. While volunteer and regular units from other states were briefly stationed in Missouri and upon occasion engaged guerrillas, the primary forces that fought there were militia: Missouri Militia, Missouri State Militia, Enrolled Missouri Militia, Provisional Enrolled Missouri Militia—all with very similar names, all vastly different in their formation and mission. Hildebrand fought against them all, as is detailed and explained in my annotations.

I have also tried to identify as many individuals mentioned by Hildebrand as possible. This has proven difficult in many cases—consider, for example, that my annotations provide profiles of three different men named Thomas Haile, all of whom lived in the same county. In addition, the same name often had more than one spelling, "Hildebrand" being the most prominent example with literally around a dozen versions. In looking through various records, my imagination has often been put to the test in determining all possible variations. In addition, simply locating a particular soldier in a particular unit did not bring research to an end. In Missouri it was the rare combatant, Federal or Confederate, who served in only one unit. Most of those who served did so in two or three or even four units. While those belonging to Federal units generally made a structured movement from one unit to another, Confederates moved much more freely; it is not uncommon to see the word *deserted* on a military card (a word that did not have the same stigma attached as it might in a unit further east). At least in part, this is due to the fact that an active Confederate in Missouri who was not attached to a formal unit could easily find himself standing in front of a firing squad. Consequently, enlistment for these men was often not so much a commitment as a mere detail.

The inconsistent spelling, punctuation and grammar used in the text of the *Autobiography* are faithful to the 1870 publication. These idiosyncrasies were retained to stay true to Hildebrand's narrative style. In addition, six sketches from the original memoir are interspersed throughout this reprint, and a photograph of the Hildebrand cave, taken from a late-nineteenth/early-twentieth-century postcard, have been added. The captions on them are from the originals. A map, drafted especially for this reprint, has also been added.

To this day Hildebrand evokes strong emotions in southeast Missouri, his story a compelling one in and of itself. With this annotated edition, it is hoped that his story will be made even more compelling by being placed in the fuller context of the lives Samuel Hildebrand affected as he conducted his personal war against his personal enemies while the War of the Rebellion raged about him.

Editor's Preface—1870

The public having been grossly imposed upon by several spurious productions purporting to be the "Life of Sam Hildebrand," we have no apology to offer for presenting the reader with his authentic narrative.

His confession was faithfully written down from his own lips, as the forgoing certificates abundantly prove.

From this copious manuscript we have prepared his autobiography for the press, with a scrupulous care to give it literally, so far as the arbitrary rules of language would permit. Sam Hildebrand and the authors of this work were raised up from boyhood together, in the same neighborhood, and we are confident that no material facts have been suppressed by Hildebrand in his confession.

The whole narrative is given to the reader without any effort upon our part either to justify or condemn his acts. Our design was to give the genuine autobiography of Sam Hildebrand; this we have done.

The book, as a record of bloody deeds, dare-devil exploits and thrilling adventures, will have no rival in the catalogue of wonders; for it at once unfolds, with minute accuracy, the exploits of Hildebrand, of which one-half had never yet been told. Without this record the world would forever remain in ignorance of the *night history* of his astounding audacity.

We here tender our thanks to those of our friends who have kindly assisted us in this work, prominent among whom is Miss Hilda F. Sharp, of Jefferson City, Mo., who furnished us with those beautiful pencil sketches from which our engravings were made.

James W. Evans
A. Wendell Keith, M.D.
Big River Mills, MO, June, 1870

Chapter One

Introduction.—Yankee Fiction.—
Reasons for making a full confession.

SINCE THE CLOSE of the late rebellion, knowing that I had taken a very active part during its progress several of my friends have solicited me to have my history written out in full. This anxiety to obtain the history of an individual so humble as myself, may be attributed to the fact, that never perhaps since the world began, have such efforts been put forth by a government for the suppression of one man alone, as have been used for my capture, both during the war and since its termination. The extensive military operations carried on by the Federal government in South-east Missouri, were in a great measure designed for my special destruction.[1]

Since the close of the rebellion, while others are permitted to remain at home in peace, the war, without any abatement whatever, has continued against me with a vindictiveness and a lavish expenditure of money that has no parallel on this continent; but through it all, single-handed, have I come out unscathed and unconquered.[2]

My enemies have thrust notoriety upon me, and have excited the public mind at a distance with a desire to know who I am and what I have done. Taking advantage of this popular inquiry, some enterprising individual in an eastern state has issued two or three novels purporting to be my history, but they are not even founded on fact, and miss the mark about as far as if they were designed for the Life of Queen Victoria.[3] I seriously object to the use of my name in any such manner. Any writer, of course, who is afflicted with an irresistible desire to write fiction, has a perfect right to do so, but he should select a fictitious name for the hero of his novels, that his works may stand or fall, according to their own intrinsic merit, rather than the name of an individual whose notoriety alone would insure the popularity of his books. But an attempt to palm a novel on the inquiring public as a history of my life, containing as it does a catalogue of criminal acts unknown to me in all my career, is not only a slander upon myself, but a glaring fraud upon the public.

Much of our misfortune as a nation may be attributed to the pernicious influence of the intolerant, intermeddling, irrepressible writers of falsehood.[4] In a community where the spirit of fiction pervades every department of literature and all the social relations of life, writers become so habituated to false coloring and deception, that plain unadorned truth has seldom been known to eminate from their perverted brains; it would be just as impossible for them to write down a naked fact as it would for the Prince of Darkness to write a volume of psalms.

The friend who has finally succeeded in tracing me to my quiet retreat in the wild solitudes of the down trodden South, is requesting me to make public the whole history of my life, without any attempt at palliation, concealment or apology. This I shall now proceed to do, in utter disregard to a perverted public opinion, and without the least desire or expectation of receiving justice, or sympathy from those who are destitute of that ingredient. The necessity that was forced upon me to act the part I did during the reign of terror in Missouri, is all that I regret. It has deprived me of a happy home and the joys of domestic peace and quietude; it has driven me from the associations of childhood, and all the scenes of early life that so sweetly cling to the memory of man; it has caused my kind and indulgent mother to go down into her grave sorrowing; it has robbed me of three affectionate brothers who were brutally murdered and left weltering in their own innocent blood; it has reduced me and my family to absolute want and suffering, and has left us without a home, and I might almost say, without a country.[5]

A necessity as implacable as the decrees of Fate, was forced upon me by the Union party to espouse the opposite side; and all the horrors of a merciless war were waged unceasingly against me for many months before I attempted to raise my hand in self defense. But fight I must, and fight I did! War was the object and war it was. I never engage in but one business at a time—my business during the war was killing enemies. It is a very difficult matter to carry on a war for four years without some one getting hurt. If I did kill over a hundred men during the war, it was only because I was in earnest and supposed that everybody else was. My name is cast out as evil because I adopted the military tactics not in use among large armies. They were encumbered with artillery and fought where they had ample room to use it, I had no artillery and generally fought in the woods; my plan was the most successful, for in the regular army the rebels did not kill more than one man each during the war.

Chapter Two

Early History of the Hildebrand family.—Settled in St. Francois county, Missouri.—Sam Hildebrand born.—Troublesome Neighbors.—Union Sentiments.

IN REGARD TO the early history of the Hildebrand family, I can only state what tradition has handed down from one generation to another. As I have no education, and can neither read in English nor Dutch, I am not able to give any of the outlines of history bearing upon the origin or acts of the Hildebrands in remote ages. This task I leave for others, with this remark, that tradition connects our family with the Hildebrands who figured in the German history up to the very origin of the Dutch language. The branch of the family to which I belong were driven from Bavaria into Netherlands two hundred years ago, where they remained about forty years, and then emigrated to Pennsylvania at the first settlement of that portion of America.

They were a hardy race of people and always shunned a city life, or being cooped up in thickly settled districts; they kept on the outskirts of aggressive civilization as it pressed the redman still back into the wild solitudes of the West, thus occupying the middle ground or twilight of refinement. Hence, they continually breathed the pure, fresh air of our country's morning, trod through the dewy vales of pioneer life, and drank at Freedom's shady fountains among the unclaimed hills.

They were literally a race of backwoodsmen inured to hardship, and delighted in nothing so much as a wild adventure and personal danger. They explored the hills rather than the dull pages of history, pursued the wild deer instead of tame literature, and enjoyed their own thoughts rather than the dreamy notions eminating from the feverish brain of philosophy. In 1832 my father and mother, George and Rebecca Hildebrand, settled in St. Francois county, Missouri, on a stream called Big River, one of the tributaries of the Meramec which empties into the Mississippi about twenty miles below St. Louis.

The bottom lands on Big River are remarkably fertile and my father was so fortunate as to secure one of the best bodies of land in that county. Timber grew in abundance, both on the hills and in the valleys, consequently, it took a great deal of hard labor to open a farm; but after a few years of close attention, father, by the assistance of his boys who were growing up, succeeded in opening a very large one. He built a large stone dwelling home two stories high, and finished it off in beautiful style, besides other buildings—barns, cribs and stables necessary on every well regulated farm.

Father and mother raised a family of ten children, consisting of seven boys and three girls. I was the fifth one in the family, and was born at the old homestead on Big River, St. Francois county, Missouri, on the 6th day of January, 1836.[1]

The facilities for acquiring an education in that neighborhood were very slim indeed, besides I never felt inclined to go to school even when I had a chance; I was too fond of hunting and fishing, or playing around the majestic bluffs that wall in one side or the other of Big River, the whole length of that crooked and very romantic stream. One day's schooling was all that I ever got in my life; that day was sufficient for me, it gave me a distaste to the very sight of a school house. I only learned the names of two letters, one shaped like the gable end of a house roof, and the other shaped like an ox yoke standing on end. At recess in the afternoon the boys got to picking at me while the teacher was gone to dinner, and I had them every one to whip. When the old tyrant came back from dinner and commenced talking saucy, I gave him a good cursing and broke for home. My father very generously gave me my choice, either to go to school or to work on the farm. I gladly accepted the latter, redoubled my energy and always afterwards took particular pains to please my father in all things, because he was so kind as to not compel me to attend school. A threat to send me to school was all the whipping that I ever required to insure obedience; I was more afraid of that than I was of old "Raw-head-and-bloody-bones" or even the old scratch himself.

In 1850, my father died, but I still remained at the homestead, working for the support of my mother and the rest of the family, until I had reached the age of nineteen years, then, on the 30th day of October, 1854, I married Miss Margaret Hampton, the daughter of a highly esteemed citizen of St. Francois county. I built a neat log house, opened a farm for myself, within half a mile of the old homestead, and we went to housekeeping for ourselves.[2]

From the time that my father first settled on Big River, we had an abundance of stock, and especially hogs. The range was always good, and as the uplands and hills constituted an endless forest of oaks, the inexhaustible supply of acorns afforded all the food that our hogs required; they roamed in the woods, and of course, many of them became as wild as deer; the wild ones remained among the hills and increased until they became very numerous. Whenever they were fat enough for pork, we were in the habit of going into the woods with our guns and dogs and killing as many of them as we could.

A few years after my father had settled there, a colony of Pennsylvania Dutch had established themselves in our neighborhood; they were very numerous and constituted about two-thirds of the population of our township. They soon set up "wild hog claims," declaring that some of their hogs had also run wild; this led to disputes and quarrels, and to some "fist and skull fighting," in which my brothers and myself soon won the reputation of "bullies." Finding that they had no show at this game, they next resorted to the law, and we had many little law suits before our justice of the peace. The Dutch *out swore* us, and we soon found the Hildebrand family branded by them with the very unjust and unpleasant epithet of "hog thieves," but we went in on the muscle and still held the woods.

As our part of the country became more thickly settled and new neighbors came in, they in turn were prejudiced against us; and the rising generation seemed to cling to the same idea, that the Hildebrands seemed to love pork a little too well and needed watching.[3] Unfortunately for me, my old neighbors were union men; all my sympathies too, were decidedly for the union. I heard with alarm the mutterings of war in the distance, like the deep tones of thunder beyond the frowning hills. I had never made politics my study; I had no education whatever, and had to rely exclusively on what others told me. Of course, I was easily imposed upon by political tricksters, yet from my heart I deplored the necessity of a resort to arms, if such a necessity did exist, and whether it did or not was more than I could divine.

While my union neighbors and enemies were making the necessary preparations for leaving their families in comfortable circumstances before taking up arms in defense of their country, there were a few shrewed southern men around to magnify and distort the grievances of the southern people. In many cases the men whom they obtained had nothing in the world at stake, no useful object in view, no visible means of acquiring an honest livelihood, and were even without a horse to ride. This, however, only afforded them a pretext for practicing what they called "pressing horses," which was done on a large scale. Neither political principles, patriotic motives, nor love of country prompted this abominable system of horse stealing. It was not confined to either party, and it was a remarkable co-incident how invariably the political sentiments of a horse-pressing renegade would differ from the neighbor who happened to have the fastest horses.

Chapter Three

Determination to take no part in the War.—Mr. Ringer killed by Rebels.—The cunning device of Allen Roan.—Vigilance Committee organized.—The baseness of Mobocracy.—Attacked by the Mob.—Escape to Flat Woods.

IN THE SPRING of 1861, the war of the Great Rebellion was inaugurated, and during the following summer was carried on in great fury in many places, but I shall only speak of those occurrences which had a particular bearing upon myself.[1]

I called on some good citizens who were not republicans, and whom I knew to be well posted in the current events of the day, to ask them what course it was best for me to pursue during the unnatural struggle.[2] They advised me to stay at home and attend to my own business. This I determined to do, so I paid no further attention to what was going on, put in my crop of corn at the usual season and cultivated it during the summer.

On the 9th day of August the popular excitement in St. Francois county was greatly increased by the killing of Mr. Ringer, a union man, who was shot at his own house for no other cause than his political principles. He was killed, as I afterwards learned, by Allen Roan and Tom Cooper.[3] It should be borne in mind that Roan was a relative of mine with whom I was on friendly terms. I was not implicated in the death of Ringer in any manner, shape, or form, but suspicion rested upon me; the "Hildebrand gang" were branded with the murder.[4]

I could not check Roan in the rash course he was pursuing; but in all sincerity, I determined to follow the advice given me by a certain union friend, who told me to take no part in the cause that would in the end bring disaster upon myself.[5] It was good advice; why then did I not follow it? In the presence of that Being who shall judge the quick and the dead, I shall truthfully and in a few words explain the whole matter. I had no sooner made up my mind fully what course to pursue, than I was caught in a cunningly devised trap that settled my destiny forever.

One evening, Allen Roan came to my field where I was plowing and proposed swapping horses with me; the horse which he said he had bought was a better one than my own, so I consented to make the exchange; finding afterwards that the horse would not work in harness, I swapped him off the next day to Mr. Rogers.

Prior to this time my neighbors had organized themselves into what they called a Vigilance Committee, and were moving in squads night and day to put down horse stealing.[6] Only a few of the committee were dangerous men, but Firman McIlvaine, who was put at the head of the gang was influenced by the worst element in the community; it became a political machine for oppression and bloodshed under the guidance of James Craig, John House, Joe McGahan, John Dunwoody, William Patton, and others, who were swearing death to every man implicated in any way with the southern recruits who were pressing horses.[7]

The horse I had traded for from Allen Roan and which Rogers obtained from me, proved to be the property of Dunwoody. I was apprised of the fact by a friend at night, and told also that they had threatened me and my brother Frank with death if they could find us, and notwithstanding our entire innocence in the matter, we were compelled to hide out. We knew that when the law is wrested from the civil authorities by such men as they were, that anything like a trial would not be permitted. We secreted ourselves in the woods, hoping that matters would take a different turn in a short time; each night I was posted in regard to their threats. I would willingly have surrendered myself to the civil authorities with a guarantee of a fair trial; but to fall into the hands of an unscrupulous mob who were acting in violation of law, particularly when law and order was broken up by the heavy tramp of war, was what we were compelled by all means to avoid. We had no alternative but to elude their search.

It is a fact well known, that in the upheaval of popular passion for the overthrow of law and order under any pretext whatever, a nucleus is formed, around which the most vile, the most turbulent, and the most cowardly instinctively flee. Cowardly villains invariably join in with every mob that comes within their reach; personal enmity and spite is frequently their controlling motive, the possible opportunity of redressing some supposed grievance without incurring danger to themselves is their incentive for swelling the mob. A person guilty of any particular crime, to avoid suspicion, is always the most clamorous for blood when some one else stands accused of the same offense. In the Vigilance Committee were found the same materials existing in all mobs. No brave man was ever a tyrant, but no coward ever failed to be one when he had the power. They still kept up the search for me and my brother with an energy worthy of a better cause.

It was now October, the nights were cold and we suffered much for the want of blankets and even for food. We were both unaccustomed to sleeping out at night and were chilled by the cold wind that whistled through the trees. After we had thus continued in the woods about three weeks, I concluded to venture in one night to see my family and to get something to eat, and some bed clothes to keep me more comfortable at night.

I had heard no unusual noise in the woods that day, had seen no one pass, nor heard the tramp of horses feet in any direction.

It was about eleven o'clock at night when I got within sight of the house, no light was burning within; I heard no noise of any kind, and believing that all was right I crept up to the house and whispered "Margaret" through a crack. My wife heard me, and recognizing my voice she noiselessly opened the door and let me in. We talked only in whispers and in a few minutes she placed my supper upon the table. Just as I was going to eat I heard the top rail fall off my yard fence. The noise did not suit me, so I took my gun in one hand, a loaf of corn bread in the other, and instantly stepped out into the yard by a back door.

McIlvaine and his vigilantes were also in the yard, and were approaching the house from all sides in a regular line. In an instant I detected a gap in their ranks and dashed though it. As they commenced firing I dodged behind a molasses mill that fortunately stood in the yard, it caught nine of their bullets and without doubt saved my life. After the first volley I struck for the woods, a distance of about two hundred yards. Though their firing did not cease, I stopped midway to shoot at their fire of flame, but a thought struck me that it would too well indicate my whereabouts in the open field, so I hastened on until I had gained the edge of the woods, and there I sat down to listen at what was going on at the house. I heard Firman McIlvaine's name called several times, and very distinctly heard his replies and knew his voice. This satisfied me beyond all doubt that the marauders were none other than the self-styled Vigilance Committee.

I was fortunate in my escape, and had a deep sense of gratitude to heaven for my miraculous preservation. Though I had not made my condition much better by my visit, yet I gnawed away, at intervals, upon my loaf of corn bread, and tried to reconcile myself as much as possible to the terrible state of affairs then existing. I saw very plainly that my enemies would not permit me to remain in that vicinity; but the idea of being compelled to leave my dear home where I was born and raised, and strike out into the unknown world with my family without a dollar in my pocket, without anything except one horse and the clothing we had upon our backs, was anything in the world but cheering. However, I had no alternative; to take care of my dependent and suffering family, was the motive uppermost in my mind at all times.

After the mob had apparently left, my wife came out to me in the woods. Our plans were soon formed; after dressing the children, five in number, as quietly and speedily as possible, she brought them to me at a designated point among the hills in the dark forest. She returned to the house alone, and with as little noise as possible saddled up my horse, and after packing him with what bed clothing and provisions she conveniently could, she circled around among the hills and rejoined me at a place I had named in the deep forest about five miles from our once happy home. Daylight soon made its appearance and enabled me to pick out a place of tolerable security.

We remained concealed until the re-appearance of night and then proceeded on our cheerless wandering. In silence we trudged along in the woods as best we could, avoiding the mud and occasional pools of water. I carried my gun on my shoulder and one of the children on my hip; my wife, packing the baby in her arms, walked quietly by my side. I never was before so deeply impressed with the faith, energy and confiding spirit of woman. As the moon would occasionally peep forth from the drifting clouds and strike upon the pale features of my uncomplaining wife, I thought I could detect a look of cheerfulness in her countenance, and more than once I thought I heard a suppressed titter when either of us got tangled up in the brush. When daylight appeared we were on Wolf creek, a few miles south of Farmington; here we stopped in the woods to cook our breakfast and to rest a while. During the day we proceeded on to what is called Flat Woods, eight miles from Farmington, in the southern part of St. Francois county, and about ten miles north from Fredericktown. From Mr. Griffin I obtained the use of a log cabin in a retired locality, and in a few minutes we were duly installed in our new house.

Chapter Four

McIlvaine's Vigilance Mob.—Treachery of Castleman.—Frank Hildebrand hung by Mob.—Organization of the Mob into a Militia Company.

THE VIGILANCE COMMITTEE, with Firman McIlvaine at its head, was formed ostensibly for the mutual protection against plunderers; yet some bad men were in it. By their influence it became a machine of oppression, a shield for cowards, and the headquarters for tyranny.

After I left Big River my brother Frank continued to conceal himself in the woods until about the middle of November; the weather now grew so cold that he could stand it no longer; he took the advice of Franklin Murphy and made his way to Potosi, and in order to silence all suspicion in regard to his loyalty, he went to Captain Castleman and offered to join the Home Guards. Castleman being intimate with Firman McIlvaine, detained Frank until he had time to send McIlvaine word, and then basely betrayed him into the merciless hands of the vigilant mob.[1]

In order to obtain a shadow of legalty for his proceedings, McIlvaine took brother Frank before Franklin Murphy, who at the time was the justice of the peace on Big River.[2] Frank was anxious that the justice might try the case; but when Murphy told them that all the authority he had would only enable him to commit him to jail for trial in the proper court, even if the charges were sustained, they were dissatisfied at this, and in order to take the matter out of the hands of the justice and make it beyond his jurisdiction, they declared that he had stolen a horse in Ste. Genevieve county.

The mob then took Frank to Punjaub, in that county, before Justice R. M. Cole, who told them that he was a sworn officer of the law, and that if they should produce sufficient evidence against their prisoner, he could only commit him to jail. This of course did not satisfy the mob; to take the case out of his hands, they stated that the offense he had committed was that of stealing a mule in Jefferson county. They stated also that Frank and Sam Anderson had gone in the night to the house of Mr. Carney to steal his mare; that Mrs. Carney on hearing them at the gate, went out and told them that Mr. Carney was absent and had rode the mare; that they then compelled Mrs. Carney to go with them a quarter of a mile in her night clothes to show them where Mr. Becket lived; and finally that they went there and stole his horse. Failing however to obtain the cooperation of the Justice in carrying out their lawless designs, the mob left with their prisoner, declaring that they were going to take him to Jefferson county for trial.

The sad termination of the affair is soon told. The mob took my kind, inoffensive brother about five miles and hung him without any trial whatever, after which they threw his body in a sink-hole thirty feet in depth, and there his body laid for more than a month before it was found.[3] A few weeks after this cold blooded murder took place, Firman McIlvaine had the audacity to boast of the deed, declaring positively that Frank had been hung by his express orders. This murder took place on the 20th day of November, 1861, about a month after I had been driven from Big River.

A few nights after my arrival at Flat Woods I made my way back to my old home in order to bring away some more of my property, but on arriving there I found that my house had been robbed and all my property either taken away or destroyed. I soon learned from a friend that the Vigilance Com-

FRANK HILDEBRAND HUNG BY THE MOB.

mittee had wantonly destroyed everything they did not want. I returned to Flat Woods in a very despondent mood. I was completely broken up.

The union men were making war upon me, but I was making no war upon them, for I still wished to take no part in the national struggle. I considered it "a rich man's war and a poor man's fight." But a sense of my wrongs bore heavily upon me; I had been reduced to absolute poverty (to say nothing of the murder of my brother) by the unrelenting cruelty of Firman McIlvaine who was a rich man, drowned in luxury and surrounded by all the comforts of life that the eye could wish, or a cultivated appetite could desire.[4]

The war was now raging with great fury in many sections of the country; yet I remained at home intent on making a living for my family, provided I could do so without being molested, but during all the time I was at work, I had to keep a sharp lookout for my enemies.

That leprous plague spot—the Vigilance Committee—finally ripened and culminated in the formation of a company of militia on Big River, with James Craig for Captain and Joe McGahan for First Lieutenant.[5] The very act for which they were so anxious to punish others, on mere suspicion, they themselves now committed with a high hand.

They were ordered to disarm southern sympathizers and to seize on articles contraband of war, such as arms and ammunition. This gave them great latitude; the cry of "disloyal" could be very easily raised against any man who happened to have a superabundance of property. "Arms" was construed also to include *arm chairs* and their *arms full of* everything they could get their hands on; "guns" included *Gunn's Domestic Medicine*; a fine claybank mare was confiscated because she looked so *fiery*, and a spotted mule because it had so many *colors*; they took a gun from Mr. Metts merely because he lived on the *south side* of Big River; they dipped heavily into the estate of Dick Poston, deceased, by killing the cattle for beef and dividing it among themselves, under the pretext that if Dick Poston had been living, he most undoubtedly would have been a rebel.

Chapter Five

His House at Flat Woods attacked by Eighty Soldiers.—Wounded.—Miraculous Escape.—Captain Bolin.—Arrival in Green County, Arkansas.

IN APRIL, 1862, after we had lived at Flat Woods during six months of perfect tranquility, that same irrepressible Vigilance Committee, or some men who had composed it, learned finally that I was living at Flat Woods. Firman McIlvaine and Joe McGahan succeeded in getting eighty soldiers from Ironton to aid in my capture. I had been hauling wood; as soon as I unloaded the wagon I stepped into the house, and the first thing I knew, the eighty soldiers and the vigilantes were within gunshot and coming under full charge. I seized my gun and dashed through a gap in their lines that Heaven had again left open for my escape. They commenced firing upon me as soon as I was out of the house. The brush being very thick not far off, I saw that my only chance was to gain the woods, and that as soon as possible. I ran through the garden and jumped over a picket fence—this stopped the cavalry for a moment. I made through the brush; but out of the hundreds of bullets sent after me, one struck my leg below the knee and broke a bone. I held up by the bushes as well as I could, to keep them from knowing that I was wounded. While they had to stop to throw down a fence, I scrambled along about two hundred yards further, and crouched in a gully that happened to be half full of leaves; I quickly buried myself completely from sight. The soldiers were all around in a short time and scoured the woods in every direction; then they went back and burned the house and everything we had, after which they left and I saw them no more.

Sixteen of Captain Bolin's men on the day before had been seen to cross the gravel road; this probably, was why the federal soldiers did not remain longer. Captain Bolin was a brave rebel officer, whose headquarters were in

Green county, Arkansas, and under whose command some of the most daring spirits who figured in the war, were led on to deeds of heroism scarcely ever equaled.[1]

Our condition was truly deplorable; there I lay in the gully covered up with leaves, with one leg rendered useless, without even the consolation of being allowed to groan: my family, too, were again without shelter; the soldiers had burned everything—clothes, bedding and provisions.

As I lay in that gully, suffering with my wounds inflicted by United States soldiers, I declared war. I determined to fight it out with them, and by the assistance of my faithful gun "Kill-devil," to destroy as many of my bloodthirsty enemies as I possibly could. To submit to further wrong from their hands would be an insult to the Being who gave me the power of resistance.

After the soldiers left, my wife came in search of me, believing that I was wounded from the manner in which I seemed to run. I told her to go back, that I was not hurt very bad, and that when she was satisfied that no one was watching around, to come at night and dress my leg. She went, however, in search of some friend on whom we could rely for assistance. Fortunately, she came across Mr. Pigg, to whom she related the whole circumstance, and he came immediately to my relief. He was a man of the right stripe; regardless of consequences, he did everything in his power to relieve my suffering and to supply my family with bedding and provisions. He removed us by night to a place of safety, and liberally gave us all we needed. While I thus lay nursing my wound, my place of concealment was known only to a few men whom we could easily trust.

In my hours of loneliness I had much time for reflection. The terrible strait in which I found myself, naturally led me to the mental inquiry: "Have I the brand of Cain, that the hands of men should be turned against me? What have I done to merit the persecution so cruel and so persistent?" I could not solve the questions; in the sight of a just God I felt that I did not merit such treatment. Sometimes I half resolved to go into some other State on purpose to avoid the war; but I was constantly warned by my friends who were southern men, (the only men with whom I could hold communication at present,) that it would be unsafe to think of doing so, and that my only safety lay in my flight to the southern army. The vigilance mob had nearly destroyed every vestige of sympathy or good feeling I had for the union people. They had reported me, both to the civil and military authorities, as being a horse thief, and withal, a very dangerous man.

On thinking the matter over I lost all hope of ever being able to reinstate myself in their favor and being permitted to enjoy the peaceful privileges of a quiet citizen. The die was cast—for the sake of revenge, I pronounced myself a Rebel.

I remained very quietly at my place of concealment while my wife doctored my wounded leg for a week before my friend had an opportunity of sending word to any of Captain Bolin's men to come to my relief. As soon as my case was made known to them, however, a man was dispatched to see me for the purpose of learning all the particulars in the case. He came and asked me a great many questions, but answered none. When he arose to depart he only said, "alright—rest easy."

The next night I was placed in a light spring wagon among some boxes of drugs and medicines, was told that my wife and family would be taken to Bloomfield by Captain Bolin in a short time, and protected until I could come after them. A guard of two men accompanied us, and rode the whole night without speaking a word to any one. Nearly the whole route was through the woods, and although the driver was very watchful and used every precaution against making noise, yet in the darkness of the night I was tumbled about among the boxes pretty roughly.

When daylight came we halted in a desolate looking country, inhabited only by wild animals of the forest. We had traveled down on the western side of St. Francis River and were now camped near the most western bend of that river near the southern line of Madison County; we remained all day at that point, and I spent most of my time in sleeping. When the sun had dipped behind the western hills we again commenced our journey. Our course seemed to bear more to the eastward than it did the night before, and as we were then in a country not so badly infested with Federals, we traveled a good part of our time in narrow, crooked roads, but they were rough beyond all description, and I was extremely glad when about eight o'clock in the morning we halted for breakfast on the western bank of St. Francis River, about midway between Bloomfield, in Stoddard county, and Crane creek, in Butler.[2]

While resting here a scouting party from General Jeff. Thompson's camp came riding up.[3]

"Well boys! what have you in your wagon?"

"Drugs and medicines for Captain Bolin's camp."

On hearing this they dismounted and kept up a lively conversation around the camp fire. Among their number was a jovial fellow who kept the rest all laughing. I thought I knew the voice, and as I turned over to peep through a hole in the wagon bed, he heard me and sprang to his feet. "Who in thunderation have you in the wagon?"

"Some fellow from St. Francois county, wounded and driven off by the Federals."

"The devil! why that is my native county. I'll take a look at that fellow. It's Sam Hildebrand as I live! How do you do, old rapscallion?"

"Well, well, if I haven't run across Tom Haile, the dare-devil of the swamps!"[4]

"Old 'drugs and medicines' what are you doing down here? Trying to pass yourself off for a great medicinal root I suppose. Do you feel tolerable better? I'm afraid you are poison. Say, Sam, did you bring some good horses down with you?"

"Hush Tom! if they find out that I'm not a horse thief, they will drum me out of camp!"

The party soon prepared to start; the first man who attempted to mount came near being dashed to the ground in consequence of the rattling of a tin cup some one had tied to his spur. Tom said it was a perfect shame to treat any man in that way: the man seemed to think so too, judging from the glance he cast at Tom. But they mounted, dashed through a sheet of muddy water, then over a rocky point, and soon were far away amid the dim blue hills.

We started on, and after traveling until about midnight, we reached the State line between Missouri and Arkansas. There we remained until morning; on starting again we were in Green county, Arkansas, and sometime during the day we arrived safely at the Headquarters of Captain Bolin, and I was welcomely received into the little community of families, who were here assembled for mutual protection—most of them were the families of Captain Bolin's men. I received every attention from them that my necessities required, and as my wound seemed to be doing well, I felt for a time quite at home.

Chapter Six

Interview with Gen. Jeff. Thompson.—Receives a Major's Commission.—Interview with Captain Bolin.—Joins the "Bushwhacking Department."

CAPTAIN BOLIN WITH most of his forces were somewhere in the vicinity of Bloomfield, Missouri, and as I was anxious to identify myself with the army, I got the use of a horse as soon as I was able to ride, and in company with several others proceeded across the swampy country east of the St. Francis river, for the purpose of joining General Jeff. Thompson. I reached his headquarters in safety, and stayed about camp, frequently meeting acquaintances from Missouri and occasionally getting news from home. As soon as I could gain admission to the General's headquarters I did so, and he received me very kindly. He listened very attentively to me as I proceeded to state my case to him—how my brother had been murdered, how I had barely escaped the same fate, and how I had finally been driven from the country.

General Thompson reflected a few moments, then seizing a pen he rapidly wrote off a few lines and handing it to me he said, "here, I give you a Major's commission; go where you please, take what men you can pick up, fight on your own hook, and report to me every six months." I took the paper and crammed it down into my pantaloon's pocket and walked out. I could not read my commission, but I was determined to ask no one to read it for me, for that would be rather degrading to my new honor.[1]

I retired a little distance from camp and taking my seat on an old cypress log, I reflected how the name of "Major Sam Hildebrand" would look in history. I did not feel comfortable over the new and very unexpected position in which I had been placed. I knew nothing of military tactics; I was not certain whether he was merely a bottle washer under a Captain. I determined that if the latter was the case, that I would return to Green county and serve under Captain Bolin.[2]

As I had no money with which to buy shoulder-straps, I determined to fight without them. I was rather scarce of money just at that time; if steamboats were selling at a dollar a piece, I did not have money enough to buy a canoe paddle. I stayed in camp, however, several days taking lessons, and hearing tales of blood and pillage from the scouts as they came in from various directions.

By this time my wound felt somewhat easier, so I mounted my horse and made my way back to Green county, and arrived safely at Captain Bolin's headquarters. The Captain was at home, and I immediately presented myself before him. He said he had heard of me from one of his scouts, and was highly gratified that one of his men had seen proper to have me conveyed to his headquarters.

"I presume," said he, "that you have been to the headquarters of General Jeff. Thompson. Did you see the 'Old Swamp Fox?'"

"I did."

"What did he do for you?"

Here I pulled my commission from my pocket, that now looked more like a piece of gunwadding than anything else, and handed it to the Captain.

"Well, Major Hildebrand—"

"Sam, if you please."

"Very well then, what do you propose to do?"

"I propose to fight."

"But Major—"

"Sam, if you please."

"All right sir! Sam, I see that you have the commission of a Major."

"Well, Captain, I can explain that matter: he formed me into an independent company of my own—to pick up a few men if I can get them—go where I please—when I please—and when I go against my old personal enemies up in Missouri, I am expected to do a *Major* part of the fighting myself."

At this the Captain laughed heartily, and after rummaging the contents of an old box he drew forth something that looked to me very much like a bottle. After this ceremony was over he remarked:

"Well, sir, the commission I obtained is of the same kind. I have one hundred and twenty-five men, and we are what is denominated 'Bushwhackers'; we carry on a war against our enemies by shooting them; my men are from various sections of the country, and each one perhaps has some grievance to redress at home; in order to enable him to do this effectually we give him all the aid that he may require; after he sets things to right in his section of country, he promptly comes back to help the others in return; we thus swap work like the farmers usually do in harvest time. If you wish an interest in this joint stock mode of fighting you can unite your destiny with ours, and be entitled to all our privileges."

Captain Bolin's proposition was precisely what I so ardently desired. Of the real merits of this war I knew but little and cared still less. To belong to a large army and be under strict military discipline, was not pleasing to my mind; to be brought up in a strong column numbering several thousands, and be hurled in regular order against a mass of men covering three or four miles square, against whom I had no personal spite, would not satisfy my spirit of revenge. Even in a fierce battle fought between two large opposing armies, not more than one man out of ten can succeed in killing his man; in a battle of that kind he would have no more weight than a gnat on a bull's horn.

I was fully satisfied that the "Bushwhacking department" was the place for me, with the continent for a battlefield and everlasting woods for my headquarters.

Chapter Seven

Trip to Missouri.—Kills George Cornecious for reporting on him.—Kills Firman McIlvaine.—Attempt to kill McGahan and House.—Returns to Arkansas.

MY WOUND KEPT ME at headquarters for about six weeks after my arrival in Arkansas.[1] During all this time I could not hear a word from my family, for the Federals had possession of every town in that section of country, together with all the roads leading from one county to another.[2]

On the 1st day of June, 1862, having been furnished a horse, I took my faithful gun, "Kill-devil," and started on my first trip back to Missouri. As my success would depend altogether on the secrecy of my movements, I went alone. I traveled altogether in the night, and most of the time through the woods. From Captain Bolin's men I had learned the names of Southern sympathizers along the whole route, so I made it convenient to travel slowly in order to favor my wounds and to get acquainted with our friends.

I arrived in the vicinity of Flat Woods, in St. Francois county, Missouri, on the 12th day of June, and immediately commenced searching for George Cornecious, the man who reported my whereabouts to McIlvaine and the soldiers, thereby causing me to be wounded and expelled from Flat Woods. After searching two days and two nights I succeeded in shooting him; he was the first man I ever killed; a little notch was cut in the stock of my gun to commemorate the deed.[3]

To avoid implicating my family in any way with my transactions, I satisfied myself with exchanging words with my wife through a friend who was thought by his neighbors to be a Union man. My family resided in a little cabin on Back creek and my wife was cultivating a garden.

To carry out the daring object I had in view—that of killing Firman McIlvaine—I went to Flat River, and after remaining several days, I took a pone of bread for my rations and walked to his farm on Big River after night.

I passed through his fields, but finding no place where harvesting was going on, I crossed Big River on a fish-trap dam and ranged over the Baker farm on the opposite side of the river, about a mile above Big River Mills, where the McIlvaine family now resided.

I found where harvesting had just commenced in a field which formed the southwestern corner of the farm. This field is on the top of a perpendicular bluff, about one hundred feet high, and is detached from the main farm by a road leading from Ste. Genevieve to Potosi.

A portion of the grain had already been cut on the western side of the field, near the woods; there I took my station in the fence corner, early in the morning thinking that McIlvaine would probably shock the grain while the negroes were cradling. In this I was mistaken, for I saw him swinging his cradle in another part of the field, beyond the range of my gun.

I next attempted to crawl along the edge of the bluff among the stunted cedars, but had to abandon the attempt because the negroes stopped in the shade of the cedars every time they came around. Then I went back into the woods, and passed down under the bluff, along the edge of the river, until I got opposite the place where they were at work; but found no place where I could ascend the high rock. I went around the lower end of the bluff, and crawled up to the field on the other side, but I was at too great a distance to get a shot. Finally, I went down to the river and was resting myself near a large flat rock that projected out into the river, where some persons had been recently fishing, when suddenly Firman McIlvaine rode down to the river and watered his horse at a ford about sixty yards below me. I tried to draw a bead on him, but the limb of a tree prevented me, and when he started back he rode too fast for my purpose.

At night I crept under a projecting rock and slept soundly; but very early in the morning I ascended the bluff and secreted myself at a convenient distance from where they had left off cradling. But I was again doomed to disappointment for as the negroes were cradling, McIlvaine was shocking the grain in another part of the field.

In the evening, as soon as they had finished cutting the grain, all hands left, and I did not know where they were. I next stationed myself at a short distance from the river, and watched for him to water his horse; but his father presently passed along leading the horse to water.

I again slept under the overhanging rock; and on the next morning (June 23rd) I crossed the river on the fish dam, and went to the lower part of McIlvaine's farm. There I found the negroes cutting down a field of rye.

They cut away for several hours, until they got it all down within one hundred yards of the fence, before McIlvaine made his first round. On getting a little past me, he stopped to whet his scythe; as soon as he had done so he lowered the cradle to the ground, and for a moment stood resting on the handle.

I fired, and he fell dead.[4]

Nothing but a series of wrongs long continued could ever have induced me to take the life of that highly accomplished young man.[5]

After the outbreak of the war, while others were losing horses, a fine mare was stolen from him. The theft was not committed by me, but my personal enemies probably succeeded in making him believe that I had committed the act.

He was goaded on by evil advisers to take the law into his own hands; my brother Frank was hung without a trial, and his body thrown into a sinkhole, to moulder like that of a beast; my own life had been sought time and again; my wife and tender family were forced to pass through hardships and suffering seldom witnessed in the annals of history. The mangled features of my poor brother; the pale face of my confiding wife; the tearful eyes of my fond children—all would seem to turn reprovingly upon me in my midnight dreams, as if demanding retributive justice. My revenge was reluctant and long delayed, but it came at last.

KILLING McILVAINE.

I remained in the woods, near the residence of a friend for a day or two, and then I concluded to silence Joe McGahan and John House before returning to Arkansas.[6] I proceeded to the residence of the former, who had been very officious in the Vigilance mob, and posted myself in some woods in the field within one hundred yards of the house, just as daylight began to appear. I kept a vigilant watch for him all day, but he did not make his appearance until it had commenced getting dark; then he rode up and went immediately into his house. By this time it was too dark for me to shoot at such a distance. I moved to the garden fence, and in a few minutes he made his appearance in the door with a little child in his arms. The fence prevented me from shooting him below the child, and I could not shoot him in the breast for fear of killing it.

He remained in the door only a minute or two, and then retired into the house; and while I was thinking the matter over, without noticing closely for his reappearance, I presently discovered him riding off. I went into a thicket in his field and slept until nearly day, when I again took my position near the house, and watched until night again set in, but fortunately for him he did not make his appearance.

I now went about four miles to the residence of John House, selected a suitable place for my camp, and slept soundly until daybreak. I watched closely all day, but saw nothing of my enemy. As soon as it was dark I went back to Flat River, and on the next night I mounted my horse and started back to Green county, Arkansas, without being discovered by any one except by those friends whom I called on for provisions.

Chapter Eight

Vigilance mob drives his mother from home.—Three companies of troops sent to Big River.—Captain Flanche murders Washington Hildebrand and Landusky.—Captain Esroger murders John Roan.—Capt. Adolph burns the Hildebrand homestead and murders Henry Hildebrand.

I SHALL NOW give a brief account of the fresh enormities committed against the Hildebrand family. The same vindictive policy inaugurated by the Vigilance mob was still pursued by them until they succeeded, by misrepresentation, in obtaining the assistance of the State and Federal troops for the accomplishment of their designs.

A Dutch company, stationed at North Big River Bridge, under Capt. Esroger; a Dutch company stationed at Cadet, under Capt. Adolph; and a French company at the Iron Mountain, under Capt. Flanche, were all sent to Big River to crush out the Hildebrand family.

Emboldened by their success in obtaining troops, the Vigilance mob marched boldly up to the Hildebrand homestead and notified my mother, who they found reading her Bible, that she must immediately leave the county, for it was their intention to burn her house and destroy all her property.

My mother was a true Christian; she was kind and affectionate to everybody; her hand was always ready to relieve the distressed, and smooth the pillow for the afflicted; the last sight seen upon earth by eyes swimming in death has often been the pitying face of my mother, as she hovered over the bed of sickness.

I appeal to all her neighbors—I appeal to everybody who knew her—to say whether my mother ever had a superior in this respect.

When ordered to leave her cherished home, to leave the house built by her departed husband, to leave the quiet homestead where she had brought up a large family, and where every object was rendered dear by a thousand sweet associations that clung to her memory, she turned her mind inwardly, but found nothing there to reproach her; then to her God she silently committed herself.

She hastily took her Bible and one bed from the house—but nothing more. She had arrangements made to have her bed taken to the house of her brother, Harvey McKee, living on Dry Creek, in Jefferson county, distant about thirty-five miles. Then, taking her family Bible in her arms, she burst into a flood of tears, walked slowly out of the little gate, and left her home forever!

I will here state that I was the only one of the Hildebrand family who espoused the Rebel cause. After the murder of my brother Frank, I had but three brothers left: William, Washington, and Henry. William joined the Union army and fought until the close of the war; Washington took no part in the war, neither directly or indirectly.[1] Never, perhaps, was there a more peaceable, quiet and law-abiding citizen than he was; he never spoke a word that could be construed into a sympathy for the Southern cause, and I defy any man to produce the least evidence against his loyalty, either in word or act. While the war was raging, he paid no attention to it whatever, but was busily engaged in lead mining in the St. Joseph Lead Mines, three miles from Big River Mills, and about six miles from the old homestead. In partnership with him was a young man by the name of Landusky, a kind, industrious, inoffensive man, whose loyalty had never once been doubted. My sister Mary was his affianced bride, but her death prevented the marriage.[2]

My brother Henry was a mere boy, only thirteen years of age. Of course he was too young to have any political principles; he was never accused of being a Rebel; no accusation of any kind had ever been made against him; he was peaceable and quiet, and, like a good boy, he was living with his mother, and doing the best he could toward supporting her. True, he was very young to have the charge of such a farm, but he was a remarkable boy. Turning a deaf ear to all the rumors and excitements around him, he industriously applied himself to the accomplishment of one object, that of taking care of his mother.

On the 6th day of July, 1862, while my brother Washington and Mr. Landusky were working in a drift underground, Capt. Flanche and his company of cavalry called a halt at the mine, and ordered them to come up; which they did immediately.

No questions were asked them, and no explanations were given. Flanche merely ordered them to walk off a few steps toward a tree, which they did;

he then gave the word "fire!" and the whole company fired at them, literally tearing them to pieces![3]

I would ask the enlightened world if there ever was committed a more diabolical deed? If, in all the annals of cruelty, or in the world's wide history, a murder more cold-blooded and cruel could be found?

A citizen who happened to be present ventured to ask in astonishment why this was done, to which Flanche merely replied, as he rode off, "they bees the friends of Sam Hildebrass!"[4]

It was now Capt. Esroger's time to commit some deed of atrocity, to place himself on an equality with Capt. Flanche; so after a moment's reflection, he concluded that the murder of my uncle, John Roan, would be sufficient to place his brutality beyond all question.[5]

John Roan was a man about fifty years of age, was proverbial for his honesty, always paid his debts, and kept himself entirely aloof from either side during the war, but against his loyalty nothing had ever been produced, or even attempted.[6]

One of his sons was in the Union army, and another was a Rebel.[7]

Being my uncle, and the father of Allen Roan, however, was a sufficient pretext for the display of military brutality.

His house was situated about three miles from St. Joseph Lead Mines and about the same distance from the Hildebrand estate.

On the 10th day of July, Capt. Esroger and his company rode up to his house, and the old man came out onto the porch, with his white locks

FEDERAL ATROCITY.

streaming in the wind, but never once did he dream of treachery. Esroger told him that he "vos one tam prisoner," and detailed six men to guard him and to march along slowly until they should get behind.

They did so until they got about a mile from his house; there they made him step off six paces, and while his eyes were turned towards Heaven, and his hands were slightly raised in the attitude of prayer, the fatal word "fire" was given, and he fell to the earth a mangled corpse.[8]

There was still another actor in this bloody tragedy, who had to tax his ingenuity to the utmost to select a part in which to out do, if possible, the acts of atrocity committed by the others. This was Capt. Adolph.[9]

On the 23rd day of July, Capt. Adolph and his company with an intermixture of the Vigilance mob, went to my mother's house—the Hildebrand homestead—for the purpose of burning it up. The house was two stories high, built of nice cut stone, and all finished within, making it altogether one of the best houses in the county.

The soldiers proceeded to break down the picket fence, and to pitch it into the house for kindling. They refused to let anything be taken out of the house, being determined to burn up the furniture, clothing, bedding, provisions, and everything else connected with it.

All things being now ready, the house was set on fire within, and the flames spread rapidly from room to room then through the upper floor, and finally out through the roof. The house, with all the outer buildings was soon wrapped in a sheet of fire.

My little brother Henry and an orphan boy about fourteen years of age, whom my mother had hired to assist Henry in cultivating the farm, were present at the conflagration and stood looking on in mute astonishment. Esroger ordered brother Henry to leave, but whether he knew it was their intention to shoot him after getting him a short distance from the house, as was their custom, it is impossible for me to say. Probably feeling an inward consciousness of never having committed an act to which they could take exceptions, he did not think that they would persist in making him go; so he remained and silently gazed at the burning house, which was the only home he had ever known.

When ordered again to leave, he seemed to be stupefied with wonder at the enormity of the scene before him. Franklin Murphy being present told him it was best to leave; so he mounted his horse and started, but before he got two hundred yards from the house, he was shot and he dropped dead from the horse. Thus perished the poor innocent boy, who could not be induced to believe that the men were base enough to kill him, innocent and inoffensive as he was. But alas! how greatly was he mistaken in them!

They next burned the large frame barn, also the different cribs and stables on the premises; then taking the orphan boy as a prisoner they left.[10]

Some neighbors, a few days afterwards found the body of my little brother and buried him.

This was the crowning act of Federal barbarity toward me and the Hildebrand family, instigated by the low cunning of the infamous Vigilance mob.

I make no apology to mankind for my acts of retaliation; I make no whining appeal to the world for sympathy. I sought revenge and I found it; the key of hell was not suffered to rust in the lock while I was on the war path.

I pity the poor miserable, sniveling creature who would tamely have submitted to it all.

Such a man would be so low in the scale of human conception; so far beneath the lowest grade of humanity, that the head even of an Indian would grow dizzy in looking down upon him.

Chapter Nine

Trip with Burlap and Cato.—Killed a spy near Bloomfield.—Visits his Mother on Dry Creek.—Interview with his Uncle.—Sees the burning of the homestead at a distance.

AS YET, I had heard nothing about the atrocities committed against the remaining members of the Hildebrand family; but in order to stir up my old enemies in that quarter, I selected two good men, John Burlap and James Cato, to accompany me in another excursion to St. Francois county, Missouri.[1]

They, too, had been badly treated at the outbreak of the war, and had several grievances to redress, for which purpose I promised them my future aid. We procured Federal uniforms, and started late in the afternoon of July 13th, 1862; but on arriving at St. Francis river, we found it out of its banks from the heavy rains that had fallen the day previous.

My comrades were rather reluctant about venturing into the turbid stream amid the floating driftwood; but I had ever been impressed with the truth of the old adage, that it was "bad luck to turn back." I plunged my horse into the stream and made the opposite shore without much difficulty. I was followed by Burlap and Cato, who got across safely, but were somewhat scratched by the driftwood. We built a fire, dried our clothes, took a "snort" from our black bottle and camped until morning.

Nothing of interest occurred until we reached the vicinity of Bloomfield, in Stoddard county, Missouri, when we met a man in citizen's dress, whom we accosted in a very familiar manner, asking him if there were any Rebels in that vicinity. He stated that there was a party of Rebels in Bloomfield, and that we had better make our way back to Greenville to the command, otherwise we would be sure to fall into their hands. He stated that he had been with them all day, pretending that he wanted to enlist; that he had learned all about their plans, and thought that about tomorrow night they would all be taken in. I inquired if they had not suspicioned him a spy? He answered that they had not; that he had completely deceived them. I then asked him if he did not want to ride behind me and my companions, by turns, until we reached Greenville? He signified his assent by springing up behind me. I let him ride about two miles, but not exactly in the direction of Greenville, for I told him that I was aiming to strike a certain cross road, which seemed to satisfy his mind. He had much to tell us about his exploits as a spy, and that he had learned the names of all the Rebels in Greenville and Fredericktown. By this time we had enough. I told him that I was Sam Hildebrand, knocked him off my horse, and then shot him.

I felt no compunction of conscience for having ended the days of such a scoundrel. A little notch underneath the stock of old "Kill-devil" was made, to indicate the probability that he would fail to report.

On the rest of our trip we traveled altogether in the night, and avoided the commission of any act that would be likely to create a disturbance. We arrived safely at the house of my brother-in-law on Flat River who lives within ten miles of the Hildebrand homestead.

Here, for the first time, I heard of the murder of my brother, Washington, also that of my uncle, John Roan. Mother's house had not yet been burned, but she had been peremptorily driven from it, and had sought refuge with her brother, in Jefferson county. The country was full of soldiers, and the Vigilance mob were in their glory. Their deeds would blacken the name of John A. Murrel, the great land pirate of America, for he never robbed a lady, nor took the bread from orphan children; while they unblushingly did both.

On learning these particulars, I determined to go to Dry Creek for the purpose of seeing my mother, although the soldiers were scouring the country in every direction for fifty miles for my destruction. We started at night, but having to travel a circuitous route, daylight overtook us when within six miles of my uncle's. We made a circuit, as was my custom, around a hillside, and then camped in such a position that we would be close to our pursuers for half an hour before they could find us.

My companions took a nap while I kept watch. They had not been asleep long before I discovered a party of men winding their way slowly in the semi-circle we had made. There were ten of them, all dressed in Federal uniforms. I awakened my companions, and they took a peep at them as they were slowly tracking us, at a distance of three hundred yards. We could hardly refrain from making war upon them, the chances being so good for game and a little fun, but my object was to see my mother; so we let them pass on to the place where our tracks would lead them out of sight for a few minutes, then we mounted our horses and rode on to another ridge, making a circuit as before, and camping within a quarter of a mile of our first ambush. On coming to that place, the Federals struck off in another direction, probably finding our tracks a little too fresh for their safety.

When night came, we made our way cautiously through the woods to within a few hundred yards of my uncle's house. I dismounted, and leaving my horse with my comrades, approached the house carefully, and climbed upon a bee-gum to peep through the window. I discovered that there were two strange men in the room, and I got a glimpse of another man around in a corner; but as I leaned a little to one side to get a better view, my bee-gum tilted over, and I fell with a desperate crash on a pile of clapboards. I got up in somewhat of a hurry, and, at about three bounds cleared the picket fence, and deposited myself in the corner of the garden to await the result.

The noise, of course, aroused the inmates of the house, and they were soon out with a light, but with no utensils of war except a short double-barreled shot-gun, in the hands of my uncle. He inspected the damage done to his favorite bee-stand, and breathed out some rough threats against the villains who had attempted to steal his honey. After ordering his family and the two strangers back into the house, he posted himself in a fence corner against the offenders, should they attempt to renew the attack.

The night not being very dark, I was fearful that if I attempted to climb over the picket fence, the old man might pepper me with shot. So I moved myself cautiously around to the back part of the garden, and found an opening where a picket was missing. Through this aperture I succeeded in squeezing myself, and then crawled around to the rail fence where my uncle was, until I got within two panels of the old man, when I ventured to call him by name, in a very low tone. He knew my voice, and said: "Is that you Sam?" My answer in the affirmative brought him to where I was, and although the fence was between us, we took a hearty shake of the hand through a crack. He told me that the two men in the house were Union neighbors, who came over to tell him that the trail of a band of bushwhackers had been discovered about six miles from there, and that on tomorrow the whole country would be out in search of them. He told me to go back until his neighbors took their leave, and then to come in and see my mother, who was well, but grieving continually about her son "Sam."

I fell back to my companions, reported progress, and again took my stand in the fence corner. As soon as the two neighbors were gone, my uncle made known to my mother, and to his wife and daughters, the cause of the disturbance; the younger members of the family having retired early in the night, were all fast asleep. As soon as my uncle thought it prudent to do so, he came out and invited us in. Although my mother had received the news of my visit with a quiet composure, yet, on my approach, she arose silently and started toward me with a firm step, but in a moment she tottered and would have fallen, but I caught her in my arms; she lay with her head on my bosom for some minutes, weeping like a child, and I must confess that now, for the first time since I was a boy, I could not restrain my tears. My mother broke the silence by uttering, in broken sentences: "Oh, my dear son! Have you indeed come to see your mother? I thought I would go down with sorrow to my grave, as I never expected to see you again on earth!" How my manhood and my iron will left me at that moment! How gladly would I have left war and revenge to the beast of the forest, and secreted myself in some quiet corner of the earth, that there, with my mother and my family, I might once more delight in the sweet songs of birds, and in the tranquil scenes of life, like those I enjoyed in my younger days!

My mother became more tranquil, and we talked over matters with a great deal of satisfaction; and my uncle, to drive our minds from a subject too serious, occasionally poked fun at me, by accusing me of trying to steal his bee-gum, in which he was joined by my two comrades. His two daughters were flying around in the kitchen, and presently announced a supper for us all. We enjoyed ourselves finely until two o'clock in the night at which time we were compelled to leave, in order to secure a safe retreat from the vigilant search to be made for us during the following day.

On starting, we rode back on our old trail half a mile, to where we had crossed a small creek, down which we rode, keeping all the time in the water, for about three miles, to a public road leading south, which we followed about six miles; then, on coming to a rocky place where our horses would make no tracks, we left the road at right angles and traveled in the woods about two miles; here we made a semi-circle around a hill, and camped in a commanding position. My comrades did picket duty while I slept nearly all day. At night we went to a friend who lived near my old residence, and from him we learned that our trail had been discovered on our way up, that the whole militia force, composed almost exclusively of my old enemies, together with some Dutch regulars, were quartered at Big River Mills; that the woods were being constantly scoured; that each ford on Big River was guarded night and day, and that they considered my escape impossible.

Before the approach of daylight we secreted our horses in a deep ravine, covered with brush and briars, and then hid ourselves underneath a shelving rock near the top of a high bluff, from which, at a long distance, we had a view of my mother's house—the homestead of the Hildebrand family. We remained here all day, during which time the house was surrounded by soldiers, how many I could not tell, but they seemed to fill the yard and the adjoining enclosures. Presently, I saw a dense column of smoke arise from the house, which told me too plainly that the Vandals were burning up the home of my childhood.

The flames presently burst forth through the roof and lapped out their long fiery tongues at every window. The roof fell in, and all that remained of the superb house was the blackened walls of massive stone.

Gladly would I have thrown myself among those Vandals, and fought them while I had a drop of blood remaining, but it would have been madness for I would have been killed too soon, and my revenge would have been ended, while my enemies would still live to enjoy their pillage.

Immediately after dark we returned to our horses and commenced our retreat to Arkansas; but instead of going south we traveled west about twenty miles until we struck on a creek called Forche á Renault, in Washington County; then turning south, we traveled over the wild pine hills west from Potosi, and camped in a secure place between Caledonia and Webster.

We started on in the evening, and just before sunset made a raid on a store, getting all we wanted, including several bottles of "burst-head." We traveled mostly in the night, followed Black River down to Current River, crossed at Carter's Ferry, and made our way safely to Green County, Arkansas.

Chapter Ten

Trip with two men.—Killed Stokes for informing on him.—Secreted in a cave on Big River.—Vows of vengeance.—Watched for McGahan.—Tom Haile pleas for Franklin Murphy.—Tongue-lashed and whipped out by a woman.

AFTER REMAINING a few days at headquarters I commenced making preparations for another trip against my enemies on Big River. I was yet ignorant of the murder of my brother, Henry, and knew nothing about the burning of my mother's house, except what I saw at the distance of a mile, a few hours before I started back to Arkansas. I was now fully determined to use the same weapons upon some of my enemies, and to retaliate by any and all means placed in my power. I told the boys my plan. Among those who were present was Thomas Haile, or "devilish Tom," as he was called, and as usual, he was spinning some of his laughable yarns; but when I spoke the name of Franklin Murphy as probably connected with the house burning, he stopped short in his conversation, and after a moment's reflection he proposed to go with me to see some of his old friends. To this I readily consented, and after selecting another man, we started on our way. We passed through Stoddard and then into Wayne county after a man by name of Stokes. He had fed me on my previous trips, inducing me to believe that he was a substantial Southern man; I learned shortly afterwards that he was laying plans for my capture, and had, more than once, put the Federals on my trail. Notwithstanding I had these statements from good authority, I was unwilling to take his life until I knew to my own certain knowledge that he was guilty. I did not wish to fall into the error, so common among the Federals, of killing an innocent man to gratify the personal enmity of some informer.

Just after dark I went to his house alone, he greeted me in a very cordial manner and remarked:

"Well, Mr. Hildebrand, I'm glad to see you—hope you are well—and are yet too smart for the Feds."

"Are there any Feds in Greenville?"

"None, sir, none at all; I was there today, the place is entirely clear of the scamps. By the way Mr. Hildebrand, are you alone?"

"Oh yes; I am taking this trip by myself."

"Glad to assist you, Sir, you must stay with me tonight. I'll hide you tomorrow in a safe place; can go on tomorrow night if you like; would like for you to stay longer."

I thanked him for his proffered assistance, but told him that as I had troubled him so often, I would go to a neighbor's about a mile off and stay until the next night. I went back a short distance to where my men were and waited about an hour.

My two men after putting on the Federal uniform, rode around the place and approached the house from another direction; they rode up in a great hurry and called Mr. Stokes out. Tom Haile in a very confidential tone commenced:

"Well sir! we are on the hot track of Sam Hildebrand! he is here again; he robbed a man down on the Greenville road, five miles below here, about sunset; he came in this direction, and we concluded to ride down to your house thinking that you might have seen or heard something of him!"

"I reckon I have, by George! Sam Hildebrand was here not more than an hour ago, and I tried to detain him; he was alone and said he was going to stay until tomorrow night at a certain house; I know the place; hold on a minute! I'll get my gun and coat and will go with you—we've got him this time, sure!"

"All right," said Tom, "come along; we are always glad to meet a man of your stripe."

He marched along with the boys until they came to where I was waiting for them; Stokes had forgotten to ask many questions, but on coming up to me in the dim moonlight he asked, "how many men have you?" one of my men answered "twelve." He at once began laying plans for my capture, and related what he had done on previous occasions "to capture Sam Hildebrand, but that Sam was too sharp for him." When I thought that he had said enough I stopped him with the remark—"I am Sam Hildebrand myself!" and emptied old "Kill-devil" into his bosom.

We then proceeded on, traveling altogether in the night, until about day-break; one morning we got near the ruins of the old Hildebrand homestead, and called at the house of a friend. Knowing that we were in an enemy's country and liable to be trailed, we could not sleep. Nor could we travel in the day-time, considering the fact that if our enemies got after us we would have to run about one hundred and fifty miles to get out of their lines, and that the government had no less than four thousand men in active employment all the time for the special purpose of capturing me. We secreted our horses in a thicket under a bluff and entered a cave near by, which was afterwards called by my name.[1] Our friend remained in the cave a few minutes with us, and it was from him I learned the particulars of the atrocities committed by the Federal troops, in the murder of my poor innocent brother Henry.

I shall not attempt to describe my feelings, when the truth flashed across my mind that all my brothers had been slain in cold blood—Frank, first, and now the other two—leaving me not a brother upon earth except my brother William, who was in the Federal army, but whose well known loyalty was not sufficient to shield his natural brothers from an indiscriminate butchery.[2] For several hours I remained quietly in the cave, studying the matter over; but finally my mind was made up. I determined to sell my life as dearly as possible, and from that moment wage a war of fire and blood against my persecutors, while one should last, or until I was numbered with the dead.

I hastily gathered my arms; only one word escaped my lips: "Revenge!" sounded and reechoed from the deepest recesses of the cavern, and with one wild rush I made for the mouth of the cave; but my men happening to be there, sprang to their feet and choked up the passage; but near it was another outlet—I dashed through it, and down the steep declivity I hastily made my way, and mounted my horse. But Haile was close after me, and before I could pass around a fallen tree he had my horse by the bridle.

"Hold on, Sam! Don't be a fool. If you are going to throw your life away, you cannot expect to kill a dozen; if you take your own time you may kill a thousand! If I go back without you, what could I tell your wife and children? Come, Sam, you must not forget your duty to them. See how they have clung to you! 'Light now, and go with me to the cave."

I have but a faint recollection of going back to our retreat; but when I awoke it was nearly sunset, and Tom soon had me laughing in spite of myself.

When night came we moved our position about five miles, to the residence of William Patton, as he was a man whom I particularly wanted; but we were unsuccessful; he was at home when we first went there, but by some means he succeeded in eluding our grasp. We left there, and before daylight we had secreted our horses in a thicket on Turkey Run, a small creek emptying into Big River above Addison Murphy's, and had stationed ourselves near the residence of Joe McGahan, on the different roads leading to his house. About eight o'clock in the morning I concluded that it was fruitless to watch for him any longer; so I proposed to repair to Franklin Murphy's residence, which was not more than a mile from where we were; but Tom suggested that we must now return to our horses and consult as to our future movements.

We found our horses all right; but when I expressed a desire to stir up Franklin Murphy for being present at the burning of my mother's house, and several other little incidents that led me to think strangely of his conduct, Tom Haile replied:

"I do not believe that he sanctioned, in any manner, the outrages of which you speak; he could not rescue your brother from the hands of a mob who seemed to have the sanction of public opinion; he could not prevent an army of soldiers, acting under the command of another man, from burning the house, nor from killing your brother Henry. Once for all, let me tell you that it will never do for you to attempt to harm that man. He is a member of a certain Order, that dates back for thousands of years; the members are bound together by an obligation to watch over each other's interests, and to shield each other, as much as possible, from any impending danger."

Tom was so sincere, and looked so serious—which was not common with him—that I told him I would never harm one of them, if I knew it, unless it was in self-defense.

We now thought it best to make our way back to Arkansas. We passed through Farmington and Fredericktown on the following night, and then camped in the woods until evening. We started before night, in order to capture some fresh horses.

Dressed in Federal uniforms, we were riding along the road in Madison county, when on passing a farm, I saw a fine looking horse in a lot near the house. I halted my men, dismounted and went up to the horse to catch him, but he was a little shy, and kept his head as far from me as possible.

While I was thus trying to get a halter on the spirited animal, a woman stepped onto the porch and bawled out:

"See here! What are you trying to do?"

"I'm trying to catch this horse."

"Let him alone, you good-for-nothing! Don't you look pretty, you miserable scamp, trying to steal my only horse?"

"Yes, madam, but I'm afraid you are a rebel."

"I am a rebel, sir, and I'm proud of it! I have two sons in the rebel army, and if I had six more they should all be in it. You white-livered, insignificant scum of creation! You had better let him alone. Why, you are worse than Sam Hildebrand! He wouldn't take the last horse from a poor widow woman!"

By this time I had caught the horse, but as soon as the woman made that last remark, I pulled the halter off, begged her pardon and left.

On getting to headquarters, Tom never let me rest about that adventure.

Chapter Eleven

Another trip to Missouri.—Fight near Fredericktown.—Horse shot from under him.—Killed four Soldiers.—Went into their camp at Fredericktown and stole four horses.—Flight toward the South.—Robbed "Old Crusty."—Return to Arkansas.

WHILE I WAS recruiting at our headquarters in Green County, Arkansas, Capt. Bolin and most of his men returned to rest themselves for a while. Of course our time passed off agreeably, for we all had so much to say, and so much to listen to, that the mind was actively engaged at all the time, rendering it impossible for time to drag heavily.

Having thoroughly rested myself, on the 25th day of August I selected three men, and we started on a trip to St. Francois County, Missouri. Nothing unusual occurred until we arrived in Madison County. On getting within about eight miles of Fredericktown, daylight overtook us, and we stopped at an old friend's house for breakfast, who had always treated us kindly, for I had stopped with him several times on my previous trips. He stated to us that there were no troops in Fredericktown. Upon receiving this information, from a source, as we supposed, so reliable, we felt quite free, and resolved to make our journey on that day to my old home on Big River. So, after getting our breakfast and feeding our horses, we made our way quietly to our usual place of crossing the gravel road leading from the Pilot Knob to Fredericktown, when we were suddenly fired on from the brush by about fifty soldiers. Fortunately for us, we had not kept the usually traveled path that crossed the road at the place where the soldiers were stationed in ambush; consequently, we were about two hundred yards from them, and none of us were hurt, though my horse was shot from under me; the ball that pierced his chest, passing through my pantaloons, slightly burning my knee.

At the word from me my three men whirled into the brush, and we retreated back in the direction from which we came, my men on horses and myself on foot. I was still lame from the effects of the wound received at Flat Woods, but we made good time, and effected our escape. On getting about a mile, I ordered my men to hitch their horses in a thicket, and we would hold the place if they undertook to follow us. After waiting for some time and not hearing from them, we concluded to make our way cautiously back to where we had been fired upon, and try to get a shot. We crept slowly up, and saw six or seven men near the place, but we could not get close enough from the side we were on; so we made our way in the direction of Pilot Knob about a mile, crossed the gravel road behind a hill, and came up on the opposite side.

We got in sight of them just in time to see a party ride up, leading our three horses; at this, I concluded to try one of them at long range, seeing distinctly from our position that we could get no closer without exposing ourselves too much. I pulled off old "Kill-devil" at one of them who wore shoulder-straps; at the crack of the gun the gentleman got a very hard fall, which, I am fearful, killed him. At this they concluded to follow us into our native woods, for which they paid very dearly. They made a dash on us, which caused us to scatter in different directions, to divide their party up into several squads. Each of us took a course through the woods in the roughest places we could find, which rendered it very difficult for them to follow. I stopped at every place, such as fallen timber, steep banks and high rocks, to get a pop at them, and would be off again in a different direction. Sometimes I was in front, sometimes at one side, and frequently in the rear. I was pleased to see them have so much pluck, for it afforded old "Kill-devil" an opportunity to howl from every knob and dense thicket in the wild woods until one o'clock in the evening, when they gave up the chase and quit the unequal fight.

On meeting my men, at dark, on the top of a certain high hill designated by me in the morning, I had four new notches in the stock of old "Kill-devil," indicating by that rough record that four more of my enemies had gone to that land where the righteous would cease from troubling them or making them afraid. Two of my men had killed a man apiece, and the other had made what we call in fishing "a water haul." I suppose, however, that he took himself into some secure corner to meditate on the uncertainty of all human affairs until the danger was over.

The Federals, on the next day, started in search of us with three or four hundred men; but their numbers being so great, we did not make war upon them that day. At night it rained very hard, and whilst it was raining we went into Fredericktown; finding all things quiet about camp, we managed to steal a horse apiece from them, but did not get the saddles and bridles, as we were in a hurry. We got about thirty miles on our way back to Arkansas before morning—each of my men riding bare-back, with only a halter for a bridle. I stopped, however, at the old gentleman's where we had got breakfast, for the purpose of having a small settlement with him, as he had deceived us in regard to the soldiers at Fredericktown, and, as we believed, had reported us, for we noticed that his son, a lad about fifteen years old, had rode off while we were eating our breakfast on that morning. I stopped, but the old man was not at home, so I took an old saddle and bridle from him, and went on to Arkansas, leaving the Federals to hunt for us, which we were told they kept up about ten days.

Before reaching Arkansas, however, for the purpose of laying in our winter's supplies, we diverged about twenty miles from our usual course to pay our respects to an old Union man living at the crossroads, who had caused the expulsion of two families from the neighborhood by reporting on them.

He still had the remnants of what had once been a full country store. No Federal soldiers happened to be near the premises at the time, so we rode up to his house about sunset, and while I left one man at his door to prevent any one from leaving the house, we went with the old crusty fellow to the store. He was not disposed to be accommodating, but we bought everything that we could put upon our horses and upon a mule that we borrowed of him, and, after telling him to charge it to Uncle Sam, with the Big River mob for security, we left, and before morning were out of the reach of danger. On reaching camp, we relieved the needy, not forgetting the two families that "Old Crusty" had driven from his neighborhood.

Chapter Twelve

Trip with three men.—Captured a Spy and shot him.—Shot Scaggs.—At night charged a Federal camp of one hundred men.—Killed nine men.—Had one man wounded.—Came near shooting James Craig.—Robbed Bean's store and returned to Arkansas.

MY FAMILY STILL remained in Cook settlement, in St. Francois County, Mo., and as they were in the enemy's country, I did not think it prudent to pay them a visit, knowing that it would only bring ruin upon them if the fact of my visit should ever become known to the Unionists in that county. But I determined by some means or other to effect their escape to Arkansas as soon as it would be prudent to make the attempt. Capt. Bolin and his men had promised me their cooperation if called upon for that purpose; but I was well aware that our whole force would be insufficient for the accomplishment of the object, if attempted by force of arms, for two or three thousand men could be brought against me in less than twenty-four hours.

To keep myself well posted in regard to the strength of the enemy along the route, I selected three of Quantril's men, and in the latter part of September, started on another raid into Missouri.[1] On arriving at the St. Francis River we found it swimming, but made no halt on that account, having by this time become inured to all kinds of hardships and dangers.

On the second day after we started we left the main road and diverged several miles to our right, for the purpose of traveling in day time. On getting within sight of a house we discovered some one run into the yard, and immediately afterwards we saw a little boy running toward a barn. The movement being a little suspicious, we dashed forward and were soon on each side of the barn. We discovered a man through a crack, and demanded his surrender; he came to the door and threw up his hands. On taking him back into the barn, we discovered his bundle to contain a complete Federal uniform, and when we noticed that the citizen's dress which he had on was much too small for him, we at once pronounced him a Federal spy. We found a letter in his pocket, written by a man by the name of Scaggs, to the authorities at Fredericktown, containing names of his rebel neighbors, whom he was desirous of having burned out. One of the men on the list I happened to know, and by that means I knew that Scaggs lived about seven miles from there. We took the spy half a mile and shot him, then, changing our course, we started on the hunt for Scaggs, whose residence, however, we did not find until after dark. Dressed in Federal uniform, we rode up to the gate and called him out. On arresting him we took him to the house of a friend, who told us that Scaggs had already made two widows in that neighborhood by reporting their husbands. We took him with us until daylight appeared, hung him to a limb in the woods, and made our way toward Castor creek, in Madison County.[2]

The next night, on crossing Castor Creek, we discovered a camp of Federals; judging them to be about twenty or thirty strong, we concluded to charge them for a few minutes; but on getting into their camp we found that there were three or four times as many as we expected; so we charged on through as quickly as possible, still two of our horses were killed and one of my men was slightly wounded in the fleshy part of his thigh. After getting through their camp, we captured the four pickets who were placed in a lane on the opposite side. As we came from the wrong direction, they mistook us for their own men, until we had taken them in. My two men who had lost their horses, now mounted those taken from the pickets. As soon as the pickets told us that they were Leeper's men, we shot them and hurried on.[3]

On our return, at another time, we were told by the citizens that we killed five and wounded several more in our charge through their camp; making nine men killed, including the pickets.[4]

My wounded man could not be kept in Missouri with any degree of safety, and according to the usage of the petty tyrants who commanded the little squads of Federals, it would have been death to any man under whose roof the wounded man might have taken refuge; the man, without any questions asked, would have been shot, his house and property burned, and his wife and children turned out into the world, houseless, forlorn and destitute. To avoid the infliction of such a calamity upon any of our friends, my wounded man was under the necessity of making his way alone back into Arkansas.

My other two men and myself traveled the remainder of the night in the direction of my old home in St. Francois County. I learned that a prolonged effort was made in the following day to trail us up to our camp in the woods; but a rain having fallen about daylight, our tracks were entirely destroyed. On the following night we made our way to the house of a friend, near the ruins of my once happy home. Here I remained, resting myself and scouting over the country on foot, two whole days and nights, trying to shoot some of the miscreants who had belonged to the old mob, but they kept themselves so closely huddled that I had no chance at them.

On the second day, however, while lying near the road, James Craig, captain of the mob—which by this time had assumed the name of Militia—with two men whom I did not recognize, came along, riding very fast. I got a bead on Craig, but my gun did not fire; and I will say here, that this was the only time during the war that old "Kill-devil" deceived me.[5]

On returning to my friend near my old home, he stated to me that our horses, which we had concealed in a nook in one of the bluffs of Big River, had been discovered by some boys who were hunting, and that they had gone to report to the militia. Upon receiving this intelligence, we started at once to our horses, found them alright, and, not being satisfied with the results of our trip, we concluded to obtain some supplies from our good Union friends before leaving. We got in Flat River about the middle of the afternoon, and rode up to a store kept by the sons of John Bean, one of whom belonged to the Vigilance mob—but he was not there.[6]

The boys had sense enough to make no demonstration, so, without damaging anything whatever, I took such things as we needed, in part payment for my property which the mob had destroyed.

The boys looked a little displeased; they considered us bad customers and did not even take the trouble to book the articles against us.

The militia, having received the report of the boys, mustered their whole force and, on the following day, struck our trail and overtook us between Pilot Knob and Fredericktown; they followed us about ten miles, but only got sight of us occasionally on the tops of hills we had to pass over. Night came, and we neither saw nor heard them any more. We traveled all night and about daylight we rode up to the house of a man named Slater, in the southern part of Wayne County, Missouri, for whom we had been watching for some time. He had made himself very busy ever since the beginning of the war by reporting Southern men. He succeeded in having several of them imprisoned, and their families impoverished. We found him at home; his manhood wilted like a cabbage leaf; we took him about a mile from home and shot him.

We then pursued our way home to Green County, Arkansas, and divided our spoils amongst the destitute families driven there by the ruthless hands of Northern sympathizers.

Chapter Thirteen

The Militia mob robs the Hildebrand estate.—Trip with ten men.—Attacks a Government train with an escort of twenty men.—Killed two and put the others to flight.

DIRECTLY AFTER the termination of my last trip, certain events transpired in St. Francois County of which it is necessary that the readers should be informed. I have already stated that the infamous Vigilance mob finally came to a head by the organization of its worst material into a militia company with James Craig for captain and Joe McGahan for first Lieutenant. As Craig could neither read nor write, and did not know his alphabet from a spotted mule, the lieutenant was actually the head and front of the marauders. Their design in assuming the form and style of a militia company was merely for the purpose of legalizing their acts of plunder. They did not pretend to take the field against the Rebels, or to strike a single blow in defense of the State or anything else. While drawing their pay from the government, they spent their time hunting hogs, sheep, and cattle belonging to other people.

Having killed all my brothers but one (and he was in the Union army where they could not reach him), they proceeded to divide the property of the Hildebrand estate among themselves. Mother, though decidedly a Union woman originally, they had long since driven off to Jefferson County, with nothing but her bed and Bible. The homestead had been burned, yet there was an abundance of stock belonging to the estate, and a large field of standing corn.

They collected the stock and gathered the corn, and then proceeded to divide it among themselves. In this division they disagreed very much; a question arose whether an officer was entitled to any more than a private, and a few of them went home declaring that they would not have anything if they could not get their share.

At the very time this valorous militia company had stacked their muskets against the fence and were chasing mother's sheep and pigs around through the dog fennel, I was capturing a government train and getting my supplies in an honorable manner.

About the first of November, 1862, having learned that the Federals were in the habit of hauling their army supplies to Bloomfield from Cape Girardeau on the Mississippi River, Capt. Bolin and myself determined to lay in our supplies from the same source.

We took ten men and started with about ten days' rations. Arriving on a stream called White Water, which, with Castor Creek, forms the Eastern fork of St. Francis River, we concealed ourselves in an unfrequented part of the woods. It was necessary that we should be thoroughly posted in regard to the expected time of the arrival of the train, and the probable strength of the escort.

I undertook this delicate mission disguised as a country farmer, in search of a stray mule. Without my gun I made my way on foot to the vicinity of a mill and there concealed myself near a road to await the arrival of some one going to mill. Presently a man came along with a cart and oxen, but I let him pass, fearing that my questions might arouse his suspicions.

I remained there nearly an hour for some boy to pass; at length I saw one at a distance coming slowly along, riding on his sack and whistling little fragments of "John Brown." I stepped into the road before he got near me and walked along until I met him. I asked about my mule, but of course he knew nothing about him. I told him that I had concluded to hunt no further, but that I was anxious to return to Bloomfield if I could only meet with a conveyance for I was tired of walking so much. He told me that the government wagons would pass there on the following day and perhaps I could get a ride. I told him that I would be afraid to do that for the Rebels might capture me; he said that there was no danger of that, for twenty soldiers always went with the wagons.

I returned to my comrades with all the information we wanted, and we soon settled all our preliminary arrangements for the attack. After dark we took the road along which we knew they were to pass; we selected a place called the Round Pond, and secreted ourselves in a clump of heavy timber through which the soldiers could not see, in order that they might imagine the woods full of Rebels.

Night passed and the morning hours wore away, when at length we saw two government wagons coming, and in the sunlight sure enough twenty bayonets were gleaming.

We suddenly broke from the woods with a great shout, and dashed in among them with all the noise we could make. We fired a few shots, killing two and causing the remainder to break for the woods in every direction. The sole object of our trip being to get supplies of clothing, ammunition, etc., we felt no disposition to hunt them down, but let them continue their flight without any pursuers.

We unhitched the horses and packed them with such things as we needed; after which we burned the wagons and everything else we could not take with us.[1]

On starting back we went through Mingo Swamp and made our way safely to St. Francis River, which we found out of its banks. With a great deal of difficulty we succeeded in swimming the river with our train, but with the loss of one man named Banks, who unfortunately was drowned. Becoming entangled in a drift of grape vines and brush, he drowned before we could render him any assistance.

Chapter Fourteen

Federal cruelties.—A defense of "Bushwhacking."—Trip with Capt. Bolin and nine men.—Fight at West Prairie.—Started with two men to St. Francois County.—Killed a Federal soldier.—Killed Ad. Cunningham.—Capt. Walker kills Capt. Barnes and Hildebrand kills Capt. Walker.

ON ARRIVING AT headquarters we busied ourselves for several weeks in building houses to render ourselves as comfortable as possible during the coming winter. Our headquarters were on Crawley's Ridge, between the St. Francis River and Cash Creek, in Green County, Arkansas. It was a place well adapted to our purpose, affording as it did a safe retreat from a large army encumbered with artillery.

Many of Capt. Bolin's men had their families with them, and our little community soon presented a considerable degree of neatness and comfort. I could have contented myself longer at this quiet place, but our scouts were constantly bringing us rumors of fresh barbarities committed by the different Federal bands who were infesting the country in Southeast Missouri, making it their especial aim to arrest, burn out, shoot and destroy all those peaceable citizens who from the beginning had taken no part in the war.[1]

They were especially marked out for destruction who had been known to shelter "Sam Hildebrand, the Bushwhacker," as they were pleased to call me. If any man should happen to see me passing along the road, and then should fail to report the same at headquarters, regardless of the distance, he was taken out from his house and shot, without even the shadow of a trial to ascertain whether he was guilty or not. An old man, with his head silvered over by the frosts of seventy winters, who had served his country in many a hard fought battle before his tormentors were born, and who now hoped to go down the declivity of life in peace and security, found himself suddenly condemned and shot for disloyalty, because he generously took a stranger into his house for the night, who afterwards proved to be "the notorious Sam Hildebrand."

These same miscreants, however, would call at any house they pleased, and, by threats, compel even women, in the absence of their husbands, to cook the last morsel of food in the house, scraped together by poor feeble women to keep their children from starving to death.

Did I ever do that? No, never! Did I ever punish a man for feeding a Federal? Did I ever shoot a man for not reporting to me the fact of having seen a Federal pass along the road? If that was really my mode of proceeding, I would deserve the stigma cast upon my name.

My enemies say that I am a "Bushwhacker." Very well, what is a "Bushwhacker?" He is a man who shoots his enemies. What is a regular army but a conglomerate mass of Bushwhackers? But we frequently conceal ourselves in the woods, and take every advantage! So do the regular armies. But a Bushwhacker will slip up and shoot a man in the night! Certainly, and a regular army will slip up and shoot a thousand.

But a Bushwhacker lives by plundering his enemies! So did Sherman in Georgia, and a host of others, with this difference: That I never charged my government with a single ration, while they did so at all times.[2] Besides, I never made war upon women and children, neither did I ever burn a house; while the great marching, house-burning, no battle hero, turned his attention to nothing else.[3]

In fact, the "Independent Bushwhacking Department" is an essential aid in warfare, particularly in a war like ours proved to be. There are a class of cowardly sneaks, a gang of petty oppressors—like the Big River mob—who can be reached in no other way. A large regular army might pass through where they were a dozen times without ever finding one of them.

As I stated before, barbarities were committed by a certain band of Federals, that warranted our interference.

Capt. Bolin, myself and nine other men mounted our horses and started on another trip, about the first day of December, 1862.

We crossed the St. Francis, and traveled several nights, until we reached West Prairie, in Scott County, Missouri, where we came upon a squad of Federals, thirty in number, like an old-fashioned earthquake.

Imagining themselves perfectly safe, they had placed out no pickets; so we ran suddenly on them, and before they had time to do any fighting they were so badly demoralized they knew not how to fight.

We killed four, wounded several more, and charged on through their camp, as was our custom; in half an hour we returned to renew the attack, but found nobody to fight.

In our first charge, we caused several of their horses to break loose, which we afterwards got. We had one man wounded, having been shot through the thigh with a Minnie ball. Capt. Bolin and six men took the wounded man back with them to Arkansas, while Henry Resinger, George Lasiter and myself started on a trip to St. Francois county.[4]

One morning, just at daylight, we found ourselves on the gravel road leading from Pilot Knob to Fredericktown, and about seven miles from the latter place. We concealed ourselves in a thicket and watched the road until evening before we saw an enemy. A squad of eight Federals came suddenly in sight, riding very fast. I hailed them, to cause a momentary halt, and we fired. One fell to the ground, but the others hastened on until they were all out of sight. While we were examining our game (the dead man), we discovered three more in the distance, who seemed to have got behind the party, and were riding rapidly to overtake them; at this we divided, taking our stations in two different places for the purpose of taking them in. On coming nearer we discovered that they were not dressed in Federal uniform. We took them prisoners and ascertained that they were Southern sympathizers from near Fredericktown, who had been imprisoned at the Knob for several weeks, but having been released they were on their way home. While we were thus parleying with them, asking questions relative to the forces at the different military posts in the country, the party we had fired into now returned with a much larger force, and suddenly we found ourselves nearly surrounded by a broken and scattered line on three sides of us, at a distance of only one hundred yards. The odds were rather against us, being about sixty men against three. I called quickly to my men to follow me, and we dashed for the uncompleted part of their circle. On seeing this movement they dashed rapidly toward that part and closed the line; but when I started toward that point it was the least of my intentions to get out at that place; I wheeled suddenly around and went out in the rear, contrary to their expectations, followed by my men, shooting as we ran until we gained some distance in the woods; having the advantage of the darkness that was now closing in upon us, and being on foot, we escaped from the cavalry, who were tangled up in the brush, and were making the woods resound with their noise.

We luckily escaped unhurt, although there were at least fifty shots fired at us. I received two bullet holes through the brim of my hat, and one through the sleeve of my coat, and one of my men got a notch in his whiskers. We were not certain of having hurt any of the Federals as we passed out of their lines. We kept together and returned to our horses; after a short consultation we mounted and rode back to get a few more shots at them, at long range; but when we got to the battlefield we found no one there. Toward Fredericktown we then made our way, until we got in sight of the place, but saw nothing of the soldiers. During the night we visited several friends, and several who were not friends, but did no harm to any one, there being only two men at that time in the vicinity whom we wanted to hang, and they were not at home. On the next day we tore down the telegraph wire on the road to Pilot Knob, and stationed ourselves about a mile from town for the purpose of bushwhacking the Federals when they should come to fix it up; but they were getting cunning, and sent out some Southern sympathizers for that purpose, and we did not hurt them. But I made a contract with one of them for ammunition, and in the evening, when we again torn the wire down, he came out to fix it up, and brought me a good supply of powder and lead.

From him we learned that a general movement against us was to be made by the troops, both at Fredericktown and the Knob, on the following day.

I knew that the whole country between there and Arkansas was in the hands of the Federals. I knew also that they had learned my trick of invariably making a back movement toward Arkansas, immediately after creating an excitement.

As they seemed not likely to hunt the same country over twice, I concluded to go north of the road and wait a few days until the southern woods were completely scoured, and thus rendered safe for our return.

While waiting for this to be done, I thought it a good opportunity to hunt up a man by the name of Cunningham, who had been living in the vicinity of Bloomfield. During the early part of the war he professed to be a strong Southern man, and had been of some service to our cause as a spy; but during the second year of the rebellion he changed his plans and became to us a very dangerous enemy, and was very zealous in reporting both citizens and soldiers to the Federal authorities.

Our intention on this trip was to arrest and take him to Col. Jeffries' camp, ten miles south of Bloomfield, that he might be dealt with by the Colonel as he might see proper.[5]

On gaining the vicinity of Farmington, where Cunningham now lived, we learned that he was carrying on his oppressive measures with a high hand, and was very abusive to those whom he had in his power.

It is said that he even robbed his own brother Burril Cunningham, and suffered him to be abused unmercifully by the squad of men under his command. On reaching the Valle Forge we struck his trail and followed on toward Farmington; but some Federals got upon our trail, and would have overtaken us before we reached town, if a friend had not deceived them in regard to the course we had taken.

We found Cunningham at his own house, and when we approached the door I demanded his surrender; he attempted to draw a revolver, and I shot him through the heart.[6]

Having accomplished our object, we now returned to Bloomfield and reported to Col. Jeffries. We remained there about three weeks.

On the 5th day of January, 1863, Capt. Reuben Barnes requested me and my two men to assist him in capturing a man by the name of Capt. Walker, who had a command in the Federal army, and was now supposed to be at his home, about six miles from there.

On approaching the house, Walker ran out, holding his pistol in his hands. As we were near enough, we ordered him to surrender, at which he turned around and faced us. On getting a little nearer, he suddenly shot Capt. Barnes, and started to run. Our chase was soon ended, for I shot him dead.[7]

We took Capt. Barnes back to Bloomfield, where he died the same day.[8] We then returned to Green county, Arkansas, and went into winter quarters.

Chapter Fifteen

Started alone.—Rode off a bluff and killed his horse.—Fell in with twenty-five Rebels under Lieutenant Childs.—Went with them.—Attacked one hundred and fifty Federals at Bollinger's Mill.—Henry Resinger killed.—William Cato.—Went back to Fredericktown.—Killed a man.—Robbed Albright's store.

ON THE 23rd day of January, 1863, I started alone on a trip to Missouri, for the purpose of making some arrangements for the escape of my family to Arkansas.[1] I got along very well until the second night; then as I was riding over a brushy ridge I was suddenly hailed by "Who comes there?"

I halted and in an instant became aware of my close proximity to a Federal camp. I instantly wheeled my horse in the woods to the right, dashed furiously down a steep hill side for a short distance, and then in the darkness plunged over a precipice eight or ten feet high. My horse fell among some rocks and was killed, but I was precipitated a few feet further into a deep hole of water in some creek.

I was a little confused in my ideas for a while, but I had sense enough to crawl up out of the deep water; as I stood there with my dripping clothes I heard some of the soldiers coming down the hill toward me; so I crossed the creek and took up the hill on the other side. I was now completely out of their clutches and could easily have made my escape; but I had left my gun in the deep hole, and the thought of leaving "Kill-devil" in that predicament was more than I could bear.

In a few minutes the soldiers left and went back up the hill. I now slipped back cautiously and got into the water to recover my gun. The water was deep and cold; however, I waded in nearly up to my chin and felt around with my feet for the gun. I got my foot under it finally and raised it up; but I had no sooner got it into my hands than I saw five or six soldiers returning with a light. As they were making their way down through a crevice in the bluff, some ten steps above the rock from which I had been precipitated I had just time to wade down the creek, which was now only a few inches deep in places, and secrete myself behind a cluster of willows that hung over the edge of the steep bank about twenty yards below.

The Federals remained ten or fifteen minutes, walking around my dead horse, and around the hole of water. They threw the glare of their lantern in every direction, and though I was completely hid from their observation, I must acknowledge that as I stood there in the water, shivering with cold, holding my dripping gun, I felt more like anything else in the world than a major. Finally they struck the trail that I had made up the hill with my dripping clothes and each one of them went in pursuit.

Taking this opportunity I slowly left my retreat and waded down the creek for a long distance. I climbed up the hill on the same side on which the Federals were camped; I made a wide circuit around them and came into the road, some four or five miles ahead. I walked rapidly to keep myself warm, and just before the break of day I arrived at the house of a friend, wet, hungry, and on foot. I was soon supplied with everything I wanted; my gun was well attended to, and when morning came "Kill-devil" looked rather brighter than usual.

I started on in the direction of Fredericktown and fell in with twenty-five Rebel boys, commanded by Lieut. Childs, who asked me to take command of his men and give the Federals a "Whack" at Bollinger's Mill, on Castor creek.

That locality for some time had been a place of rendezvous for Southern recruits; that fact being well-known, the Federals concluded to station some men there. They were known to be about one hundred and fifty strong, but I consented on condition that his men all take an oath never to surrender under any circumstances. After the oath was administered we marched to the place above mentioned, arriving there about eleven o'clock at night, on the 4th of February. We succeeded in capturing their pickets, made a charge on their camp, fought them for about five minutes (or until they got ready to fight); killed twenty-two of their number as we were informed afterwards, and at the word we marched out on double-quick time.[2] We took four prisoners with us and got some important information from them, but finding that they were not McNeal's men we released them all.[3]

We lost one man killed, Henry Resinger, and three badly wounded, who recovered.

We carried the wounded with us in our retreat, and at daylight we all started for Mingo Swamp.[4]

The Federals followed us, and as our march was retarded by our wounded; they made their way around, and charged us, striking our columns at right angles they divided our line—cutting off seven of my men, whom they took prisoners.

In this little skirmish I lost one man, and killed three of the Federals, at which they left our trail and permitted us to make our way to St. Francis River, which we were compelled to swim.

We got one horse drowned, but got over safely without any other accident, struck camp and commenced getting our breakfast, dinner, and supper, all the same meal. Presently some one from the opposite shore called for us to bring him a horse. From his voice we knew him to be William Cato, one of the seven who had been taken as a prisoner.[5] One of my men swam over to him with a horse, and when he had arrived safely in camp, he informed us that six of the prisoners were shot, and that he had made his escape by dodging them in the brush. He was barefooted, and had torn nearly all his clothing off.[6]

We afterwards learned that the officer in command at Bollinger's Mill was Capt. Leeper from Ironton, Missouri.[7]

Not being satisfied with my trip, I did not remain but one week in camp, before I selected two men and started back to Missouri to make another effort towards getting my family to Arkansas. On getting to Fredericktown we found the place full of soldiers. In that town there lived a Dutchman, whose meddlesome disposition led him to be very zealous in the cause of putting soldiers on the track of private citizens. It seems that he never left town, and that it would be impossible to kill him unless it were done in public.

After night I layed off my coat, and gathering up a saw buck, which I found at a wood pile, I walked straight across a street or two, until I reached the door, thinking thereby not to attract any particular attention; but on being told that he was not at home, I carried myself out of town as soon as circumstances would permit, got with my two men and started on toward Farmington. When morning began to approach we left the road several miles and secreted ourselves on a certain hill, for a friend on whom we had called during the night told us that the military authorities were aware of my presence in the neighborhood, and that they had secured the services of two or three good woodsmen to aid in tracking me up.

About one o'clock in the afternoon we discovered a man tracking us slowly around our steep hill, looking cautiously ahead, holding his gun in a position to raise and fire in an instant. The ground was hard and our horses were not easily trailed, but our pursuer kept moving along very slowly. We were at a loss to know whether he was really a brave man or a natural fool. Not coming to any definite conclusion however, I concluded to make my way down the hill a little to gratify his curiosity by letting him find me. I wounded him severely on purpose to let him see me, but he yelled so loud that I had to kill him with my knife, for I wanted "peace" about that time.

We heard some horsemen coming, so we hastened away from there and secreted ourselves in a thicket on Wolf Creek, near the residence of John Griffin. Here I learned that my wife had procured a little wagon and a small yoke of oxen, with which to move to Arkansas; that she started with the family on the 16th day of February, and by this time was in the vicinity of Bloomfield.

At night we went out on the plank road leading from Farmington to Ste. Genevieve and fired into a camp of Federals; we could not get near enough to do them any harm, but wished to draw them out to hunt for us; but in this we failed and had to abandon the project.

From there we went to the junction of the Pilot Knob and Iron Mountain roads, and robbed a store belonging to a Dutchman by the name of Albright. We patronized him very liberally and started back to Arkansas with all the goods we could pack.

At this stage of the war the Federals held possession of all the principal places in Southeast Missouri. Bloomfield was also held by them, and there was no doubt in my mind but what my family was now in their hands.[8]

While passing through Stoddard County, the Federals overtook us, and run us so close that we were compelled to throw off a part of our loads; on arriving at St. Francis River we found it guarded. Our only chance was to whip the Federals, and we determined to try it. We retreated into a dense cane brake and then commenced upon them. We killed three of their men on the second round and then they fled. We got home safely and were again prepared "to clothe the naked and feed the hungry."

Chapter Sixteen

Started to Bloomfield with three men.—Fight at St. Francis River.—Starts on alone.—Meets his wife and family.—They had been ordered off from Bloomfield.—Capture and release of Mrs. Hildebrand.—Fight in Stoddard County.—Arrival in Arkansas.

FOR THE PURPOSE of getting my family to Arkansas, it was necessary that I should make a trip to Bloomfield, although that place was now held by a large Federal force under McNeal.[1]

I started with three good men, crossed the St. Francis River at a shoal, but we had not proceeded more than ten miles when we ran into a company of McNeal's men, who instantly fired upon us, slightly wounding one of my men in the fleshy part of the arm.

We thought it best for four men to retreat from the fire of nearly one hundred, which we did, in double-quick time. They pursued us very closely, but we were at too great a distance for them to shoot us.

Wishing to get a few shots at them, we concluded to cross the river and give them a fight from the other side; so we plunged our horses in the deep water at the nearest point, were swimming, and had nearly gained the opposite shore, when the Federals ran onto the bank we had just left and fired a volley at us with their muskets; but their shots were all too high.

We reached the bank where the willows were very thick, jumped off our horses and returned the fire. From our place of concealment we could easily see that three of their number were killed. They kept up a random fire at the willow thicket, in which they wounded three of our horses and caused them to run up into the woods, terribly affrighted. By this time they had ceased firing and had taken refuge behind trees and were watching for our movements; in this position they stood two rounds from our rifles, in which four of them fell, having been shot through the head. Before we could get another shot we discovered a portion of the men making their way up the river, and I understood at once that their intention was to engage our attention at that place, while a part of the command would make their way around and take us in; so we retreated in good order to a place of safety, and remained all night.

The next morning we crossed the river in company with several others; and found that the Federals during the night after the fight had gone to Bloomfield. They procured a wagon and team from an old man living near for the purpose of hauling off their dead. The old man stated to us that there were seven killed and two wounded.[2]

I now decided to change my tactics, and try my luck alone and on foot. I thought that by stealthy movements I could find my family and get them off to Arkansas much better than with a small company of men.

In a few days I met my family about twenty miles south from Bloomfield on their way to Arkansas, in an old wagon pulled by a small yoke of oxen, which my wife was driving. I learned from her that some of Capt. Bolin's men had removed her from Flat Woods to Bloomfield, in Stoddard County, Missouri, but that McNeal, on taking possession of the town, had ordered her to leave, adding that the wife and family of that "desperado, Sam Hildebrand," could not remain within one hundred miles of his headquarters.

With the wagon and oxen furnished her by a friend to our cause, she took the children and some provisions and started out upon the road, and when I met them she was making her way as best she could, but was just preparing to camp for the night in the lone woods. She cautioned me very particularly about the Federals, and said that she had seen two or three squads that day. On the following morning we resumed our journey, and about ten o'clock I met six Union soldiers, who came suddenly upon me at a short turn in the road, but, being dressed in Federal uniform, they did not suspicion me as being a Rebel. They asked me to what command I belonged, and I answered them to Capt. Rice's, stationed at that time in Fredericktown; at this they seemed satisfied, and passed on, swearing vengeance against any Rebels that might fall in their way.[3]

As soon as they were out of sight, I told my wife to drive on, while I traveled through the brush awhile. I had scarcely got out of the road when I discovered a whole regiment of Federal soldiers, not more than half a mile off, who were coming directly toward us. I soon gained an eminence in the woods, from which I could observe their maneuvers. They stopped at the wagon, and after parleying with my wife for several minutes, they turned her team around and took my family along.

At this juncture it is needless to say that I became enraged, and knowing an old rebel citizen about two miles off, I resolved at once to go to him, thinking that perhaps I might hear from some of our boys, for I was sure that if there were any in the neighborhood the old man would know it. I was overjoyed when he told me that James Cato and Wash Nabors were taking a nap in the barn, while he was standing on the lookout. I repaired to the barn at once, told them the fate of my family, and that I wanted their assistance that we might amuse ourselves in bushwhacking them.[4]

After getting something to eat, and some provisions to take along with us, we started through the dense forest, and got in sight of them about sundown. Before darkness set in we killed a man apiece, and then lurked around the camp all night. About every two hours, Cato, Nabors and myself would meet at a certain hill, designated before dark, and report progress. I made a great many random shots, but I think that during the night I killed as many as fifteen men. My comrades thought that they both together killed as many more. I learned afterwards that the number we killed during the night was just thirty; none were wounded that I ever could hear of.

Morning began to approach, and we fell back to a high hill, until they began to move toward Bloomfield. Throughout the day they kept their skirmish lines so strong that we could do nothing; however, we got several shots, at long range, at their scouts, but during the entire day I was not certain of killing more than two men.[5]

We kept in the woods, as near the troops we could, until we had followed them into the very suburbs of Bloomfield; then we started back along the road about dark, intending to pick up stragglers. Judge of my surprise and joy when, on going back, I came across my wife and children sitting by the roadside, where the Federals had left them about noon, but without the oxen and wagon, and without any provisions, bedding or change of clothing.

The capture of my wife had proved rather fatal to them, and her detention among them had produced nothing but disaster and death.

It reminded me of a passage of Scripture that I once heard my mother read from the Book of Samuel, giving an account of the Philistines having captured the ark of the covenant; they took it from one place to another, but a plague was produced wherever it was detained, until many thousands were dead. Finally, to get it out of their hands, they hitched up a yoke of cattle to a cart, and without any driver started it out of the country. The Federals, however, varied somewhat from the Philistines, for, instead of giving her a cart and oxen, and loading her down with presents of gold, they took her wagon and oxen and everything else she had, and left her by the roadside in an unknown wilderness.

On seeing me my family was greatly relieved in mind, yet they were in a starving condition, and we had nothing to divide with them. Believing that the "ark" might have been left there for the purpose of trapping me, I took my position about two hundred yards from my family, and remained while my two comrades were gone after something for them to eat. After their return I made a fire for my wife in the woods, and gave her directions in regard to the course she must travel in the morning, in order to reach the house of our old friend and requested him to meet my family as early as possible, and convey them to his house. He did so; and in the evening of the same day, having procured the use of a team, we started on for Arkansas.

Col. McNeal sent out a party from Bloomfield, under Capt. Hicks, who followed us to the St. Francis River, but we had got across, and they did not venture very close to the bank, having learned a lesson from me on my upward trip a short time before.[6]

We arrived safely at Capt. Bolin's camp, and my family was soon safely housed and supplied with the necessities of life, in the charming little community where a score of pleasant families resided.

Chapter Seventeen

Put in a crop.—Took another trip to Missouri with six men.—Surrounded in a tobacco barn.—Killed two men in escaping.—Killed Wammack for informing on him.—Captures some Federals and releases them on conditions.—Went to Big River Mills.—Robbed Highley's and Bean's stores.

HAVING SUCCEEDED IN getting my family to Green County, Arkansas, I settled on a piece of land whose owner had left for parts unknown, intending to hold the same until the owner should return. During the month of April, 1863, I was an "honest farmer," and by the 10th of May I finished planting a field of corn, while at the same time my wife put in a large garden.

At this occupation I enjoyed myself very well for a while; I got some chickens, a few pigs, and a milk cow, so that my family could get along without materially interfering with my main object in life—that of killing my enemies.

The boys were now anxious to make another trip to Missouri; so I took six men and started for Castor Creek, in Madison County, after some notorious scamps who had been giving us trouble on previous trips, by putting the Federals on our trail, besides the constant annoyance they gave Southern citizens in that county, by reporting them to the Federals.

We passed west of Bloomfield through the Southern part of Madison County, arriving in the neighborhood about daylight on the morning of the fourth day from home, secreted our horses, leaving three men to guard them, while myself and the others proceeded to spy out the men for whom we had come in search. We did not succeed in finding any of them, and after returning to our camp in the woods at sunset, we went to an old friend's about three miles distant, where we could get a night's sleep, and something to eat for ourselves and horses.

On arriving, our old friend received us kindly, but told us that as he was not well we would be under the necessity of taking care of our own horses which we were very willing to do. After supper we tied our horses in a neighboring thicket; but as the weather was rather inclement, we repaired to an old tobacco barn for shelter; it was about one hundred yards from the woods on one side, and about two hundred on the other. Here we slept soundly, keeping one man on watch all the time, but as we had not slept more than one hour in each twenty-four since starting, our sentinel fell asleep. In the morning I went out to take a peep at the weather, and was saluted by a shot that struck a board just above my head. I sprang into the barn, raised the alarm, and took a peep at the position of our enemies. They were about thirty strong, and had completely surrounded the barn, posting themselves behind stumps and old trees, but at a distance of about one hundred and fifty yards.

The extent of their circle made their lines very weak, and perceiving that they were much the strongest in front of the barn, I ordered my men to remove the underpinning from one place in the rear of the house. We crept through this aperture, and lay on the ground at the back of the building, being protected from observation by a pile of rubbish. I proposed taking the lead, and directed my men to follow in a straight line, but to keep twenty or thirty feet apart. I arose and started at full speed; but before I got fifty yards, all the Federals who were in sight of me, fired off their guns; yet I was not killed, but felt a stinging sensation on the point of my shoulder, which afterwards proved to be a slight abrasion, caused by a musket ball. On reaching the line, I shot the two men with my revolver who were guarding that point, without making the least halt; but I could not help feeling a thrill of pity for them and wished that they were again alive and on my side, for they were brave men and faced the music nobly, but missed their aim.

My men followed me through to the woods unhurt, save one poor fellow, who was pierced by a musket ball just as he reached the edge of the timber.

On reaching the woods, which were very thick, we felt much relieved, and were quite at home. We reached our horses, and fearing that the Federals might find them, we mounted and rode back to give them a little brush; but finding them all gone, we made our way around to our friend in whose barn we had slept, but found that the Federals had killed him, and had committed many other depredations about the place before leaving. Our kind lady, who had thus so unexpectedly been made a widow, was suffering the pangs of uncontrolled sorrow, but from her broken sentences we learned that a citizen by the name of Wammack was with the soldiers, and was probably the informant at whose instigation the whole tragedy had been brought about, and that as the soldiers left in the direction of Fredericktown, he took the road toward his house. We concluded to try, and if possible, to get Wammack. I ordered three of my men to take the horses out of the neighborhood, to travel over ground where they would occasionally make plain tracks, until they got to a certain creek, eight or ten miles off, then to turn back, keeping in the creek some distance, and then to secret themselves in the bushes near the residence of one Mr. Honn. Our arrangements having been completed, we separated; myself and my two men had not proceeded far, keeping all the time near the road, before we discovered three men coming from the direction of Wammack's house. When they were near us, we hailed them, and leaving our guns, we stepped out into the road where they were and inquired the way to Cape Girardeau. We told them that we had obtained furloughs at Ironton the day before, and were on our way to Illinois to see our families, but that a few miles back we met some soldiers, who stated that they had got into a skirmish with the bushwhackers and were going to Fredericktown to bring out the whole force; so we concluded to hide in the woods until they returned.

They mistook us for Federal soldiers, sure enough, and one of them related the whole circumstance in a very jubilant manner, stating that he was with the soldiers at the time, that they had killed four of the bushwhackers and the old Rebel who had harbored them, and that if he had his way he would burn up the whole premises. I suggested that we had better go to the main road and wait until the force came; but he objected, for the reason that he wished to see who buried the dead bushwhackers.

By this time I thought I could venture to ask him his name, and after telling me that his name was Wammack, and that he was "all right," he made a motion to proceed, at which we drew our revolvers and told him that he was a prisoner. The other two having answered a sign which I made while talking to Wammack, I saw that they were "all right" instead of him. I told them that they could go, but requested them to bury the dead, which they cheerfully agreed to do.

Just as this conversation ended, Wammack suddenly jerked out his revolver and attempted to shoot one of the men and broke to run; the movement was so sudden and so unexpected that he got nearly forty yards before we succeeded in killing him.

We then left that part of the country and went to Wayne County; while stopping there for supper at the house of an old Rebel, a young man came in and stated that about five miles from there, on Lost creek, he saw some Federals putting up for the night; on receiving this pleasing information, we determined to go and take them "out of the wet," as one of my boys expressed it, and after feeding our horses and taking our rations, we were soon on our way for that purpose.[1]

We found the place without much difficulty, made our way to the house and knocked at the door. The man of the house came, and in answer to our questions, stated that there were five Federals sleeping in the stable loft, and that their horses were in the stable. After telling the old man who we were, and ordering him not to leave the house, we proceeded to surround the stable, which stood in the middle of a lot of perhaps about half an acre. Our positions having been taken I set fire to a hay stack that stood in the corner of the lot, nearly in front of the stable door. When the hay blazed up, the light shone so suddenly on the Federals that they sprang to their arms in great fright. I hailed them, demanding their surrender, and told them that I was Sam Hildebrand, and that I and my twenty men had them completely in our clutches, but that if they would surrender without firing a gun, I would let them off on easy terms. To this they gladly acceded, and coming down from the loft, they piled their arms in the lot. I ordered two of my men to extinguish the fire that had caught in the fence, and then proceeded to negotiate with our prisoners, which was done in a friendly and satisfactory manner. Rough jokes were passed back and forth with perfect freedom, and they repeated some of the many tales of blood circulated in camps about me, in which I was represented as a hero more daring and dreadful than "Jack the Giant Killer."

At this time there were two of Capt. Bolin's men in prison at Ironton who had been captured while on a scout up Black River in Reynolds county, Missouri; and as my prisoners belonged to the command stationed at that place, I proposed to them that if they would pledge themselves that by some means or other they would manage to let the two boys escape, we would release them, and permit each one to retain his private property. To this they agreed; they retained their pistols, but gave up their guns and horses.

We all stayed until morning, took breakfast together with the old man, who seemed highly pleased at the turn matters had taken, and occasionally contributed to our fun by some of his timely jokes.

After breakfast we separated, the Federals making their way on foot, carrying a pass from me, written by one of my men, to prevent any of our boys from molesting them on their way, should they happen to fall into their hands.

After a short consultation with my men, we concluded that it was about time to make our enemies in St. Francois County pay their taxes to the Southern Confederacy. On the evening of the last day of May, we rode into the little town at Big River Mills, and made a haul on the store of John B. Highley, but not being certain of his politics, we were very light on him. We then went six miles further to John Bean's store on Flat River, arriving there about 11 o'clock in the night. We knew him to be a strong Union man, and we knew also that one of his sons belonged to the Big River mob. We supplied ourselves with such articles as were needed by the families at Capt. Bolin's camp.[2]

In a few days after our arrival in Green County, the two boys who had been in prison at Ironton, came in, and related to us that the guards who permitted them to escape, told them all about the contract they had entered into with me. Those Federals deserve much credit for keeping their word.

Chapter Eighteen

Took seven men.—Went to Negro Swamp.—Attacked fifteen or twenty Federals.—A running fight.—Killed three.—Killed Crane.—Betrayed by a Dutchman.—Hemmed in a house by Federals.—Fight and escape.—Killed eight soldiers.—Caught and hung the Dutchman.

CONCLUDING TO TAKE a trip to Negro-Wool Swamp, I selected seven good men, and struck out; making our way slowly, we visited our Southern friends, and passed off the time very pleasantly with them. We made but few miles a day until nearing the point to which we had started, the object of our trip being to take in a couple of very noisy Union men, for the purpose of giving them a nice necktie of our own make, manufactured from the textile fabric of nature's own production that we occasionally stripped from the thrifty young hickories in the shady woods. But while we were on the lookout for them, a scout of Yankees, fifteen or twenty in number, came into the neighborhood, and we concluded to let the two meddlesome Unionists rest for the present and to give the Federals a chase. We ascertained their exact locality, and at sundown I gave one of them a dead shot from old "Kill-devil," which was all that was necessary to give them a start, and I assure you it was "a running start."

Seeing the course they took, we knew that they were bound for Bloomfield, so we mounted and started in pursuit; but they knew so well who was after them that they gave us no show for a fight; however, being much better acquainted with the country than they were, I made my way, with one of my men, across on a nearer route, and got in ahead of them, while my other boys kept up the chase. We did not beat them much, for when we had gained the point, we heard them coming at full speed, and as they passed, we both fired at the same time; only one man fell, and as "old Kill-devil" was in the habit of tearing a tolerable large hole, we had no dispute about who did it. From there on to within a few miles of Bloomfield, our chase was in vain; a streak of greased lightning could hardly have caught them. Knowing that a considerable force would now be sent out into the vicinity of Negro-Wool Swamp to clear that country of bushwhackers, we concluded not to return to that place, but wound our way around south of Bloomfield, and ran suddenly on to a man by the name of Crane, for whom one of Capt. Bolin's men had been hunting for more than a year; as he was not along, and we were acting as a band of brothers, I took it upon myself to shoot the *fowl.* After having done so, we made our way into Wayne County, where we remained several days, enjoying the rich luxuries placed at our disposal by our friends in that county. We then took a scout on Black River, and stopped with a German, who had always professed great friendship for us, and who, on this occasion, greeted us very warmly, and seemed to put himself to a great deal of inconvenience to make us comfortable; he stood watch for us, as usual, while we slept in an unoccupied house. Our minds being free from suspicion, we slept quite soundly for three or four hours, but I was aroused by the sound of horses' feet; and by the time I had awakened my men, and made ready for our escape, we were completely surrounded. Through a crack I took a hasty peep, and saw our old friend, the German on horseback and in the line of the Federal soldiers.

FEDERAL STAMPEDE

At this juncture, two of my men were in favor of surrendering; I answered by telling them to follow me. There being a dense forest in front of the house, not more than one hundred and fifty yards off, I made for it in my fleetest manner, holding my gun in my left hand and my revolver in my right; I would have killed the Dutchman as I ran, but he was on the opposite side of the house; a whole volley was fired at us as we went, killing one of my men and wounding two more slightly, but not sufficiently to disable them from duty, and giving me four very slight wounds. As we passed out, we fired two or three shots a piece with our revolvers, killing two of their horses, and wounding one man seriously in the face.[1]

On gaining the woods we felt very well over our narrow escape, and made our way for a gap in the bluff, about half a mile off, through which we gained the point, and stopped to rest ourselves, and reloaded our pistols; after which we made our way to the top of the bluff, and discovered through the thick brush, at a distance of not more than two hundred yards, the Federals approaching slowly and cautiously toward us. I gave my men orders to fire in the same order in which they lay, that is for our extremes to fire on theirs, so that no two men would fire at the same Federal.

When fairly within gun shot I gave the word and we fired; four of them fell dead, and one fellow, badly wounded, broke down the hill calling loudly on the name of the Lord. Our rifles were quickly reloaded and we followed cautiously after them in the direction of our friend's house where we came so near being taken in; on gaining the edge of the woods we discovered them sitting on their horses, near the house from which we had escaped. They seemed to be holding a council of war; one of them who had on shoulder-straps, appeared to be making a speech. The distance being about one hundred and fifty yards some of my men objected to shooting, but I answered by giving the word slowly, "ready—aim—fire!" At the discharge of our rifles, four of them fell, and the gentleman with shoulder-straps was helped from his horse. At this juncture, they began to form themselves into about twenty different lines, with only one abreast, each man being in advance, and each one bringing up his own rear. It was a novel military position, a kind of "nix cum rous," but it worked well and in almost an instant they seemed to be spirited away, and we saw no more of them.

We made our way down Black River about two miles and camped for the night, and the next morning about sunrise I went to the house of a friend, who lived back in the woods to obtain provisions for my men. He told me that the Federals had left for Greenville immediately after our second round at them, and had given orders to some citizens to bury their dead, and on the following day to send the horses to Patterson, which they left in their care, and which included those they had captured from us; at which place they would meet them with a large force and proceed to exterminate the Bushwhackers.

I obtained what provisions we wanted and hastened back to camp. After eating we hurried over to the Patterson road, selected a good position, and waited impatiently for the men to come along with the horses. About ten o'clock in the forenoon an old man about sixty years of age, and three little boys came slowly along with them. After they had approached sufficiently near, we stepped out and I addressed the old man in a very friendly manner, and stated our business, at which he made some serious objections, remarking as he removed his old cobpipe, that it was rather against his orders, "to deliver the horses up to Sam Hildebrand." As the old man gave the horses up, I could easily perceive a smile of secret satisfaction lurking about his face. The little boys, however, were badly scared, and seemed to realize the fact that Sam Hildebrand had them. We took possession of the horses, fourteen in number, and according to previous arrangements, five of the boys struck for Green County, Arkansas, with them, while one of them stayed with me, on foot, for the purpose of killing the German who had betrayed us, and thus came so near having us taken in, and who had caused one of the bravest men in the Southern Confederacy, to be killed. After sending the old man and the boys away I took leave of my men, and with my comrade repaired to a neighboring hill, rested and slept by turns, until near sunset.[2]

From the position we occupied I had a fair view of the surrounding country, and particularly the main road leading to Patterson. But during the day all was quiet, save a citizen would occasionally pass along the road.

As night approached we became restless from inaction, and before the sun had shed its last rays upon the neighboring hills we were on our way to the scene of our tragedy the day before.

Arriving there before it was entirely dark we took our position in the fence corner near the house, and here we lay in silent impatience until the gray horizon warned us that our watch for the present was ended. We quietly retired to the house of a friend for our breakfast, not having eaten anything except a piece of corn bread since the morning before. Having partaken heartily of our friend's rough but substantial fare, we again repaired to the house of our treacherous German enemy, having sworn in our wrath to take his life before leaving the country, and succeeded in gaining a position within one hundred yards of his house and directly in front of the door. Here we remained all day, during which time the family seemed to be discharging their domestic duties very cheerfully. About four o'clock in the afternoon two strange men rode up to the house and held a conversation with the lady for several minutes and then rode off in the direction they came; this gave us some hope that the Dutchman would soon be at home. It was evident that as he had left with the Federals the day before in their retreat, and in great haste, that he had made no arrangements for a long absence; and it was more than probable that those two men only came to see whether or not the way was clear. We felt indeed that our most sanguine expectations were soon to be realized; but the hour passed slowly on; we changed our position after dark to a place in the fence corner, near the woodpile, and here we remained until the night was half spent. Then we were made glad by the sound of horses' feet coming from the direction of Patterson; as the sound came nearer we could easily perceive that the noise was made by only one horse.

Advancing slowly, the Dutchman approached the house, alighted at the woodpile and tied his horse to the end of one of the limbs within a few feet of us. Just then we arose and demanded his surrender. The old fellow was very badly alarmed and called alternately on the Almighty and Mr. Hildebrand for mercy; but I gave him to understand that it was useless for him to beg for mercy; that he was a prisoner and that we expected to take him to headquarters as a prisoner of war. His wife came out to the fence immediately on his arrival, and it was her presence alone that prevented us from shooting him on the ground.

I guarded him while my comrade went to the stable to look for another horse; but finding nothing there but an old mule, he came back leading it with a blind bridle.

I requested the lady to loan me a saddle, and she soon returned with her own saddle, and remarked that it was the only saddle on the place. I told her I could not rob a lady; to keep the saddle, and that I was sorry from my heart to be compelled to give her uneasiness or trouble; that war had no mercy, and that through it all I hoped that she would be protected from harm.

We tied the old man's hands behind him, and then tied him on the mule without any saddle; at which the mule humped up his back, gave us a specimen of mule melody on a base note that re-echoed among the hills, and then became more quiet. We started on leading the horse and mule, but we had to stop several times to let the mule finish braying, for he would not budge an inch until he got entirely through. We went about a mile and then proceeded to hang the Dutchman. He spoke only once and then the mule chimed in, and before he had finished, the Dutchman was swinging to a limb. To render his duplicity still more apparent, it should be borne in mind that he was now completely dressed in Federal uniform, having probably enlisted during his absence. Previous to the hanging, we had taken from him his pocket book and a revolver.

We now mounted the horse and mule, and went on about two miles, stopped at the house of a friend and called for something to eat. Our friend, on hearing what had taken place, plead manfully for the lady whom we had so lately made a widow, stating that she was a good woman, recounted many good deeds she had performed, and finished by adding that she would now be entirely dependent on the charity of the community for support, and insisted on us having the horse and mule sent back.

We readily consented to this, and told him also that we would much rather she had the pocket book also, for on counting the money we found that it contained forty dollars.

No one could deliver the mule, horse and money to her without being considered in some measure implicated. Finally it was agreed for our friend to take the horse and mule back while it was yet night; to leave them near the premises and to throw the pocket book over the gate into the yard. All things being arranged we started on foot for our homes in Arkansas, and arrived there safely.

Chapter Nineteen

Took eight men.—Attacked a Federal camp near Bollinger's Mill at night.—Lost two men killed and one wounded.—His men returned to Arkansas.—He went alone to St. Francois County.—Watched the farm of R. M. Cole to kill him.—Was checked by conscience.

I REMAINED TWO weeks at home plowing, and then went on a scout to the vicinity of Mingo Swamp with eight men. We watched around for several days to capture some infamous scamps in that country who had been giving our friends trouble from the beginning of the war. Being too cowardly to go into the army, they were staying at home and were constantly annoying peaceable citizens by making false reports against them of every kind.[1]

Having failed to get any of them, we concluded to make another trip over onto Castor Creek, for my men were always anxious to go to parts of the country frequented by the Federals. We had been on Castor but one day and night when a party of Federals came along, making their way through the country, and camping within a short distance of Bollinger's Mill. We were quietly enjoying ourselves in the nook of rocky range of brushy hills when a runner came to inform us of the fact. Of the exact number of Federals he did not know.

It was with some difficulty that I restrained my men to wait until a proper hour of the night before making the attack, but finally about ten o'clock I gave the word to get ready, which was done in a very few minutes. Going around the hills we struck the main road about a mile from their camp. We rode very slowly until we routed the pickets, then dashed on and crowded them into camp; but the locality of their camp and the position in which they had taken up quarters, had not been stated to us correctly; consequently we came out somewhat worsted.

They had chosen a narrow place in the road, and had turned their wagons across it, so that in our attempt to dash through their camp, as was our custom, we found our progress suddenly stopped; this bothered us so badly that they opened a heavy fire on us, killing two of my men and wounding another slightly before we had time to retreat. We were not certain of having killed any of them, but were afterwards told by a citizen that we wounded three, one of whom died next morning.[2] After this unfortunate mistake my remaining men wanted to go back to Green County, Arkansas, where our wounded companions could be properly cared for; to which I consented, and bidding them adieu I started alone to St. Francois County, Missouri.

I now thought this a favorable opportunity to take vengeance upon R. M. Cole for the course he had taken at the time my brother Frank was hung by the Big River mob. That matter had never yet been redressed, and my mind was yet harassed by conflicting impressions concerning his guilt or innocence in the matter. That he was a Southern man I very well knew, but that it was his duty, as a civil officer, to wrest my brother from the clutches of a merciless mob I knew equally well. I will here remark that all my evil impressions concerning his complicity in the hanging of my brother have long since been entirely removed from my mind; but at time of which I am now writing, I finally adopted the unwelcome conclusion that he was evidently guilty. I escaped the vigilance of my enemies, and of the hundreds of soldiers whose especial duty it was to watch out for me; and unobserved by any one who would be likely to inform against me, I succeeded in reaching his farm, on Flat River, and found to my joy that he had not yet finished plowing. I went around to the back part of the farm, hitched old Charley to a sapling in the woods, and taking old "Kill-devil" in my hand, I cautiously approached the cornfield where I had seen him plowing from a distance, and about sunset I secreted myself in a fence corner about ten rows from where he had plowed the last furrow. I waited until I became satisfied that he had taken out for the night. It was now about dark.

I went back to where I had hitched my horse, unsaddled him and went in search of feed. I soon found an abundance of oats already cut in the field. On my way back I chanced to cross a splendid melon patch; on the ripe melons I made out my supper, feeling thankful for my good luck so far.

My only chance now was to wait until morning, which I did, making myself as comfortable as possible during the night.

In the morning I took my station again in the fence corner with old "Kill-devil" already cocked. After a long delay, as I thought it, he made his appearance, following along behind the plow and singing most merrily. I was a little flustered by his merry mood, and a strange weakness kept me from firing. I thought I would let him plow one more round. I chuckled to myself as he walked deliberately away from me as if nothing was about to go wrong with him. He came around again as merrily as before. I once more raised old "Kill-devil" to my face and was in the act of pulling the trigger, when I heard a stick crack in the woods just as he was turning. This and some other imaginary noises caused me to delay until he was too far off to make a sure shot. Here was a good chance lost. This I thought would never do, for I was becoming quite nervous; I bit my fingers as I usually do to stop what hunters call the "buck ague," but it seemed to do me no good.

The more I thought of the matter, the more nervous I got, and I must acknowledge that I never felt that way before when I was in a just cause, and a thought struck me that there might be something wrong in this matter after all. I knew that it would never do to remain squatting in the fence corner any longer; that I must either shoot or leave.

Can it be possible that he is innocent of the charge brought against him by my friends, and that my suspicions are groundless?

It may be so! I began to think about letting the man live; but the thought of riding several hundred miles for the express purpose of killing a man, and then go back without doing it, after having had such a good chance was a thought that I did not like.

While these thoughts were revolving in my mind I still set as quietly as a mouse. Once I would have got up and left, but the man was now making his third round, and was too close for me to do so without being seen. I deliberately raised my gun and took a bead on him to make my decision while he was completely in my power—"live on, sir! live on!" was my decision, and as soon as I thought he was out of sight among the corn I rode away, and never before in my life did I feel so happy as I did when I passed opposite the row he was in. I bade him silent farewell, and mentally told him to rest easy, for that he never should be hurt by my hand.

On my homeward trip I stopped in the vicinity of Bloomfield (which was still in the hands of the Federals) in order to pay my respects to Captain Hicks. He was the commander of the company which followed me and my family to the St. Francis River; and boasted that he was the man who shot me at Flat Woods. Not being disposed to rob him of his honors, I was willing to admit that he did the act, and to govern myself accordingly.

I lay around his residence four days and nights, getting my provisions out of his smokehouse, before he made his appearance.

On the evening of the fourth day he rode up to his house, and in a few minutes walked out with his wife into the garden.

I walked up to the garden fence and spoke to him; he seemed agitated and started toward the house; I raised my gun, halted him, and told him to come to me as I wanted to talk a little to him. He halted and with some reluctance walked toward me, and on getting within a few paces he asked me who I was. I told him that I was Sam Hildebrand; that I understood he had been hunting for me for some time, and I thought I would come by and see what he wanted. At this he made a lick at me with a hoe which he held in his hand, and came very near hitting me; but in a moment I ended his existence by shooting him. I eluded all search and effected my escape to Arkansas.[3]

Chapter Twenty

Trip to Hamburg with fifteen men.—Hung a Dutchman and shot another.—Attacked some Federals in Hamburg, but got gloriously whipped.—Retreated to Coon Island.—Returned to St. Francis River.—Killed Oller at Flat Woods.—Robbed Bean's store at Irondale.

ABOUT THE MIDDLE of August 1863, at the solicitation of two brave boys who had kindly assisted me on several trips to St. Francois County, and expected my assistance in return, I started to a small place called Hamburg, with fifteen men under my command.[1]

We wished to take in three or four Dutchmen who had given the relatives of my two men a great deal of trouble, causing them to be robbed, and in some instances imprisoned.

We crossed into Butler county, and then into Stoddard; passing south and east of Bloomfield, we crossed Little River above Buffington and entered Scott County. By traveling together in the night we created no disturbance until we got near the point to which we were aiming.

About ten o'clock in the forenoon we rode up and surrounded the house of one of the men whom we were after. He recognized us as Union soldiers and came out without being called. He commenced addressing us in Dutch, but I told him that we did not belong to that persuasion; he then began speaking broken English and still advancing toward us. When in the act of extending his hand toward one of my men who was nearest to him, he suddenly discovered his unfortunate mistake, and called to his wife who was yet in the house. The whole family came out, placed themselves in a group near us and implored us in broken English to spare their father. To the bottom of my heart I cursed the man who first invented war; but as war on one side and mercy on the other would only lead to death, we marched our Dutchman off about a mile and hung him to a lean tree. About one hour afterwards we came to the house of another of those cunning informers; he broke out at a back door and ran so fast that we all had to fire before we brought him down.

We now pushed on to get a couple more who lived at Hamburg, but on entering the place were met by a volley of musket shots which made our ears ring. One of my men was killed on the spot, at which we charged the enemy, seeing that their numbers were only about twelve. They took refuge behind an old dilapidated frame house; and while I placed some of my men in positions to command both ends of the building, others marched up to the front of the house and set it on fire.[2]

By this time the shooting had attracted the attention of other Federals in the vicinity, who came to the rescue, and before we were aware of their presence we were nearly surrounded. We made a dash to clear their lines, and in the attempt four of my men were badly wounded, but none of them killed.

I began to think that I had met with more than our match, for as we retreated they followed us in a solid phalanx. Our horses were put to the utmost of their speed, our wounded were left behind, the chase after us was gloriously exciting; we probably gained a little after we had gone about two miles, but they did not by any means give up the chase, for we were not allowed to enjoy anything that had the least resemblance to peace and tranquility, until we had gained Little River and swam across to Coon Island. We lost nearly everything we had except our horses and they were badly injured; some of my men lost their guns, and others lost every bit of fight that they formerly had in them. The Federals made no attempt to cross the river, but left us to brood over the sad result of our rash and inconsiderate adventure. The whole matter looked to me a great deal like a defeat, and I must confess that I viewed it rather in that light, but if it had been the Army of the Potomac they would have called it "a strategic movement—merely a change of base."

We lost one man killed and four wounded, prisoners whom we supposed would be shot. In justice to General Steele, however, I can proudly say that in this case he did us more than justice by retaining our men as prisoners of war and treating them well.[3] Their wounds were healed, and in three months they were exchanged and returned to our Green County Confederacy.

On leaving Coon Island we struck the St. Francis River at Twelve Mile Creek, and remained there several days recruiting our horses. Not wishing to be idle, I concluded that while my men and horses were resting, I would take a trip on foot to Flat Woods and pay my respects to George F. Oller, who was so intent on bushwhacking me that he spent most of his time in the woods watching for my appearance on my accustomed routes.

Aside from his many boisterous threats against me he was in the habit of marking out "Old Sam," as he called me, on trees and shooting at the figure at various distances. His vindictive spirit was not manifested against me alone, but even against the children of Southern sympathizers. At one time he went to St. Francis River where some Southern boys were in the habit of bathing, and at the high rock from which they were fond of plunging, he drove some cedar stakes and sharpened the upper ends which were just under the water.

Fortunately when the boys next went there to bathe the water had fallen a few inches, and the ends of the stakes exposed so that the boys discovered them before making the fatal leap. Oller of course did all this for the patriotic motive of subjugating the South; but the result was that the little boys were saved and the country lost.

On arriving in the neighborhood I learned from a very kind German lady whom I happened to meet and who mistook me for a Federal, that the hunt for me was still going on.[4]

I learned also that Oller's zeal for the good of the Union cause was not in the least abated by his many failures to hit my figure which he had cut on a large oak near his house, nor by his failure to kill the innocent children whom he was afraid would be Rebels at some future time.

At night I went and inspected his premises, and before daylight I took my position; but the day passed off and he didn't make his appearance. When night came I repaired to the house of a friend, obtained two days' rations, returned to my ambush, and slept until the first peep of day. I was again doomed to disappointment; but on the third day, late in the evening, as I lay brooding over the many failures I had made to inflict justice upon those who were seeking my blood, Mr. Oller made his appearance.

He walked slowly up to the premises with his gun on his shoulder. On getting to a pig pen he got over the fence and commenced marking a pig. I shot him through and hastily left the place; on gaining the top of a small hill a few hundred yards off I heard the pig squealing, for Mr. Oller had fallen across it, and it was not able to extricate itself from the trap.

On getting back to my men I selected five of them to go with me, and permitted the rest to return to Arkansas.

As soon as it was dark I started with my five men for Irondale, on the St. Louis and Iron Mountain Railroad.

Just after dark on one evening in the early part of September, we entered the town. We saw no soldiers in the streets, and no one else, except Dr. Poston, a citizen of the place. We compelled him to knock at the door of Bean's store and ask for admittance; when this was done we entered without any trouble, took all the goods we could conveniently pack, and returned to Arkansas by the way of Black River.[5]

Chapter Twenty-one

Started with six men for Springfield, Missouri.—Deceived by a Federal Spy.—Was captured through mistake by Rebels.—Surprised on Panther Creek.—Returned home on foot.

I WAS UNDER obligation to assist some of my boys in a trip to the neighborhood from which they had been driven, in return for their services on several of my trips.

About the middle of September, after having only rested about a week, I started with six men from near Springfield, Missouri, to make a raid in the vicinity of that city. Not being acquainted with the country over which we designed traveling, I had but little to say in regard to the programme of our intended raid. After our plans were arranged, we started, taking with us "neither purse nor script," for we intended to rely altogether on our good fortune for our supplies.

From Green County, Ark., we traveled through Randolph and entered Missouri in Ripley County. Here we were detained, for one of my men had the misfortune to lose his horse. Having reached a part of the country known as the Irish Wilderness, we concluded to rest a day and hunt.

In the evening before we struck camp, a young man, dressed in citizen's clothes, who claimed to be going to the Rebel army, joined us, and asked permission to stop with us until morning. He professed to be going to Arkansas, and we readily consented to entertain him as best we could.

After the confusion incident to striking camp, making fires, attending to our horses, etc., was over, our new companion began a series of interrogatories relative to the part of the country through which we had operated, since the beginning of the war. After having posted him thoroughly in regard to the field of our operations, we related to him many thrilling incidents and daring adventures connected with our history; to all of which he listened with intense interest, and at the amusing parts of our story he laughed most heartily. After we grew tired of relating our many dangerous feats and bloody deeds, he began his narrative of hair breadth escapes and heroic adventures. The field of his operations having been Kentucky, we were very pleasantly entertained by receiving the full accounts of several incidents of which we had heard some rumors.

We had scarcely marked the transition from twilight to Egyptian darkness, so much we were pleased with our new companion's pleasant stories, when one of my men remarked that "the last hour of the day was melting away into the eventful past." Our programme for the day following had been made by our new comrade and heartily approved by us all, that we would take an old fashioned deer hunt, among the wild hills surrounding us.

Our quiet slumbers were scarcely disturbed even by the intermission of rolling over, until "Old Sol" was looking us fair in the face, as if to read the guilt of our hearts.

Upon awakening, one word loudly spoken was sufficient to bring the whole squad to a half recumbent position; and as we went through the antiquated performance of rubbing our eyes, the attention of each one seemed to be turned to the spot where our new comrade had deposited himself for a sleep a few hours before. He was gone! The fragment of an old log, that had served him as a pillow, was all that was left of him or his bed. But this was not all;—one of our best horses was gone! We cared but little for the horse, so far as his real value was concerned, for we had some experience in "raising horses," and knew that we could get another on very easy terms, but we did not like the idea of having been gulled by a young adventurous loyalist, in the face of the fact, too, that we considered ourselves "shark proof."

Neither were we certain that our misfortunes would end here, for our "Sharper" had succeeded in getting our plans for the entire trip.

During the preparation of our morning meal, the subject of our misfortune was freely discussed, with many conjectures in regard to who our deceiver was, and the probable result of his acquired information.

A majority of the men were in favor of continuing our journey, while only one man joined me in opposing any further movement in the direction of Springfield.

However, as it was not my own trip, I did not feel at liberty to say much about it; not wishing to appear obstinate, I contented myself with making them a "humbug" speech, for I must confess that the recollection of our unfortunate adventure at the place, seemed as though it would haunt me to the grave. All my arguments, however, did no good, they would not be convinced against their own will; so I submitted cheerfully to the good old democratic rule of going with the majority.

During the day, myself and two others, rode over to the edge of the settlements to get a horse for our pedestrian "bushwhacker," and succeeded in finding one; but the owner was a noted Rebel; our only way to sustain ourselves in the act was to pass ourselves off for Union soldiers, this we did with a very good grace and got the horse without any resistance. In fact, he made but little objection, for he knew that the "Union savers" were terrible when irritated.

After going back two or three miles toward our camp in the Wilderness, I saw some deer on the side of an adjoining hill, and fearing that the boys in camp had failed to kill meat for our supper, selected a nice buck and shot him dead on the spot.

After having dressed the meat preparatory to carrying it into camp, we concluded to build a fire and broil some of it for our dinner. While we were thus busily engaged, all squatted around the fire, we were suddenly saluted by a remarkably boisterous mandate of "surrender!" at which we sprang to our feet with our revolvers in our hands to find ourselves confronted by five of Capt. Bolin's men, who had left Green county, Arkansas, a few days before us, and were on a visit to see some friends in the neighborhood, from one of whom we had taken the horse. We had anything else rather than a fight, for we quickly recognized each other, and a general congratulation was the only military demonstration between us.

The five "bushwhackers" were concealed near the house of the old Rebel from whom we had taken the horse, and who had really regarded us as Federals. As soon as we had left his house, he reported us to Capt. Bolin's men, who took our trail and tracked us to the wild solitudes of the Irish Wilderness. We at once decided on changing our quarters. I sent my two comrades to the camp and had the boys to move over to the edge of the settlements. The old Rebel, from whom we had taken the horse, was our best friend; we gave it back to him, and got another in that neighborhood on the following night.

The reader, without making any very extravagant draw upon his imagination, can conclude that we had a jolly time when we all got together.

Our adventure with the sharper, my attempt to steal the old Rebel's horse, and our unconditional surrender in the Wilderness while broiling the venison, were the subjects discussed. From the boys, we learned something more of our adventurous Yankee detective. He had been in that neighborhood a week or two, repeating the same story he had told us. He evidently thought that the bushwhackers were rather thick in that neighborhood, and concluded to leave it as quick as possible.

On the following morning, our whole party, with myself, took up our march for Springfield, and in the evening of the same day we reached the vicinity of Thomasville, in Oregon County. We were warned against traveling in the day time, unless we were hunting for a fight; we assured our friends that a fight was the least of our desire at the present time, the object of our trip being solely for the purpose of enabling some of our boys to avenge certain wrongs received at the hands of Union men in Greene County, Missouri.

After making a tolerable heavy draw on some of our Rebel friends for provisions and horse feed, we again resumed our journey, and the following morning found us in the woods, quartered for the day, near a small town in Howell county, called Lost Camp, where we remained all day.

A substantial old friend living near by, brought us two or three bottles of "burst-head," which produced the effect of making some of the boys believe that they had fought a great battle, and that the United States government had taken refuge in a deep cavern, the mouth of which they had stopped with a large flat rock, on top of which the boys were dancing. The only question with them seemed to be what they would do with their twenty million of prisoners.

When sable light again clad the wicked world in half mourning, we resumed our journey, and on approach of day, we were in the beautiful little town of Vera Cruz, in Douglas County; on the next night we reached Panther Creek, in Webster County. One of our men who professed to be acquainted in that neighborhood, went to a pretended Rebel friend to get supplies, but the old fellow flatly refused to give him anything. I was a little amused at the disappointment of the boys, and at the dilemma in which they were placed. I could not help thinking how different I would have acted on a raid of my own.

About ten o'clock in the forenoon we were surprised by a party of Federal soldiers, numbering perhaps about sixty men. Before we were aware of their presence they charged upon us at a most furious rate, yelling and shooting at us most fearfully. A mere glance at the party was sufficient to convince me that an attempt at resistance would be worse than folly. I sprang to my feet, yelled out to the boys to run; but having no time to mount our horses, we had to depend upon our own fleetness for our escape. In our retreat through the dense forest, we had the advantage over our enemies; I and four others managed to keep together for about a mile; not seeing any pursuers, we took our position on a high hill, and remained there until late in the evening. While keeping a vigilant watch over the surrounding country, we discovered one of our men emerging cautiously from a dense thicket in the valley at the foot of the hill.[1]

He seemed terribly frightened. I made my way down the hill to within a hundred yards of him, and then called him by name; but it was some time before he recognized me. Fortunately for us, this man was acquainted with the country through which we would have to pass in making our way back to Arkansas. The tops of the highest hills were yet basking in the sun's last lingering rays, when we started on our perilous journey of two hundred miles on foot, without any blankets, provisions, or anything else, except our pistols and one gun, for I had made my escape with old "Kill-devil" in my hand. The next morning about daylight, we ran into a gang of sheep, succeeded in catching one, and made our way down into a deep ravine, where we could not be discovered. There we built a fire and fared sumptuously. We continued on during the night, and the next day I killed a deer. On the following night we reached our friend near Vera Cruz, and here we met another one of our boys, but he was no better posted in regard to the fate of our company than myself.

I will not weary the patience of my reader by detailing the many privations incident to our trip; suffice it to say that we did get back to Arkansas; and that fortunate for me I never received an invitation to take another trip to Springfield under the command of an unexperienced leather-head.[2]

About a week after arriving in camp, another one of the boys came in, looking somewhat subjugated. I afterwards learned that two of our men were killed when we were routed, and that the others were taken prisoners, none of whom ever returned during the war.

I have cautioned the boys never again to imagine themselves dancing on the flat rock covering the prison door of the defunct Yankee nation, lest they might unexpectedly find some of them yet running at large.

Chapter Twenty-two

Started with four men.—Surrounded in a thicket near Fredericktown.—Escaped with the loss of three horses.—Stole horses from the Federals at night.—Killed two Federal soldiers.—Suffered from hunger.—Killed Fowler.—Got a horse from G. W. Murphy.—Went to Mingo Swamp.—Killed Coots for betraying him.—Killed a soldier and lost two men.

I SELECTED FOUR good men and started on another trip to St. Francois County, Missouri on the 10th of November. We traveled altogether in the night; arriving in the vicinity of Fredericktown about midnight, we stopped at the house of a well-known friend, who expressed a great deal of surprise at seeing us there, stating that the cry of "Hildebrand," had been raised in the community about ten days previous, and that the Federals, with the assistance of citizens, had been scouting the woods between that place and Farmington ever since. He was no little amused when we told him that the report was utterly false, and that we were on a scout out westward at the time.

The report of my having been in that part of the country ten days previous, I was satisfied would work favorably to the success of our present enterprise, for it was not probable that they would make another search so soon after having made one so thoroughly.

After passing Fredericktown in the night, we learned that several companies of Federals, Home Guards and Militia, were hunting for me in every direction. In fact, we came near being discovered by several squads during the night. We hastened on into St. Francois County; Tom Haile and myself being in front, we took Farmington without firing a gun long before my other men came up. As we rode in, the streets were full of people, but we only had time to take a second look when the place seemed to be entirely deserted. Not a man, woman or child could be found, at which Tom laughed heartily, and remarked that he thought cellar rent ought to be very high in that place. When my other men came up Tom told them that we had found a beautiful town not claimed by anybody, "just laying around loose," and that he was sorry we could not take it along with us until we found an owner. We did not haunt the town very long with our unholy presence, but after going into a grocery, where we had to help ourselves, we took a hearty drink of some good old liquor that had been left by the generation that once lived there; then mounting our horses we left the lonesome place. Tom remarked that as we had no wounded man to leave there to garrison the town we had better leave for the "settlements." We went on to Big River to look after our old enemies but their consciousness of having committed such a catalogue of crimes against me made them the hardest men in the world to find.[1]

From there we went to a dense thicket near the residence of Mr. North, and being very tired and sleepy, we lay down, and slept very soundly until the morning sun was looking down upon our quiet retreat. Our old friend had supplied us with two days' rations and some shelled corn for our horses, so we had a complete outfit for a good rest.

While living at Flat Woods, I became acquainted with a man named John Fowler. He professed to be a strong Southern man, and having perfect confidence in his veracity, I entrusted him with many things in regard to my plans, that I withheld from the rest of my neighbors; but about the time that I was run off from there by the Federals, my friend Fowler joined the Union army.

On receiving this intelligence, I felt much mortified, and concluded at once that he had betrayed me, notwithstanding he sent me word on several occasions that I need not fear him. His duplicity, however, was so apparent that I determined to kill him on sight; this I had some hope of doing, as he seemed to enjoy some liberties, and often came into the neighborhood, but generally in company with other soldiers. On every visit he came to my house and conversed pleasantly with my wife, but I regarded him rather as a spy.

As we were traveling along on the present occasion, I ran suddenly on him about five miles southwest from Fredericktown. We met in a narrow path, and before he hardly had time to recognize me, I shot and killed him instantly.

I will here state that I had cause to regret this act afterwards, for I ascertained that he had deserted the Federals, and was on his way South to join the "Bushwhacking department" of the Southern army.

Whilst lying lazily around our horses, planning the future of our trip, we were suddenly startled by the sound of a gun near by, which was evidently discharged at one of us. A moment, however, was sufficient to satisfy me in regard to the nature of the case; we had been spied out, our horses tracked up, and our thicket surrounded. At a bound I lit in my saddle and was soon out of the thicket in an opposite direction from where the gun was fired. On reaching the open ground, I discovered the Federals coming around the woods, not having yet completed their circle. They fired on me, but the distance was too great, and I remained unhurt. My men had not taken time to mount their horses, but as they followed me on foot, one of them received a bruise on his back from a spent ball. In a few minutes our complete escape was effected, with no damage but the loss of four good horses.[2] The Federals followed us closely for about a mile, when we got far enough ahead to give them the dodge by turning at right angles into the St. Francis River bottom. We made our way back to within a mile of Fredericktown, where we remained the rest of the day. When night came we went in quest of our pursuers; we found them camped in a lane about six miles northwest from Fredericktown.

Our object now was to get horses. We made our way on foot toward them but found that the end of the lane was guarded; we went around to the other end and found it guarded also, while the horses were in the middle, tied to one of the fences. We then went around through the field, laying down the outside fence very carefully, and approached the lane fence on the opposite side from where the horses were tied. The night was very dark, but we could distinctly see a sentinel slowly walking his beat of about fifty yards, ourselves being at the end of the beat. When his back was turned, I lay the fence down easily; we sprang to a horse a piece, cut the halters, mounted and were off at full speed before he turned on the other end of his beat.

Our hasty flight of course raised an alarm in the camp, but we saw no more of the Federals that night. Being again mounted, we resolved to give them employment for a few days in hunting us, and for that purpose we took up our quarters in a place least expected, by going within a mile of Fredericktown onto a certain eminence, after having made a circuit around the side of a hill.

On the following day we slept by turns; I killed a pig with my knife near the house of a farmer, and cooked it in a deep ravine where the fire could not be observed; during the previous night we had stolen a sufficiency of feed for our horses. I concluded to go into Fredericktown to get a supply of ammunition which I did about ten o'clock in the night, by meeting with an old friend there who bountifully supplied us with all we needed.

We moved seven or eight miles in the direction of Pilot Knob, supplying ourselves with horse feed and provisions on the move.

When morning again made its appearance, I left my men in charge of the horses, and after instructing them where to meet me again in case of trouble, I went to the gravel road for the purpose of killing a Federal or two. I concealed myself near the road, and about 10 o'clock in the day, two came along and I let old "Kill-devil" off at one of them. They wheeled suddenly around and started back in the direction of Pilot Knob; the one I shot was badly wounded and bled freely. Only an hour afterwards a squad of perhaps ten came from the direction of Fredericktown. It was a quandary in my mind whether it was best to take a pop at them, or not, a feeling of revenge settled the matter. I fired, and one fell; at this they put their horses to full speed. Soon after they were out of sight, another came along in a very great hurry as if he was endeavoring to overtake the others; on coming up to the dead man he made a momentary halt, of which I took advantage and shot him through. I now concluded that I had done enough for the day, or enough, at least, to raise an excitement, so I went back to my men and we moved about twelve miles in the direction of Farmington, and near the St. Francis River on a high bluff, which afforded us peculiar advantages in the event of a fight, where we were compelled to remain several days.

My comrade, who had received a bruise on the spine, had by this time become so disabled by that slight injury, that he could not ride. The little amusement that I had taken on the gravel road was now creating quite a stir in military circles, and their search for us was carried on with a zeal worthy of a better cause.

Having called out the forces at Pilot Knob, Fredericktown and Farmington, with a large majority of the citizens, the search was made thoroughly and in earnest.[3] Squads frequently passed in sight of us, and within easy gunshot, but none of them ascended the high bluff we occupied. On the evening of the third day our provisions and horse-feed gave out, and each night I went out in search of more. Obtaining provender for our horses was a very easy matter, but getting provisions for ourselves was not only very difficult but extremely dangerous. I knew but few men in the neighborhood, and on approaching their houses I invariably found our well-known signal of danger —a towel hung on a nail outside the door. We could easily have killed a hog or a sheep, but we could not run the risk of making a fire to cook it. After our provisions gave entirely out, we were twenty-four hours without any food. During the second night I found some bacon in somebody's smokehouse. I knew not whether he was a friend or foe, and cared still less, but I took two hams to camp, which we ate raw.

On the sixth night our comrade was able to ride, and we moved about fifteen miles, stopping south of Fredericktown. Here a friend supplied us with the necessities of life and even brought food to our camp ready cooked for our use.

Our wounded companion, who was too much disabled to take any part in a raid, now obtained leave to return to Arkansas alone, while I and my other men started on a trip to St. Francois County.

In our business of killing enemies, we met with good success everywhere but on Big River. Up to the time of the present writing, a majority of those miscreants, with hands dripping with the blood of my brothers, are yet permitted to live. For several days and nights we watched around the houses of my old enemies, but to no purpose; it was impossible to find them. One of my men made his way around through the neighborhood to ascertain their whereabouts, and reported that they were all from home except Franklin Murphy; but Tom Haile was determined that I should not kill him.[4] He exacted a promise from me long ago that I never would molest him or any of his property. Haile was a man who wielded an influence over every one with whom he came in contact. He was ever in a perfect good humor; the clouds of adversity never seemed to throw a shadow on his brow; his heart was all sunshine, and his feet ever trod in the vales of mirth and gladness.

I plainly saw that so far as killing my old enemies was concerned my present trip was a failure. During all the incidents of my previous trips to Missouri, I never for once lost sight of that one leading object of my mind. The killing of Federals, in which I had taken such an active part, only afforded me pleasure by the reflection that they were a part and parcel of the same stripe, and in sympathy with the Big River vigilance mob.

I was now much in need of a good horse, and after talking the matter over with my men, Tom Haile and myself concluded to demand a good horse, bridle and saddle, from G. W. Murphy, a man whose nature it was to be quiet and inoffensive, and who had attended strictly to his own business during all the struggle.

He was abundantly able to assist us in the matter, and we considered that he ought to contribute that much toward the Southern cause. We were raised close together from boyhood, and I had nothing against him; but as he was well able to spare me a horse, I made the demand. He complied with the request after emerging (as I believe) from a barrel of feathers. His novel appearance caused Tom Haile, who was always fond of a joke, to tell him that he must not let Jim Craig see him in that condition, or he might capture him for a spotted mule, which Murphy, in his good humored way, passed off very well. We also took a horse from Orville McIlvaine, who lived on the place known as the Baker farm.[5] I had some anxiety to see him in order to make him break his well-known rule of never parting with a green back after it got into his safe; but his retiring nature prompted him to conceal himself in the garret until we departed.

We now rejoined the other boys and started back by way of Mingo Swamp. Before we reached that place we were warned by our friends that the Federals were thick in that locality.[6] About midnight we arrived at the house of William Coots (well-known as old Bill Coots), who had heretofore invariably represented himself as a Rebel of unusual bitterness. In answer to our inquiries, he told us that there were no Federals in the neighborhood, neither had there been any for more than a month. He also told us that the men we wished to find were then at home. I felt very much gratified on hearing statements so favorable to the success of our enterprise, and requested him to supply us with a few days' rations and provender for our horses, while we camped at a certain point not more than half a mile distant.

BETRAYED BY COOTS.

He readily consented, and gave us a very pressing invitation to come and take breakfast with him about sun up. To this we agreed, and at the time designated, we all left our camp and repaired to the house of our generous host, who received us with a great deal of what might be termed "Arkansas courtesy." It may be readily supposed that the scanty fattening process we had gone through while on the St. Francis bluff had produced a streak of lean running the whole length of our mortal bodies; and that the odor from the kitchen, of coffee, ham and eggs, with other ingredients intermixed with spices, made us for a time forget all other things on these mundane shores. When breakfast was announced and we were about to seat ourselves at the table, old Coots remarked: "Here, gentlemen, you can lay your arms on the bed," but it was not our custom to take off our arms at any time, so we seated ourselves at the table with them on. We were perhaps about half done eating when a ragged looking Federal stepped up to the door, and in an exulting tone said: "Well Coots, you got them, did you?" and bawled out "surrender," at which I sprang from the table, drew my revolver and shot Coots, seized my gun which I had left near the door, and cleared the door by about fifteen feet; I shot a Federal with my revolver which I still held in my right hand, and in a few bounds gained the woods unhurt, save a slight wound on the back of my head. My men attempted to follow without their guns, two of them were killed in their attempt to escape, while the remaining one (Tom Haile) soon got with me and we made our way to our horses. Fortunately the Federals had not found them. We tarried awhile for our comrades, but as they did not come up we were fearful that they were slain. Mounting our horses and leading theirs, we made our way to a canebrake about a mile off, and sent a citizen back to ascertain the real state of affairs. After taking an old bridle in his hand, he made his way over, inquiring of each person he met for a grey mare and a black colt.[7]

On passing the house of old Bill Coots he was halted, at which he did not seem to be the least alarmed, but expressed the utmost surprise when the whole tragedy was related to him. The worst part of the whole affair was that two of my men were killed and were lying at the time in front of the house. On receiving this news we started home to get a force sufficient to clean out the Federals, but on arriving in Green county, Arkansas, nearly all of our men were out on scouting excursions, principally toward the West.[8]

Chapter Twenty-three

Took ten men.—Went to Mingo Swamp.—Went to Castor Creek.—Medicine traffic.—Attacked two companies of Federals under Capt. Cawhorn and Capt. Rhoder.—Fought them seven nights.—Dick Cowan.—Went with Capt. Reed's men.—Attacked Capt. Leeper's company.—Killed fourteen and wounded eight.—Captured forty-four guns, sixty pistols, forty horses and four hundred dollars.

ON THE 15th day of December, 1863, I started back to Mingo Swamp with ten men, and met with no obstacles on our route after swimming the St. Francis River. When we got into the neighborhood of the unfortunate tragedy of our previous trip, we ascertained from reliable sources that the Federals left for Bloomfield on the day following the skirmish at old Bill Coots', and that the men we had been looking after so long had gone into the regular army.

We visited the house of our newly made widow, Mrs. Coots, for the purpose of seeing the graves of my two brave boys. She confessed that Coots had layed plans for my capture; that the Federals were camped only one mile off at the time, and that after I had consented to come to his house for breakfast, he went to the Federal camp and notified them of the fact and made arrangements to take me in. Finding no one in that vicinity to fight, we made our way over onto Castor Creek to a well known friend, who had, since the beginning of the war, acted as an agent for us in receiving and forwarding supplies and medicines. Hearing of no Federals in that portion of the country, and there being no persons in that quarter against whom we had enmity sufficient to induce us to invest any of our capital in bark or grape vines, we obtained the medicine sent to that place from Farmington, St. Francois County, Missouri, and started back for Mingo Swamp. On our way the monotony of our journey was suddenly relieved by seeing a Federal coming toward us, apparently riding very cautiously. We only got a glimpse of him as the road took him down into a small ravine out of our sight. We were very certain that he had not discovered us, so we got out of the road until he came up; when we halted him he seemed very much frightened, but surrendered quietly.

He told us that he had been to Cairo, Illinois, to see his family, and was on his way back to his command at Fredericktown. Upon the whole he gave such a good account of himself that we only disarmed him and took his green backs, which, however, only amounted to twelve dollars.

On the following night we heard of three more Rebel boys in the country and sent for them. After they agreed to try a trip with us, we left the drugs with a friend and went back onto Castor Creek to watch for the Federals who were in the habit of passing there on their road between Fredericktown and Cape Girardeau. We had been there but one night and day when we heard of two companies of Federals near by commanded by Captains Cawhorn and Rhoder.[1] As soon as it was dark we proceeded to spy out their exact locality and take a look at the surroundings. We found from their position and numbers that it would be entirely unsafe to charge through their camp as was our custom, and concluded to bushwhack them. During the night we killed twelve and wounded several more, as we were informed afterwards. When day again made its appearance we went about two miles into a dense thicket with our horses. We put out spies watching and waiting impatiently for them to move. Instead of marching, however, they were charging around the most public places in the vicinity, threatening Southern sympathizers with annihilation, but we got no chance to bushwhack them.

During the day a squad of them went to the residence of Dick Cowan, one of my men, burned his house and other buildings, and attempted an outrage on one of his sisters who happened to be there.[2] For several days the people in the neighborhood were compelled to suffer the most glaring insults and wrongs. Each night we renewed the attack, and killed one occasionally at all hours of the night. They stood our mode of warfare six days and nights, but early on the morning of the seventh day they started on their way to Cape Girardeau. During their march we stationed ourselves at convenient places, and as they came along poured a deadly fire into their ranks and then retreated into the woods. We thought by this means to induce them to follow us, but it only seemed to hurry up their march. This we repeated three times before they reached Cape Girardeau.

By this time we were anxious to see our families and started back to Arkansas. Taking our drugs that had been left with a friend, we soon met twenty-eight of Capt. Reed's men who insisted on our taking a trip with them to Wayne County, and perhaps as far north as Iron County.[3] To this I consented, detailing two of my men to take the drugs to Arkansas, we started on our way, marching in day time. We passed about twenty miles south of Bloomfield and on to Greenville, in Wayne County, arriving there about sunset, but did not find any Federal troops in the place to protect its loyalty. Soon after arriving in town we heard of a company of Federals on Lost creek under Capt. Leeper, and taking our informant for a guide we marched at once to give them a fight.

Reaching there about sunrise the next morning we charged their camp, running their pickets in at full speed, fought them only a few minutes, when those who had not got into the brush surrendered. In the fight we lost four men killed and six wounded, the latter, however, all recovered. Of the enemy we killed fifteen, wounded eight, and took ten prisoners besides the wounded. Our booty consisted of forty-four guns, sixty pistols, forty horses, four hundred dollars in green backs, and other articles of value to us and to our families.

The subject of what disposition we would make of the prisoners came up, and in cases of the kind we were purely democratic, so we took the vote whether we would kill them or set them loose.

In consideration of the wrongs my family had received at their hands, and of their well-known cruelty, I made a speech in favor of killing them and voted accordingly.

When the whole vote was counted I found myself in the minority by just two votes; but true to my word I released them, unarmed and on foot.

In the evening before we had attacked them they had killed an old man by the name of Tom McKee and burned his house with other buildings. This fresh outrage was not known to us until they were gone, or we undoubtedly would have shot them. On being informed of this fact, however, we sent a scout after them, but they had left the main road and secreted themselves in the thick woods. The wounded, however, were at our disposal, but we did not, during the whole war get mean enough to imitate our enemies by killing wounded prisoners, but placed them at the house of a widow woman who promised to take care of them until the Federals at Pilot Knob could have them removed.

We procured a wagon and loaded it with our booty; took our six wounded men and started back to Green county, Arkansas, where we arrived without any difficulty, and found all things right at headquarters.[4]

Chapter Twenty-four

Took fifteen men.—Captured three Federals.—Hung one.—Captured a squad of Federals.—Reception of "Uncle Bill."—Hung all the prisoners.—Captured five more, and hung one.

AFTER SPENDING THE winter very agreeably, on the 10th day of March, 1864, I concluded to make a raid to the vicinity of Jackson, Cape Girardeau County, Missouri, with fifteen men, several of whom were from that county, and knew the people and county well.[1]

It was to remunerate these men for the invaluable services they had rendered me on several of my trips that I consented to go with them.

We passed through Butler County into Stoddard, leaving Bloomfield to the south a few miles, crossed the southeast corner of Bollinger and into Cape Girardeau.

Having traveled very slowly, and altogether in the night, we had created no disturbance on our way, nor interfered with any one, for it was our custom to make no demonstrations until we were ready to return.

In the latter part of the night we arrived in the vicinity of Jackson, selected a good place and camped for the day, during which time some of the boys visited their friends. One of my men who was an entire stranger in that part of the country, went into town to get whiskey, and to see what was going on.

On returning late in the evening he told me that there were three Federals in town who seemed to be well acquainted with the people, and that they were behaving very well. He wanted to take some of the boys and go back after them, to which I consented. They started off in eager haste, but soon returned with the three prisoners, having met them in the road some distance from town. Not knowing them I retained them as prisoners until the boys came in who knew them. Being governed by their statements, I released two of the Federals and kept the other as a prisoner and took him with us when we started that night for White Water, but we did not take him far before we tied him to a limb.

On White Water we remained inactive several days, receiving the kindest treatment from our Southern friends, which enabled some of my men to visit their friends and relatives.

About sunset one evening a citizen came to us and stated that about an hour before nine Federals had passed the road, and the probabilities were that they would stop for the night at the first house.

The night was now growing very dark, and we were soon under full pursuit of them. On nearing the house, however, we rode very slowly, and tied our horses in the thicket at some distance, and approached the premises very cautiously. It was a double hewed log house, with an open hall between them, with a small cooking apartment forming an ell to the main building, but separated from it by a narrow hall also.

After forming my men in a line around the house I crept to the windows and peeped into both rooms, only one of which, however was lighted, and in it I could see no one except a very old lady, who might have been a grandmother, and some little children who were grouped around the old lady, and who seemed to be holding a very earnest conversation with her in a very low tone. I went around to the kitchen window, and upon looking in to my great joy I saw the Federals eating their supper.

The position I occupied was a very easy one, and their conversation was so peculiarly interesting that I could not refrain from listening. They were using very vulgar and indecent language to the lady, who, with all the kindness and amiability characteristic of her sex, was waiting upon the ruffians while the old gentleman was seated on a box in a corner of the room exposed to the most outrageous insults, accompanied with threats of the most heinous character; but in silent fear the old man bore their criminal epithets and bitter curses without returning a word.

By this time I had heard all that my weak humanity could bear. I retreated from my position, passed around the circle, and collected my men at the entrance to the kitchen into the open hall, this being their only place of egress, and placed an equal number of my men on each side. I now stepped into the door and demanded a surrender, at which my men became impatient and rushed for the door, but I prevented them from entering. Each of the Federals pushed back his chair, at which I told them that I would shoot any man who should attempt to arise from the table with his arms, admitting my men at the same time. At this the Federals placed their revolvers on the table and retired according to my command to the fartherest end of the room and formed in a line.

By this time our little disturbance had aroused the old grandmother and the little children in the other house, who came to the scene, the children screaming in a terrible manner, and clinging to the old lady's dress for protection. On reaching the kitchen, however, the scene was quite different from what they had expected. They halted a moment at the door in dreadful suspense, then suddenly the oldest girl, who was about eight years of age, sprang suddenly into the room, exclaiming "Well, grandma! if here ain't Uncle Bill!" then seizing one of my men by the hand she sobbed aloud, "Oh Uncle Bill! don't let the soldiers kill pa!" at which the whole household greeted "Uncle Bill." The old gentleman last of all approached my man who had been recognized and greeted with so many smiles and such marked distinction, giving his hand slowly while the tears trickled down his weather-beaten cheek, and only said: "Bill, I'm glad to see you," my comrade receiving his hand and retaining it for perhaps half a minute, said nothing, but turned and introduced me as Major Hildebrand to his relative, and to the household. As I stepped forward to receive the salutation of the old gentleman of whom I had heard so much, and knew so little, I heard one of my prisoners remark, "a hell of a Major" and upon casting my eyes around I found them ready to burst into a derisive laughter, which I must confess took me a little back.

At this I ordered one of the rooms forming the main building lighted, and stationed my men properly, I marched my prisoners out of the kitchen through the little hall into the room of the main building, put a guard over them and pickets around the house, I returned to the kitchen with my man now known as "Uncle Bill," to have a talk with the old gentleman while his wife was hastily preparing a nice little supper for us all. The old man again took me by the hand, thanking me for my coincidental visit, stated that the Federals had made several trips into the neighborhood after him, but heretofore succeeded in eluding their search. He also stated that the only charge they had against him was for feeding bushwhackers, and that when the soldiers came up to his house on the present occasion, just after dark, they were in the hall before he saw them, and he had no possible way of escape except through them.

Considering his escape so very uncertain, he resolved to submit to his fate, and that when we made our timely appearance he was a prisoner, sentenced to be executed as soon as they were done supper. He wound up his statement by saying: "Well, Major Hildebrand, I must confess I am very agreeably disappointed in your general appearance; I have long been anxious to see you, and am surprised that you never called on me before, but if you had done so I should never have taken you for Sam Hildebrand. I was led to believe, by hearing of your exploits, that you certainly were a rough looking customer, a perfect 'raw-head and bloody-bones;' and that Belzebub himself would have been daunted by your ferocious appearance."

Supper being announced eight men were left to guard the prisoners while the others were eating, until all had partaken of the sumptuous repast. We were now ready for business, we marched our prisoners out to the fence in front of the house, tied their hands securely behind them, placed them on their own horses and tied their feet together underneath. Then mounting we started south, leading the horses on which the prisoners rode. Having traveled very fast we reached a part of the country as day began to approach in which we felt perfectly safe.

Leaving the road we went into a deep ravine about fifteen miles northeast of Bloomfield, covered with thick undergrowth and sheltered by heavy timber. Here we hung our prisoners. They were really brave fellows, and submitted to their fate without a murmur, and during our march that night they showed not the least sign of being conquered, but said they were McNeal's men, and that when they went into the army it was for the purpose of killing Rebels, and that some of the worst Rebels they had killed were men who were staying at home, and the most of them professing to be "loyal."[2]

After disposing of our prisoners, we secreted our horses in a dense thicket, and ten of us took our station on a road leading from Benton, Scott County, Missouri, to watch for Federals. We remained here nearly all day, without seeing any, and were thinking about giving it up as a bad job and returning to our camps; but when the sun was about an hour high, in the evening, we discovered five Federals winding their way slowly toward Bloomfield.

My men were divided into two parties, and were stationed about one hundred yards apart. We allowed them to get nearly opposite the second squad of which I was one, then we stepped suddenly into the road before them and demanded a surrender, to which they submitted, but seemed very much alarmed. On calling up my men who had been stationed farther down the road, and who stood at this time behind the prisoners, they seemed somewhat relieved as they recognized one of them as being an old acquaintance, who extended his hand cordially to all of them but one, remarking to him that he would not shake hands with him "until he met him in hell."

They now dismounted and surrendered up their arms and their horses. I then marched them out of the road to a safe distance into the woods and inquiring of my man who had recognized them, concerning their character. He reported that all of them were his acquaintances of long standing; that four of them were very clever fellows, these I released immediately; but the fifth one we hung after investigating his case.

When night came we mounted our horses, and taking our booty with us, started back to Arkansas.[3]

Chapter Twenty-five

Put in a crop.—Started to Missouri with nine men.—Killed a soldier near Dallas.—Went to St. Francois County.—Watched for Wall and Baker.—Watched near Big River Mills for McGahan.—Came near shooting Mr. Sharp.—Robbed Burges, Hughes, and Kelley of their horses.—Robbed Albright's store.—Captured some Federals on White Water.

AS WE ALL belonged to the "Independent Bushwhacking Department of the Confederate States of America," and were entirely dependent on our own exertions for a livelihood, it was necessary now that we should put in our crops.

For nearly two months, Crowley's Ridge on which we lived, and the adjacent country, looked as if it contained an industrious little community of "honest farmers."

The axe was heard in every direction; the smoke from burning brush was curling up from a thousand fires, and at night the little boys and girls were making bright fires until midnight, under the impression hinted at by their fathers that it was "such fun." All day long the women were out in full force with their hoes and their rakes, unmindful of the music of crying babies heard at nearly every cabin. Mothers were nearly always deaf while planting out onions; it is a little season of orphanage through which most children in the country have to pass once a year. We have all passed through that bitter day with red eyes, and it is no wonder that the sight of an onion in after life is so apt to bring tears in our eyes.

I put in a good crop of corn, and my wife made an excellent garden with no help but the children. I am very much tempted to brag a little on my excellent wife, but if I were to assert that I had the best wife in the world, each one of my male readers who are married would want me to except his own; this would render the exceptions so numerous that my wife would come nearly last, so I will say nothing about it, and keep my own opinion to myself.[1]

After plowing my crop over once I made preparations for another trip to Missouri, but we had all got into such a good humor while busily engaged in farming, that we were nearly two days recounting our grievances before we were mad enough to think of snatching our enemies into eternity.

Taking nine men, one of whom had served under Quantrel, we started on the 25th day of May, 1864, for another raid into Missouri.[2] Crossing the St. Francis River at the southwest corner of Stoddard county, we went into Scott county and watched three days and nights to catch some men we were after, but failing in this we went in the direction of Dallas, the county seat of Bollinger.

My men wanted to return, as nothing of an exciting interest had transpired so far; but at my earnest solicitation they agreed to go with me one more day. The next morning we were traveling in day time, and had not proceeded more than four or five miles when we discovered a party of Federals, seven in number, who had discovered us and were under full speed toward the town of Dallas, which was at that time garrisoned by about one hundred Dutch soldiers. We dashed on after them; the race was a very exciting one. When we had gone about six miles we began to gain on them, and when we got within a mile of the garrison one of their horses fell, giving the rider a thump on the ground that knocked him senseless until we were upon him. We disarmed him, and as his horse had not left, we made him mount and go with us about two miles in the woods.

The Dutchman seemed very much alarmed, and gave us enough broken English for a good sized volume; but as soon as we arrived in a thick timbered hollow between the hills, we quietly sent his spirit back to the Rhine where it never should have left. In a few hours we called at the house of a friend, fed our horses, and got some refreshments for ourselves.

To the Flat Woods, in St. Francois county, we then made our way, and remained there about twenty-four hours, after which we went to the extreme northern part of the county and concealed ourselves among the Pike Run hills. Those hills are perhaps the most rugged part of the whole State, and are covered with a dense thicket of underbrush, making it a wild, uninhabited wilderness. These hills not being far from Big River, they afforded me a secure place for my temporary headquarters while searching around for my enemies.

Early in the morning I engaged the services of a well known friend, who feigned business in several parts of the neighborhood, who returned at night and reported that only two of my persecutors were at home, whose names were James Wall and John Baker.[3]

On the following morning when the light of day again pierced through the gloom of our retreat I went and stationed myself near the house where they both resided.

I did not watch long before Wall came out onto the porch. But I had failed to get a position sufficiently near for me to kill him at the house; I was watching for them to come to the wood pile, which would only have been about one hundred yards. I could always hit a spot as large as a man's hand at that distance with old "Kill-devil."

About ten o'clock two men rode up to the house, alighted and went in; they came out again in half an hour followed by both Wall and Baker, who started off in an opposite direction from where I lay. I then changed my position to the opposite side of the house, thinking they probably would return soon.

I remained quietly until the sun had dipped behind the western hills, then I returned to camp where I again found my friend who had acted as a spy for me. He told me that he had seen Baker and Wall going in the direction of De Soto with two other men, one of whom stated to him that "Sam Hildebrand was thought to be in the country, from the fact that strange and very rough looking men had been seen at several public places, and that they were thought to be Hildebrand's men."

The reader will here understand that these unwarrantable scares were very frequent in this vicinity; one poor ragged stranger making his appearance in the neighborhood was sufficient at any time to raise the cry of "Hildebrand," at which all who had wronged me would squat like young quails.

Knowing that any further efforts to kill either Wall or Baker would be fruitless, I concluded to run the risk of watching the town of Big River Mills, which was at that time a place of rendezvous for the Militia, where they generally collected before starting out against me.

I accordingly took my station on a bluff overlooking the main road leading from the settlement of my old enemies to that place, being about a quarter of a mile below the town and fifty yards from the road. At daylight I was on the bluff and ready for business. During the day people passed the road at intervals of from fifteen minutes to half an hour; but none of them were the men I wanted to kill. From the position I occupied I could easily recognize the features of any one with whom I was formerly acquainted.

In the evening, about an hour by sun, I discovered a man riding slowly and alone toward the town, whom I recognized as Joe McGahan. A thrill of intense satisfaction pervaded my whole system, which it would be folly in me to attempt to describe. The English language from its high standard of dignity to its inexhaustible mine of seething invective would be inadequate to describe the supreme contempt I felt for that man. When I reflected that one of the men who had dipped his hands in the blood of my brothers was now within the range of my gun, my feelings of joy, mingled with a hope of success was indescribable. Nearer and nearer he came, unconscious that retributive justice was hanging over his head; and as he approached the desired point I raised my trusty rifle to my face, placed my finger on the trigger, and was nearly in the act of pulling when the man turned his face a little toward me, when I discovered the sad and almost fatal mistake, that instead of being McGahan it was a man by the name of Sharp. He was a Union man living near by, but was a worthy man and highly esteemed by all who knew him. I almost involuntarily hailed him in order to explain and apologize, but was checked instantly by the return of reason. As he passed slowly out of sight my eyes were riveted on him until a point of the bluff around which he had passed broke the spell. I was deeply absorbed in thought, and the question naturally arose in my mind, why I should have been so often thwarted in my attempts to meet out justice to one who was a scourge to the land that gave him birth, and who had not even the magnanimity of the rattlesnake whose alarm is heard before the blow is struck.

I arrived finally to the conclusion that his Satanic Majesty, who still ruled the infernal regions without a rival, was jealous of his protege upon earth where he still needed his services, and that he wished to delay the period when he would be compelled to doff his crown to a superior.

I did not remain long in ambush after I had come so near committing a terrible error; but hastened through the woods, back to my retreat among the Pike Run hills, and found my men awaiting my return with anxious impatience. As soon as it was dark we started south, and after midnight reached the pinery, southwest from Farmington, and slept there until late in the morning. Our horses were much fagged, we saw that it was best to swap them off before proceeding on our journey.

During the day we stationed ourselves near the plank road between Farmington and Pilot Knob, to watch for an opportunity of exchanging horses. A large company of Federals passed by, but they were too numerous for our purpose. Toward evening we saw three men approaching who were mounted upon fine looking horses. The names of the men were Burges, Hughes and Kelley. We lost no time in capturing the party, and to prevent them from reporting us too soon, we made them go with us several miles over the rugged hills and deep ravines.

Not understanding this movement, they seemed much alarmed, thinking probably that we designed "barking" them.

Old man Burges begged manfully for his life, and shed an occasional tear; but I told them that as they were not Federal soldiers, and that as I had no personal animosity against them, it would be barbarous in the extreme for us to harm them. We took their horses, gave them our own and then released them. They left seemingly well pleased with the arrangement, and as we had rather out-jockeyed them, we certainly had no right to complain.

We kept near the road leading to Pilot Knob until near sunset, when we came to Albright's store. Albright was a good Union Dutchman, and was not in the habit of crediting bushwhackers, so we robbed his store of all we wanted and then taking to the woods we changed our course.

Night soon overtook us, and we traveled eastward until we got into the neighborhood where Mr. Bess resided, on White Water. It was now late in the morning, and we took our position on the top of a high hill where we had a fine view of the surrounding country, and especially of the main road along which the Federals were in the habit of passing from Cape Girardeau to Fredericktown.

In the evening, while most of us were sleeping, my pickets discovered a small squad of soldiers about a half a mile off, making their way Westward. On being awakened I directed my men to follow me, went down to the road which was skirted by very thick undergrowth, where we secreted ourselves in two parties about fifty yards apart, giving orders not to fire on the Federals unless they showed fight or attempted to run. When they got near the second squad we stepped out into the road and demanded them to surrender. Our appearance was so sudden that they had no time to draw their weapons. Several of them wheeled their horses for a run, but on discovering themselves faced on that side also they threw up their hands in token of a willingness to surrender.

I made them dismount and stack their arms against a tree; after which we marched them into the woods to where our horses were and proceeded to question them.

Then I told them who I was, at which they seemed rather pleased, and remarked that they had often heard of me, and although they had no desire to fall into my hands as prisoners of war, yet they always wished to see me.

I asked them if they had not heard of me as being a bushwhacker and withal a very bad man, and that I was in the habit of killing all my prisoners. "Oh yes!" said their leader, "we have heard that you did not regard the life of a personal enemy as of any value, but we have seen several men whom you had released who told us that you were quite a different man from the fabulous blood-thirsty Hildebrand we had heard so much about in timid circles."

Upon producing papers which satisfied us that they were neither McNeal's or Leeper's men, but belonged to the command of Col. Beverage of Cape Girardeau, we released them unarmed and afoot.[4] We went on toward Bollinger's Mill, but when in that vicinity on the next morning about sunrise, we met two Federals in the road, who instantly wheeled their horses and dashed through the woods at full speed.

Being burdened with the horses and the arms we had taken from our prisoners on the day previous, all of us could not engage in pursuit. Captain Snap, myself and two men started after them at full speed, and caught them in less than half a mile. They stopped and threw up their hands before we were within two hundred yards of them. I was almost tempted to shoot them for being cowards.

After taking them back to our boys, we went on the top of an adjacent hill and camped for the day. We ascertained from the prisoners that they were new recruits, which was corroborated by some letters from their friends which they happened to have in their pockets.

Knowing that they had not been in the army long enough to have committed many depredations, we decided to release them; but as we were already burdened with horses we took them along with us to assist with our stock until we had passed Mingo Swamp, and then released them. A few days afterwards we arrived safely in Green County, Arkansas.

Chapter Twenty-six

Started to St. Francois County, Missouri.—Hung Vogus and Zimmer.—Hung George Hart.—Concealed in Pike Run Hills.—Started back.—Hung Mr. Metts' negro, and another one.—Took two deserters back and hung them.

AFTER REMAINING A few days with my family, I yielded to the solicitation of Captain Bowman to take a trip to St. Francois County, Missouri for the purpose of capturing a young man by the name of George Hart, who, on a scout with some militia, had killed Captain Bowman's brother in order to get a very fine horse that he rode.

Our company, consisting of nine men, started on the 20th day of June, 1864; we traveled altogether in the night, and on the morning of the 26th we camped for the day on Wolf Creek, about six miles from Farmington. During the day one of my men clad himself in citizens' clothes which we always carried along for such emergencies, and went into Farmington to see the sights and to get a bottle of good old "tangle-foot."

When night came our man had not made his appearance; we immediately arrested a couple of Dutchmen for the purpose of eliciting information from them concerning the military force in town thinking that probably my man had been taken in by the soldiers as a spy. The men we arrested were Henry Vogus and John Zimmer, who stated that there were no forces in town at that time, and that there had been no soldiers there for nearly a month. They affirmed that they had been there that day, and that if we did not believe them they would go with us to town and prove the matter. At this juncture my man came in and reported a company of soldiers in the town who had been there for some time. It was now evident to our minds that the Dutchmen were aiming to trap us. I will here state that during the whole war the Dutch went further, tried harder and risked more for my capture than any other people. A very short consultation was sufficient to seal the fate of our two prisoners on the present occasion; we hung them and went on our way rejoicing.[1] Passing a short distance east of Farmington, we stopped at the house of Ross Jelkyl, who was at that time Provost Marshal, and took such things as we needed.[2] Some of my men were anxious to kill him, but he had befriended me on one occasion, and I would not permit them to do so.

From there we went to the residence of Charles Hart, where we found his son George, whom we were after. We stationed men at the back door and demanded admittance at the front; the old man in a short time opened the door, and in obedience to our orders struck a light. On demanding George Hart he made his appearance, looking very much condemned. On asking him about the horse he had taken when he murdered young Bowman, he stated that he had traded him off, and that he was out of the country. We then told him that he must go with us, to which he made no objection, but was very anxious to know what we wished to do with him; we told him to wait and see. Before we had taken him far, he became satisfied that he would be killed, and made us some offers for his life, which Captain Bowman silenced in a few words by asking him if he thought he was able to pay for the life of young Bowman whom he had murdered in cold blood. We traveled about eight miles with our prisoner, during which time he made a complete confession.

Daylight began to appear; we were now about a mile from Big River Mills, and not wishing to be encumbered by a prisoner, we took some hickory bark and hung him to a dogwood sapling. One of his feet touched the ground, so we placed it in the fork of a bush, which completed the process of hanging.[3]

The main object of our trip having been accomplished, our next move was to get supplies of summer clothing for our families, which we decided on taking from an old meddlesome Union German in Jefferson County by the name of Lepp, who had a store on a small creek called Swashen. We accordingly proceeded to the place and found the old man in his store; he was closefisted and not in the habit of crediting, but we succeeded in getting all we wanted at very low figures, and after promising him our patronage in the future we started back.

Knowing that our operations about Farmington would create a great excitement, that the forces at Pilot Knob, Farmington, Potosi, Fredericktown and the Iron Mountain with the irrepressible Big River Militia, would all be put on our trail, we decided to travel by night and to get out of the country as soon as possible. But we were overruled by a power higher than our own, and our plans were in some measure thwarted.[4]

On our way to rob Lepp's store, one of my men complained of feeling unwell, and by the time we had rode ten miles on our return he became too sick to sit upon his horse. We retreated to a cave in the Pike Run hills where we could conceal ourselves, our horses and our goods while administering to the wants of our sick comrade. Our situation here was indeed a very critical one, and had it not been for the kindness of a true Southern friend, who supplied us at night with provisions and horse feed, we undoubtedly would have suffered; he risked his own life to save us, and in addition to his other acts of kindness he procured the services of a physician, who checked the disease in a few days.

It is needless to state that during all this time the country was literally flooded with Federal soldiers who hunted for me on their same old plan, of riding along the road, threatening women and children, and killing chickens.

After remaining at the Pike Run hills seven or eight days, our comrade was sufficiently recovered to mount his horse. As he was yet quite weak we thought it best to travel during daylight at the commencement of our trip. We rode slowly through the woods, and avoided the soldiers by keeping out of the public roads, and by shunning all places where liquor could be obtained. On reaching the vicinity of my brothers-in-law, on Flat River, we met old Isaac, a negro belonging to Mr. Metts, carrying a bridle around his shoulder. As we were dressed in Federal uniform he mistook us for Union soldiers, and in answer to our inquiries, made a lengthy report against the Southern men in that neighborhood, clearly implicating the Simms family as well as the Shannons and Sweeneys. He said he would have reported sooner, but that he was afraid they would suspicion him and get Sam Hildebrand to put him out of the way.

The report he made to us, if told to a squad of Federals, was sufficient to have consigned those Southern men to an ignominious death without any further evidence. The charge was this: that in his opinion "if Sam Hildebrand was to call at their houses and ask for something to eat, that they would feed him until he was as plump as a stuffed turkey." Some of my boys wanted to shoot him to prevent him from making that awful revelation to the Federal authorities; but I objected, because the sound of a gun might lead to our discovery. We quietly lashed him to a horse which we were leading, took him among the hills toward Westover's mill and hung him. On searching his pockets for a knife I found a pocket book containing sixty-four dollars. Some of the boys proposed that as they seemed to have money we should take in a few negroes until our pockets were replenished. On the next day we came suddenly across one in the woods; as we were traveling slowly it was necessary that we should get through the country without being reported. Having no spare rope, we hung the negro with hickory bark; but on searching his pockets we found nothing but a cob pipe.

Nothing else worthy of note occurred until we reached the vicinity of Greenville. While camped for the day on a high elevation, we discovered two men coming up the hill toward us. They came leisurely up the hill, walking as if they were very tired, and got within fifteen steps of our camp before they discovered it. Their first impulse was to run, but we ordered them to surrender, and they abandoned all idea of being able to make their escape. They proved to be deserters from the Federal army at Ironton, who were making their way to their homes at New Madrid. One of my men knew them well, and to him they are indebted to this day for their lives. We kept them with us until night and then permitted them to continue their journey.

We were no little amused at the many horrible tales of pillage and bloodshed that they said were reported daily at the Federal camps about my depredations. The strangest part of it was that many of those enormities were committed on the same day and in localities very remote from each other.

When night came the rest of the company proceeded on to Arkansas; but Captain Bowman, Traster and myself concluded to go into Shannon County after a couple of deserters who, in the early part of the war, had belonged to Captain Bolin's command. While with us, however, they were of no service, being too cowardly to fight and too lazy to steal; but since their desertion they were constantly reporting every squad of rebels who visited that section of country, and were in the habit of annoying Southern citizens in that neighborhood.

On reaching the neighborhood where they lived we learned that they had gone to Ironton, and the supposition was that they had gone there for the purpose of joining the Union army. But on the next day they returned; we quietly arrested them, got them out of the country without creating any alarm and marched them back to Green County, Arkansas, where we hung them in the presence of the command.

Chapter Twenty-seven

Started with nine men to St. Francois County.—Stopped in the Pike Run Hills.—Robbed the store of Christopher Lepp.—Hung Mr. Kinder's negro.—Attacked by Federals.—Killed two and lost a man.—Shot two soldiers on a furlough.—The strange camp.

I HAD NOT been at home long before I formed the acquaintance of a man by the name of Gibson, who had come to our little Green County Confederacy for the purpose of joining the "bushwhacking department." Gibson was a man possessing some superior advantages over most of Capt. Bolin's men; he had an accomplished education, and was endowed with a peculiar faculty of making all the men like him. He was the best marksman in our whole company, with one single exception; and that exception, I must modestly assert for the sake of truth, was myself.

On the 16th day of July, I selected Gibson and eight other men for another trip into St. François County. Having made so many failures in that quarter, I had some forebodings that I would again meet with disappointments; but I had long since resolved to let my old enemies have no peace while I labored under no greater disadvantages than I did. It is true that they were backed by a great nation of untold wealth, whose enemies actually in the field numbered more than one million and a half of armed men, and whose line of garrisoned territory extended one hundred and fifty miles south of their nest on Big River; yet while I thought that I was backed by the South with her armies of three hundred thousand men, I asked no better amusement than that of striking at my enemies under the ponderous wing of Federal protection.

Unlike my enemies, I had no commissary department, no steam presses running night and day striking off greenbacks, no outlet to other nations by commercial treaties, no people at my back willing to be saddled with a debt of three or four thousand million of dollars merely to carry into effect a Utopian idea. My long marches had to be made in the night and with the utmost caution and secrecy. The woods were my home, the moon my orb of light, and the hooting owls my spectators.

My enemies long since had learned to fear my name; the fear of retributive justice was sufficient to make them cower; their militia organization only assumed a tangible shape when I was absent; for on my approach they secreted themselves so securely that nothing short of the prolonged sound of Gabriel's trumpet could ever be able to bring them forth.

We passed quietly through Butler County, along the western line of Madison, then through St. Francois and across Big River to those native hills and hunting grounds of my boyhood, known as the Pike Run hills.

The reader must bear in mind that these hills possess peculiar advantages over any other part of the country between St. Louis and the Arkansas line.

They look like the fragments of a broken up world piled together in dread confusion, and terminating finally in an abrupt bluff on the margin of Big River, where nature has left a cavern half way up the perpendicular rock, now known as "The Hildebrand Cave," mouth to which cannot be seen either from the top or bottom.

Among these rugged hills, covered over by the dense forest and wild grape vines, are many yawning caverns known to some hunters, while there are doubtless many others never yet seen by the eye of man. We took up our abode in one of these caverns during the inclemency of the weather, and as the ground was too soft to venture out on horseback, for fear of leaving a trail, I went around through the Big River neighborhood on foot, for the purpose of finding some of my enemies. The only one I saw was James Craig; I discovered him one day in the act of leaving home on foot, so I made a circuit through the woods and stationed myself in advance with the intention of arresting him. I wished to take him to my cavern that my comrades also might see him hung; but he never came along, and thus I missed my game entirely.

By this time my men were tired of inaction, so we started on our march and on going about fifteen miles we came to a place called the tunnel, on the Iron Mountain railroad.

From the store of Christopher Lepp, we supplied ourselves with all the articles that we could conveniently carry, took our back track to the crossing of Big River, near the ruins of the Hildebrand homestead, and made our way toward Castor creek, for the purpose of squelching a negro belonging to Mr. Kinder. This negro had become notorious for his meddlesome nature, and his propensity for reporting white men. On the night of our arrival there, we succeeded in finding him, and to satisfy ourselves thoroughly in regard to his meanness, we passed ourselves off for Federals, and questioned him concerning his old master. He very freely and exultingly proceeded to relate the many reasons he had for believing that he was disloyal. We asked him whether or not he was willing for us to kill the old man. He told us that he would kill him himself if we would see him out in it; that the soldiers had told him two or three months ago that if he would kill him that he should have the farm, but that as yet he had not succeeded in getting a good opportunity. At this we were satisfied that he would make good food for the buzzards, so we hung him up for that purpose, and started on our way.

We were now traveling in the day time and pursuing our way very leisurely, when about four o'clock in the evening, we were trailed up and ran into by a company of Federals, who had probably been trailing us all day. They ran on to us in good earnest, and seemed very anxious for the honor of capturing or killing me. The manner of their attack is worthy of note. On getting within sight of us they held back until we were passing over the backbone of a ridge, then they made a rush, and on getting to the top of the hill were within one hundred yards of us. Their elevation caused them to over shoot all of us except one poor fellow, one of our new recruits, who was shot through the head. We dashed into the brush and went over the rough country about a mile at full speed; then giving up our horses to the other men with directions where to meet us, Gibson, myself and two others started back on foot to "bushwhack" them. On getting within two hundred yards of where our dead man lay, we saw them exulting over their victory. I directed my men to make their way around and take their positions along the road where they could get a shot, while I took it upon myself to run them back. I crawled up within one hundred yards of the party, got a bead on one of them, and when I fired he fell from his horse within a few feet of where our dead man lay. This was all that was necessary to put them on their back track, and they were off at full speed; as they passed my men they all fired in turn, Gibson brought one to the ground, but I think the other boys missed their aim although they insisted to the last that they wounded a man apiece.

We secured the horses belonging to the two men we killed, and started on our journey, and on the following morning took up quarters within eight miles of Bloomfield.[1]

During the day, myself and Bill Rucker, walked down to a plum thicket near the road, and while we were there eating plums, we discovered two Dutchmen dressed in citizens' clothes passing by.[2] We called to them to come and get some plums, which they readily consented to do. As we were dressed in Federal uniforms they seemed at once to take us for Union soldiers. We asked them to what command they belonged; who they were, and why they were not in the service. They said they belonged to Leeper's command, and were on furlough to see their uncle living at Mine La Motte, that they had on borrowed clothes and no arms in order to fool the Rebels, should they meet any. We found out a great deal about "Bolin's and Hildebrand's band of murderers and rapers," as they called us. We shot them both, and returned to camp. At night we started on, and in a few days arrived safely at our usual place of crossing the St. Francis.

We arrived on the bank of the river just after dark, and were startled by the appearance of a camp on the other side at the mouth of a little creek. We could easily perceive the reflection from several camp fires among the trees, and more than once we caught the sound of human voices.

Could it be possible that this was a camp of Federals? If so, why did they not place out their pickets? The more we studied about the matter the further we were from coming to any conclusion.

We rode back into the timbered bottom and continued our way down the country at some distance from the river, until we were about a mile below the strange looking camp, and there crossed the river by swimming it.

After continuing up the river a short distance we rode on to a high brushy point and dismounted. Then taking it on foot I proceeded to spy out the mysterious camp above us. I continued to approach cautiously, watching closely for the pickets, but I saw nothing of them. Finally I stood in the midst of perhaps a dozen little brush shanties and yet I saw not a single human being. I was more puzzled than ever. I peeped into one of the brush arbors and a lady's voice cried out: Who is that? The alarm spread, and I heard the voices of women in every direction.

Presently I heard the voice of my wife, and on going to her I soon learned the particulars of the calamity that had befallen our community in our absence.

Chapter Twenty-eight

Capt. John, with a company of Federal, burns the Headquarters in Green County, Arkansas.—He is "bushwhacked," routed and killed.—Raid into Washington County with fourteen men.—Attacked by twenty Federals.—Killed a Union man for piloting Capt. John.

A FEW DAYS before my arrival in Arkansas, our little community of women and children at headquarters, were suddenly aroused from their slumbers one morning by the firing of a gun, and found themselves surrounded by a whole company of Federals under the command of Capt. John from Ironton, Missouri.[1]

All the men were absent on different scouting expeditions, except eight men, who happened to be in camp that morning; they seized their guns and endeavored to make their escape, but seven of them were shot down, and the other made his escape unhurt. The Federals immediately commenced burning the houses after taking all the provisions and clothing they could find.[2]

The women in great consternation, gathered in their children, and in their night clothes huddled together in the center of the square; there in their helpless condition to watch the devouring flames that were fast winding around them and reducing their homes to ashes.

Before the houses were all in flames, however, Capt. John ordered his men to supply the women with what clothing they could snatch from the flames.

After their hasty toilet was concluded their terror subsided, and with perfect composure they watched the progress of the flames without betraying any emotion; they were determined that the Federals should be deprived of the satisfaction of believing that they had triumphed over their spirit of eternal enmity to the Federal cause.

Some of our boys who had been out on a hunt now returned toward the camp, and before they were aware the Federals fired upon them and killed two of their number. As the scouts were in the habit of coming in from various directions, it was impossible to give them warning before they were completely in the Federal trap.

A few hours after the tragedy commenced, the Federals had all left, and the women in squads of five or six, went in different directions and camped a few miles off to meet the scouts as they returned.[3]

My wife and her party had camped near the St. Francis River, and were living on fish when I returned. The Federals were still in the neighborhood, burning the farm houses, mills and shops.

On the same night that I learned these particulars, I sent all my men out in different directions to ferret out the enemy and to meet at a designated place before daylight. With much difficulty we succeeded in finding several squads of the Federals, from which we inferred, that finding our men mostly absent, they had divided into many little bands to finish their work of devastating the country as soon as possible.

We met at the time and place designated and concluded that our only chance was to "bushwhack" the Federals, and thus drive them out of the country as soon as possible. Two men were detailed to take a trip up Black River, to notify Capt. Bolin, and as many men as they could find, of what was going on, that they might intercept the Federals and "bushwhack" them after I should succeed in routing them from the country.

In less than an hour our company was increased to fifteen men. We hastened in foot toward the lower end of the settlement, and on getting within half a mile of a farm house, we saw about thirty Federals engaged in burning the buildings. We heard the discharge of a gun, and on looking in that direction, we saw a Federal reel in his saddle and then fall to the earth. Two soldiers on horseback immediately dashed toward the point where the shot proceeded from, and in an instant we saw a boy about thirteen years of age, crawl out of a gully and start toward the point of the hill where we were with the soldiers after him.

The boy had so much the start of them that we saw he could easily reach us before the Federals could overtake him. We lay concealed in the thick brush and let the boy pass without seeing us; the soldiers were soon in our midst; we rose up and made them surrender without creating any alarm. We tied them securely and awaited the approach of others who might be sent out in search of these two.

The boy was greatly overjoyed when he found out who we were. In about half an hour ten Federals came riding up toward us. Our prisoners had been removed back half a mile and hung to prevent an alarm. We saluted the Federals with a sudden discharge from our rifles, and six of them dropped from their horses; the others suddenly wheeled and made their escape. The other soldiers hastened on to an adjoining ridge and kept up a harmless fire against us for two or three hours; they did this to divert our attention as it appears, for before we were fully aware of the fact a fresh force of Federals, numbering perhaps forty men, commenced a deadly fire upon us in our rear, and soon drove us from our position. Our retreat was rather disorderly, and before we had succeeded in crossing a ravine and gaining the opposite ridge, four of my men were killed and two others slightly wounded. We continued our retreat for five miles, and then placed ourselves in position to take the Federals without much danger to ourselves. Here we remained for several hours, and were loth to leave the place, but it finally became apparent to us that the intention of the Federals was to burn out the neighborhood, and then to hasten back before we could collect our men together.

We wound our way through the woods toward our old headquarters. Late in the evening we heard firing in front, and in an instant we started in that direction, but were soon met by eight of our men who had just returned from a scout, without knowing what was going on. As they were on the retreat we did not feel justifiable in trying to make a stand against such superior numbers, so we diverged to the right and let the Federals pass without attracting their attention.

On the night following we succeeded in finding the Federal camp, and during the whole night continued to "bushwhack" them at intervals, until we had killed eight or ten of their pickets. The next morning they seemed to have taken up their march for Missouri, but during the whole day we annoyed them all we could, by posting ourselves in positions where we had the advantage, and thereby picked off several of them. Late in the evening they made an attempt to follow us into the woods, but we attacked the party on every side; the slaughter was terrible, and we finally put them to rout after killing Capt. John himself, and quite a number of his men.[4]

We discovered among the Federals, several citizens, who we afterwards learned had gone from Missouri for the purpose of giving all the assistance in their power toward ferreting out our headquarters.

Wearied by constant fighting, I and my men now returned to the neighborhood of our old camp leaving a fresh supply of Capt. Bolin's men to continue "bushwhacking" the Federals until they should return to their hive in Ironton.[5]

After we had completely routed Capt. John's incendiaries and driven them from the country, our condition was indeed deplorable.

Without shelter for our families save a few huts that the Federals did not consider worth burning, into each of which two or three families were huddled, without bedding or a change of clothing, and but little food, we were indeed in adverse circumstances. Several of our men were compelled to remain at headquarters several months to repair damages. Our families, in their crowded condition, became unhealthy, and several of the children died. While we were arranging matters for the comfort and convenience of our families we obtained our supplies from the border counties of Missouri by making short raids; our bedding and provisions, however, we obtained in a great measure, from our friends; but we occasionally branched out further to rob the stores and houses of Union men.

Another great difficulty under which we labored was the entire absence of surgical aid for our wounded, for the want of which many of our men who recovered were so deformed that they were forever afterward rendered unfit for active duty.

The whole available force of our community now only amounted to eighty available men, and by the time that we had rebuilt twenty houses and a temporary mill, our numbers were still further reduced by desertion, for many of them now left and went into Texas. While these repairs were going on we had a council, in which it was decided that half of our men might take the field against our enemies in Missouri, and make them pay for the damages that we had sustained. In doing this we had no intention of applying the torch to the dwellings of our Union enemies; we were never mean enough for that; we made no war upon women and children; that kind of warfare was exclusively used by our enemies of boasted civilization, refinement and magnanimity.

I started to Washington County, Missouri, with fourteen men to obtain supplies of clothing and ammunition. With a great deal of caution we made our way up Black River through Butler and Reynolds Counties, and entered Washington County on her extreme southern line, traveling only at night, and concealing ourselves each day among the rugged hills of Black River.

We visited a store and packed several horses which we had taken in the neighborhood, with shoes, domestics and calicoes; and here we found some concealed ammunition, which we appropriated. On starting back we traveled slowly; not having heard of any Federals in the neighborhood, we imagined ourselves safe, and designed traveling in the day time. As we were so familiar with all the roads and by-paths in this section of country, we generally felt safe while on our return to Arkansas, but on this occasion we were doomed to disappointment.

We had gone but a short distance into Reynolds County, when we were suddenly attacked by a party of Federals, numbering perhaps twenty or twenty-five; they had trailed us from the store we had robbed, and now they came upon us with a perfect fury.

Being heavily packed and encumbered with the horses we were leading, we could not run; at their fire one of my men was killed, when I took advantage of their empty guns, wheeled my men into the brush, dismounted and in an instant returned their fire, at which three of their number fell; I dashed forward with about half of my men and succeeded in gaining their rear. My party in front and my men in the rear now made a simultaneous charge upon them with our revolvers, killing two more and wounding several, in which two of my men were wounded, but not mortally.[6]

In the fight all the other Federals charged over us and got away, with the exception of eight prisoners, three of whom were wounded. The result of the little fight was, five dead Federals, thirteen horses, eighteen guns and ten revolvers; having lost one man killed and two wounded, but not sufficiently to keep them from traveling.[7]

After I had inspected the damages, I turned my attention to the prisoners, who were dismounted, disarmed and sitting by the roadside, under guard. On approaching them two of them arose, called me by name and asked permission to shake hands with me. After a short conversation I found that they were two of the men I had captured on Lost Creek, in Wayne County, during the month of May, 1862, whom I released after negotiating with them for the escape of two of Capt. Bolin's men in prison at Ironton. On recognizing them I again gave them my hand in reassurance that I appreciated the services they had rendered us in proving true to their word, and could not help telling them that I was glad to see them. After the ceremony incident to the renewal of our acquaintance was over, I began making preparations for the continuing of our journey after having first buried the dead.

I told our two Union friends that they were again released, together with their three wounded comrades, but that I would take the other three along with me; they, however, plead manfully for the release of their three friends, but I told them that I was compelled to have their assistance in getting along with our stock, until we reached Greenville, at which place, for their sake, I would release them, and true to my word, I did so.

We made our way to Green County with as much haste as prudence would permit; being too much burdened to "bushwhack" any of those citizens who had accompanied Capt. John into our little confederacy, we concluded to let them rest for the present; but having accidentally met one in the road, I shot him through the head and rode on. We found all things cheerful about headquarters, and soon divided our goods among the needy families.

Chapter Twenty-nine

Took a raid into Missouri with four men.—Killed a Federal.—Killed two of Capt. Milks' men.—Started to De Soto.—Routed by the Federals.—Adventure with a German.—Killed three Federals on Black River.

IN THE LATTER part of August, 1864, I selected four men and started after some of my old enemies on Big River.[1]

At this period they had all disappeared except three or four who still ventured to call their old residences their homes, but they stayed most of their time around the Federal camps anxiously waiting for the time to come when the Federal authorities would succeed, either in killing or capturing me, when a new era of peace and quiet would again bless them in the pursuit of theft and murder.

Those of the old mob who had left their homes and were now dwelling, as they supposed, in utter obscurity, were not lost sight of by me, for I kept myself posted in regard to all their movements. The especial object of this trip was to penetrate the enemies country as far as De Soto, Jefferson County, Missouri, and surprise a couple of the old mob who now lived in that vicinity, and before the authorities were aware of our unholy presence, to have our little mission of vengeance completed. On passing Bloomfield it might truthfully be said that we were within the Federal lines. A heavy military force was stationed at Pilot Knob at the beginning of the war, and smaller forces were stationed at the county seats of the various counties in Southeast Missouri; they were inactive so far as the national war was concerned, but amused themselves by marauding through the country, and occasionally killing some unarmed citizens, or indulging in the characteristics of Ben Butler.

On gaining the vicinity of Fredericktown, we obtained important information from our friends in that quarter relative to the distribution of the

Federal forces, which aided us materially in shaping our course. From this place we went east of Mine La Motte, and took up our quarters for the day in an unfrequented part of the country, about three miles south of the Cross Roads, in St. Francois County, where we remained unmolested until in the evening, when we discovered a man in Federal uniform tracking our horses slowly across an adjoining ridge. We felt very sorry for him in his lonely condition; I went down the hill a little distance toward him, and when he came within a hundred yards of me, and commenced making his circuit toward our camp I turned old "Kill-devil" loose upon him; but owing to his stooping posture as he was looking for tracks I shot him too low and broke him down in the back. He set up a hideous yelling, which was very annoying to us just at this time; so I hastened to his relief, and soon dispatched him with my revolver. Being a little fearful that we had attracted the attention of the people in the neighborhood, and that perhaps a Union force was on our track, of which the lone Federal might have been one of the number, we concluded to move. Directing our way through the most thickly wooded parts of the country during the balance of the day, we reached Wolf Creek about midnight at the plank road leading from Farmington to Ste. Genevieve.

Feeling much fatigued, and having lost much sleep, we decided on camping until the following night, having with us a sufficiency of provisions and horse feed. We slept soundly until daylight, and then did picket duty by turns until late in the evening, when I discovered two Federal soldiers in the valley below us, going toward Farmington. I at once took my position with one of my men, and as they came up talking very merrily, we surprised them by presenting our pistols in a few feet of their faces and demanding a surrender, at which they seemed somewhat alarmed but made no resistance.

After dismounting and disarming them we took them to our quiet nook in the woods, and upon inquiry we found that they belonged to a company at Ste. Genevieve under Capt. Milks.[2]

We felt very much rejoiced at getting two of this company who had formerly been stationed at Farmington, and after harassing and robbing the peaceable citizens in that community for several months they were removed to Ste. Genevieve.

On one of their scouts through the country they arrested Charles Burks, county Judge of Ste. Genevieve for compelling the Provost Marshal to deliver up some horses belonging to the judge whom the marshal had unjustly seized.[3] The old man was taken a few miles after his arrest by Milks' men and shot without any questions being asked, and without even a charge of disloyalty ever having been brought against him. On another occasion they arrested Irvin M. Haile, one of the most peaceable men in St. Francois County, under a charge made by some sneaking informer, that on one occasion he had fed me and my men. This was the whole of the accusation brought against him. He was allowed no trial, no defense; but two inhuman monsters took him a few miles, shot him through the head, then taking his horse they left his body in the woods, where it was afterwards found.[4]

The recollection of these and some other acts of atrocity committed by that company sealed the fate of my two prisoners; in the name of justice and humanity I shot them both through the head with my revolver, and ordered my men to cast them in a deep hole of water in Wolf Creek, with stones tied to their feet.[5]

As soon as it was dark we went to the house of a friend to get some feed for ourselves and horses, but on arriving there we saw a party of perhaps twenty persons who were just mounting their horses in front of the gate, and in a few minutes they rode off and were lost to us in the dim starlight. We approached the house cautiously, but found no one there except the kind lady who told us that the cause of the excitement was that "Sam Hildebrand was supposed to be in the country;" that some soldiers from Fredericktown had come up and stated positively that my trail had been followed in that direction, and that the citizens were ordered out to assist in the search.

After getting something to eat and feed for our horses we started on, and by daylight the next morning we were safely housed in a cave among the Pike Run hills, in the northern part of St. Francois county.

Here we remained but one day; as soon as darkness approached we proceeded on into Jefferson county until ten o'clock, when we stopped at the house of a friend who gave us our suppers and treated us so well that the night was half spent before we started on. Our friend warned us very pressingly against going any further in the direction of De Soto, but we determined not to retreat until real danger was apparent. But unfortunately we had consumed too much time, and did not reach the part of the country where we designed taking up quarters for the day, and while making a forced march between daylight and sunrise on an old unfrequented road near the top of a ridge where we designed taking up quarters, we suddenly ran into a company of Federal soldiers who were coming toward us.

They charged us on sight and in good earnest, firing a volley at us, but we miraculously escaped unhurt, but several of us carried off some respectable holes in our clothing. Their charge was really furious, and caused us to scatter in every direction, and after a hasty and precipitate retreat of perhaps a mile and a half, I ventured to stop and take a look at my surroundings; the last fifteen minutes of my life passed off in such a "whiz" that I hardly knew where I was, and I felt very well over the fact that there were no Federal soldiers in sight.

I was not long in planning my course; a place had been designated by me in the Pike Run hills for us to meet in an emergency of this kind, and I at once struck out for the spot, traveling very cautiously and keeping in the thickest timbered country all the time.

Arriving at the place late in the evening, I found one of my men who had gained the spot a short time before me. Here we remained waiting in anxious suspense until after dark, and had almost come to the conclusion that the other men had been captured or killed when they came up. They had got together soon after the stampede, and not being very well acquainted with the country they had been lost, and when night overtook them they pressed a pilot into their service whom they discovered passing along the road, and compelled him to accompany them to the place. The pilot I knew very well, and after deceiving him in regard to the course we designed taking, we released him under the promise that he would not report us.

As we were now destined to be hunted down like the wild beasts of the forest, we resolved to get out of the country as quickly as possible and over some country not traveled by us heretofore. We started in a westwardly direction, and after traveling a few miles stopped at the house of a friend for our suppers.

Crossing the Iron Mountain railroad south of Blackwell's Station, we gained the vicinity of the Old Mines, in Washington county, before it was yet light, where we took up quarters for the day. One of my men being acquainted in the neighborhood, we had no trouble in getting our necessary provisions and horse feed.

While we made our brief sojourn in this locality an incident worth relating occurred, which was very amusing to us, and may not be uninteresting to the reader. About ten o'clock in the forenoon, while it was my turn to stand on picket I sauntered through the thick brush down to the main road, distant about two hundred yards, and suddenly ran on to a German who was sitting near the road side, sheltered from the sun by some brush. I discovered him before he saw me. He held in his hand an old double-barreled shot gun. As he had on an old suit of Federal uniform, my first impulse was to draw my revolver, which I did in an instant. As soon as the German saw me he sprang to his feet, let his old gun fall to the ground and threw up his hands. Seeing that I was dressed in Federal uniform he immediately cried out that he was "all right," and began in a hurried, broken gibberish to give an account of himself; that he was from De Soto and was going to a saw mill west of Potosi; that he was a discharged Union soldier; that Sam Hildebrand was in the country about De Soto, and that he was afraid to stay there on that account. At this I advanced toward him and extended my hand, saying as I did so that I was really a little frightened, that I thought he was Sam Hildebrand himself when I first saw him; that I would not hurt him if he was a Union man, but that I came very near shooting him under the mistaken idea that he was Hildebrand. He laughed heartily at the coincident and was quite merry over the happy turn that the affair had taken.

I told him that I had some men stationed back in the woods on one of Hildebrand's old trails, and that he could go with me and form one of my party for the day, to which he gladly consented, manifesting a great deal of gratitude. As we made our way cautiously to the camp through the thick brush I told him that he was running a great risk in traveling through that portion of country, for it was one of Hildebrand's main passways.

On coming up to the boys in camp he did not wait for an introduction, but stepped in ahead of me and shook hands with them all in the greatest glee, telling as he did so a great many things he knew about "Sam Hildebrand."

The boys seemed to understand the matter perfectly well without any explanations from me, and humored the joke very well by asking the most absurd questions about my barbarity; but none of the questions were too hard, for he answered them all, making it appear that I was a bloodthirsty barbarian, without an equal in the world's history.

It was not until sometime during the afternoon that we undeceived him in regard to the true nature of things; it was sometime before he could comprehend the sudden change, or be made to believe that he was really in my hands. But as he gradually became convinced of the fact he began a series of lies that would have shamed "Baron Munchausen" himself.[6] We stopped him short, however, and told him that if would not report us for one month we would let him go, at which he sprang at me, seizing my hand with both of his, he pledged himself and swore by all that was holy and righteous that he never would report us while he lived. He shook hands with us all and started, looking back every ten feet until he was out of sight, then he seemed to double his speed until he was out of hearing.

While the sun was yet an hour high we started on our way, keeping in the woods until dark, then passing west of Potosi, by traveling all night, we reached a point near the town of Centreville, in Reynolds County, where we obtained feed for ourselves and horses.

In traveling down Black River late one evening we ran into a squad of Federals, six in number, whom we charged in a furious manner, firing on them with our revolvers. They did not return our fire, but ran most gloriously. We killed one and captured two more; those we captured stated that they belonged to Leeper's command; this being the case of course we shot them.[7]

We took their horses and arms, made another night's journey, and arrived safely in Green County, Arkansas. There I found a dispatch for me from Gen. Sterling Price, requesting me to take charge of the advance guard of his army, as he was "going up to possess Missouri," to which I most gladly consented on conditions that I would be released as soon as we should reach the vicinity of my old home on Big River.[8]

Chapter Thirty

Commanded the advance guard in Price's raid.—The Federals burn Doniphan.—Routed them completely.—Captured some at Patterson.—Killed Albright at Farmington.—Left Price's army.—Killed four Federals.—Maj. Montgomery storms Big River Mills.—Narrow escape from capture.

IT IS NOT my purpose to give a history of Price's raid into Missouri further than to narrate a few facts connected with my own operations.

In September, 1864, by request, I took charge of the advance guard after all arrangements were made for the grand campaign. The dispatch that came to me, having stated that General Price designed taking Missouri and holding it, I felt that a great honor was conferred upon me, and was pleased beyond measure with the prospect of being once more enabled to triumph over my enemies and to peaceably establish myself at the home of my childhood, among the blissful scenes of my earlier years.

While these day-dreams were passing through my excited imagination, I repaired to the designated point and found that my command consisted of a party of ragged Missourians, about forty in number, some of whom I knew. Keeping pace with the main body of the army, we traveled not more than fifteen miles each day. Nothing of importance occurred until we reached the town of Doniphan in Ripley County, Missouri; when, on approaching the place, we discovered large volumes of smoke arising from the town.[1] We put spurs to our horses and hastened into the place as soon as possible; finding that the Federals in evacuating the place, had set fire to every house but one, and that belonged to a Federal officer, we concluded that it had better burn also.[2] We arrived in time to save the mill which seemed to have burned very slowly. It appears that McNeal's and Leeper's men were on their way to burn up our Green County Confederacy, but ascertaining that Price was on his march for Missouri, they set fire to the town and decamped. We pursued and overtook them before they got to Greenville, had a little skirmish, lost two men killed and four wounded, captured sixteen Federals and shot them, rushed on to the town of Patterson, captured eleven negroes and seven white men in Federal uniform and shot them.[3] While the main army advanced slowly I scouted in front of it with my command; but Federals and Union men were very scarce; I still held the advance however, passing through Greenville, Bloomfield, Fredericktown and Farmington; all of which were evacuated before our arrival, and through which I passed with my force without molesting any one with one exception. On reaching Farmington no resistance was offered; the people were somewhat alarmed, but all surrendered quietly except a German, named Albright, who ran when we approached, refused to halt, and was shot of course.

Finally, reaching the Iron Mountain Railroad at Mineral Point, we tore up the road, burned several bridges, and tore down the telegraph; but finding no one to kill, I left the command, according to previous agreement, and hastened to the neighborhood of my personal enemies. Finding none of them there to kill I employed myself in recruiting for the Southern army, and succeeded in the short space of six days in getting a full company, who were sworn in, and under Capt. Holmes went into the Southern service. While laboring for the cause of the South I was at the residence of Maj. Dick Berryman at the stone house in Bogy's Lead Mines, near Big River, with a portion of Capt. Holmes' men, when four Federals who had escaped from the fort at Ironton during the siege, came along the road; with but little difficulty we effected their capture, shot them and threw their bodies into a mineral hole.[4]

The main army did not remain long in our section of the country; Gen. Price indeed was a great military chieftain, but his present campaign through Missouri seemed to lack design; from the time he entered the State until he left it, he garrisoned no post in the rear. Pilot Knob, the terminus of the railroad from St. Louis and the depot for supplies for all Southeast Missouri was taken, and then abandoned on the next day; he made his way to Missouri River and then up that stream in the direction of Kansas for several hundred miles without molestation whatever, leaving St. Louis, the great commercial key of the West, almost "spoiling to be taken." The great Missouri chieftain left St. Louis to his right, while the heavy force at that place were quietly taking possession of the abandoned posts in his rear. If he had joined the "Independent Bushwhacking Department of the Confederate States of America" with all his men, in less than thirty days there would not have been a Federal soldier west of the Mississippi. While Maj. Berryman and a few other officers stayed in St. Francois County recruiting, the main army gained the Missouri River and was quietly making a blind march in the direction of Idaho.[5]

The Federal forces took possession of the Iron Mountain railroad, and on one pleasant afternoon in October, our new recruits armed with their shot guns and squirrel rifles were run into by Maj. Montgomery of the Sixth Missouri Cavalry and completely routed, in which their loss was seven killed and all the balance missing. Montgomery also killed several citizens, whose names were Fite, Vandover, and Judge Haile, the father of Irvine M. Haile, who was previously murdered by Milks' men.[6]

On the day before Maj. Montgomery routed the new recruits at Big River Mills, I went with some men to Cadet on the railroad and took from the store of Mr. Kellerman a wagon load of goods which I delivered up to Maj. Berryman, who distributed them among his men. Maj. Montgomery, with two companies of the Sixth Missouri Cavalry, struck our trail and followed us nearly into camp; but when he ran into the pickets they obeyed the orders I had previously given, and ran in a different direction from the camp, thereby leading the Federals away from our squad of raw recruits, and giving them time to escape. I was not at Big River Mills when Montgomery stormed the place, but was at St. Joseph Lead Mines, when he passed. I was sitting on my horse talking to a lady, when the first thing that I saw of them they were within a few yards of me; I assumed an air of unconcern and continued the conversation; on discovering that they were eyeing me very closely, I turned my horse and rode within a few feet of the column in the direction they were going, talking back to the lady until I was too far off to continue the conversation. I then found myself near a lieutenant whom I addressed as captain, asking him in a very awkward manner if he was going to Big River Mills to drive the Rebels off, which he answered in the affirmative. I told him that I would like to help if I had a gun, but he told me very curtly that he wanted no men who were not drilled. My horse seemed to be a little lame and I gradually fell back, talking all the time to the man opposite me until the last one had passed. I kicked and "cussed" my horse to try to keep up but I could not do it. On getting about one hundred yards behind I availed myself of an opportunity at a turn in the road and took to the woods; the lameness of my horse was very much improved, but I could not beat them into the town; however, I knew that the pickets would lead them off some other way. They did so but were overtaken and killed at the ford above the mill pond.[7]

The new recruits were within hearing of the guns and "broke for tall timber." The short sojourn of the Confederate forces in Missouri was indeed a severe blow to the course I had marked out for myself. In my excited imagination I had raised the veil and looked down the vista of time, beheld the Southern arms triumphant, our country again restored to peace and prosperity, and my little family and my aged mother leaning upon my arm for support at the old homestead, surrounded by all the endearments of our once happy days. But I was awakened from my dream by the unhappy termination of Price's raid; it impressed my mind very forcibly with the fact that the people of Missouri were tired of the war and would sacrifice but little more at the shrine of their political convictions. In fact a large majority of them were compelled by circumstances beyond their control to remain at home and take their chances. The atrocities committed in their midst by men professing Union sentiments finally failed to elicit from them a casual remark.

When the war began, the American people were untutored in regard to the cruelties of war; in fact, I am inclined to the opinion that there was not a nation upon earth which had formed the most remote conception of the cruelties of the American people, with all their boasted moral and religious training. Even the words of political bias expressed in times of peace, many years before the war commenced, while yet almost the whole nation was of the same opinion, were treasured up and resurrected against certain citizens, for which their lives were taken.

From a contemplation of this unwelcome subject I turned my mind, and through my native woods I traveled alone to my home in Arkansas, with my fond hopes crushed, and my spirits below zero.

Chapter Thirty-one

Selected three men and went to Missouri to avenge the death of Rev. William Polk.—Got ammunition in Fredericktown.—Killed the German who informed on Polk.—Returned to Arkansas.

AFTER RECRUITING OUR horses and making all necessary arrangements for the comfort and convenience of my family in my absence, I selected three men and started to Madison County, Missouri, for the express purpose of killing the German who reported on preacher Polk, and by whose instigation his murder, by the Union soldiers, had been brought about.

That venerable Baptist minister, William Polk, was about seventy years of age, and had been preaching for about forty years. As a Christian of unquestionable piety no man ever stood higher; as a citizen his conduct was irreproachable, and as to his loyalty and patriotism it never before was brought into question. From his lips no word had ever dropped that could be construed into an expression of sympathy for the Southern rebellion.

In the latter part of October 1864, three Federal soldiers rode up to his house to rob him first and then kill him.

They demanded his money which he gave up, amounting to twenty dollars; he told them that he had no more, at which they replied that twenty dollars was not enough to save his life.

They took him out of the yard, when a Federal soldier by the name of Robert Manning shot him through the head.[1]

Believing that the German informer was the most guilty one in this transaction, I was willing to attempt his capture even at this inclement season of the year.

Camping out in the woods was disagreeable; stopping at the houses of our friends at night was extremely dangerous; and if a snow should happen to fall, thereby exposing our trail to the Federals we would be under the necessity of running a horse race for nearly two hundred miles.

On reaching the St. Francis we found it considerably swollen from rains higher up the river. I proceeded at once to swim it, and arrived safely at the opposite bank, but my three men having entered the river too near together their horses crowded each other, which caused them to beat down with the current until one of my men named Swan washed into a drift and came near being drowned before I could pull off my coat and boots and swim to his rescue. I got to him in time to pull him out on to a drift, but his horse washed under it and we saw him no more.[2]

After we had all got over we built a fire, dried our clothes and camped for the night.

Swan did not feel well the next morning; so he concluded to make an effort to get back to headquarters, while we proceeded on with our journey traveling only twenty or twenty-five miles per day, stopping with our friends on the way.

On reaching Madison County we began to look out for Federal squads, as there were two or three hundred troops quartered in Fredericktown. My ammunition was getting very scarce and I felt as though I would be compelled to stop and see my old friends in town. We secreted ourselves and horses about a mile from the place, and as daylight was near at hand we had to lay over for the day; on the following night I made my way cautiously, and crawled into an alley near the residence of my friend, when a dog spied me and tried to make me retreat; I tried to negotiate with him, offering him as I thought everything that was fair, but to no purpose. About ten o'clock, all things being favorable, I went around to the opposite side of town and started in through an open street, walking leisurely, but keeping near the buildings. When I had got fairly into town I came suddenly on a Federal picket at the corner of a block, who accosted me by inquiring: "Where are you going, Bill?" I answered in a whisper "after some whisky;" "all right" said he, "bring a fellow a snort." By this time I was out of whispering distance, and soon came to a large saloon on the corner, passed around to the other side which was closed up, and amused myself several minutes in looking in at the window. I saw quite a number of the Federals, some playing cards, some amusing themselves in various ways, and all of them seemed to be enjoying themselves very well. I made my way to the house of my friend, climbed over the plank fence, and gave a peculiar wrap at the back door which was well understood. I got a lunch, some good brandy, plenty of ammunition, rations to last two days, and some very important information. I went out through the alleys as a matter of choice, the smaller dogs being posted in the alleys and the larger ones in the streets. As the night was half spent we made our way over to the German's who was accused of laying the plot for the murder of Elder Polk.

Dressed in Federal uniform, we rode up to his house as the sun was going down, were taken for Federal soldiers and received with a great deal of cordiality. We had talked to him but a short time when the subject of "Preacher Polk" was introduced. The German in a boastful manner gave us the history of his transactions in the matter, fully confirming his complicity in the murder. We marched him off into the woods near the farm of Mr. North, where I talked all the Dutch language to him that I knew, and after giving him distinctly to understand that "hog killing time" had come, I shot him.[3]

As soon as it was dark we rode back to the suburbs of Fredericktown for the purpose of silencing a Union citizen of that place who had made himself rather officious in reporting citizens for disloyalty, and for accusing certain ones of having fed "Sam Hildebrand."

I left one of my men with the horses, and taking the other I went into town and knocked at the door, our call was answered by a lady who innocently told us that the man for whom we inquired had gone to St. Louis, at which we politely bid her good night and left the town. We hurried on to Castor creek to the house of a friend whose hospitalities we enjoyed for several days, while we were endeavoring by every means in our power to take in a certain man who lived in that neighborhood; but the excitement we had raised by squelching the German rendered our intended victim very shy. Finally we went to his house after dark one night and called for him, but his wife declared that he was not at home. We made a diligent search through every room, but not finding him we started for Cape Girardeau County for the purpose of obtaining some supplies for the winter. We succeeded in getting all that we could conveniently pack, and started for Arkansas. We saw but one squad of Federals on our homeward trip; we were passing through Stoddard County, east of Bloomfield, when a party of about ten came up behind us, but they fired upon us before they got near enough to do any harm, and by taking to the woods we made our escape. They might easily have compelled us to throw away our goods to facilitate our flight, if they had felt disposed to continue the pursuit. As it was they never got in sight of us any more, and although our horses were much jaded we made very good time until dark and then proceeded on more slowly. We swam the St. Francis without much trouble and landed home safely.

I found my wife and children well, but Mr. Swan, whom I had rescued from the turbid waters of the St. Francis had sickened and died during our absence, and had been buried a few hours before our arrival.

Chapter Thirty-two

Started with eight men on a trip to Arkansas River.—Hung a "Scallawag" on White River.—Went into Conway County.—Treachery of a negro on Point Remove.—"Foot burning" atrocities.—Started back and hung a renegade.

DURING THE EARLY part of the winter of 1864, several persons from the vicinity of Lewisburg, Arkansas came to our Headquarters and reported trouble with the negroes and scallawags in that part of the State.

Lewisburg is a small town on the north side of the Arkansas River, about fifty miles above Little Rock; the country around this place is very fertile, and before the war, was inhabited by a wealthy class of farmers of the highest cast of honor and intelligence, the most of whom owned a large number of slaves. It seemed that as soon as the ordinance emancipating the slaves was enforced in that part of the country, several scallawags from the free States, slipped in among the negroes, whose especial duty seemed to be to incite the negroes to deeds of villainy.

About Lewisburg they seemed to have been very successful in their mission as insurrectionists, and the continued reports from that quarter convinced us that a short campaign among them during the winter might be beneficial. In January, 1865, I started with eight men, we passed through Lawrence and Independence Counties, and on reaching the beautiful country bordering on White River, which had been in a high state of cultivation before the war, but now sadly neglected, we approached near the town of Batesville, when we learned that two or three of the very animals we were hunting for were in that "neck of the woods." I left six of my men with our horses in a dense thicket, and three of us started out separately to visit the negro cabins.

I had not proceeded far before I entered a dirty cabin of "colored people," whom I greeted very warmly. The household consisted of an old man and woman, each about sixty years of age, and about six others who were grown. The old man treated me with great politeness, and would persist in calling me "Massa," notwithstanding my repeated objections. I talked to them some time on the subject of their freedom; the old man gave me distinctly to understand that he considered their condition much worsted by the change; but the youngsters seemed to be in a high glee over their future prospects. I succeeded in gaining their confidence by professing intense loyalty to their cause, and ascertained beyond all doubt that a "Bosting man" had been through the neighborhood to obtain their names and their pledges to support him for Congress as soon as the war should close, with the solemn promise from him that he would have the land and property of the whites confiscated and given to them.

One of the boys showed me a paper which he said was a certificate that he was to be the owner of the Anthony House in Little Rock. On inquiring where I could find my "Bosting brother," they told me that he was "Down about Lewisburg raising money from the Rebels to build school houses for the colored people."

After intimating that I was an officer of the Freedman's Bureau, I was about to depart, when a tall, lank specimen of a genuine Eastern philanthropist made his appearance at the door. After being assured that I was "all right," he remarked that he had been in the neighborhood several days, and had made a report of all the property which would be confiscated as soon as he returned to Washington. He proceeded to draw it out from the lining of his hat and handed it to me to read, I fumbled about in my pockets for some time, and then remarked that I had lost my spectacles; he then took the paper and read it with a great deal of pomposity, commenting occasionally on the names as he read them off.

I sanctioned the report heartily, and told him that it was bound to win. He then remarked to the negroes that any assistance they could render him in the way of money matters, would be thankfully received, as he was working for their good alone. They contributed all the money they had which I think amounted to about six dollars. I arose to depart, stating that I had promised to take dinner with some colored friends about a mile from there, and insisted that my "brother missionary" accompany me, to which he readily consented.

During our walk he laid before me many of his plots and plans, which fully convinced me that he designated to excite the minds of the negroes with the hope of ultimately expelling all the white people from the State, except their immediate friends from the North.

We finally arrived at the place, but it proved to be a Rebel camp instead of a negro cabin. On coming up to the boys my missionary seemed to be badly alarmed, but made no show of resistance. We hung the scallawag to a limb, where he remained until we got our dinner, then we took him down and threw him into a hole of water, with a large stone tied to his feet. We crossed White River at a ferry several miles below Batesville, immediately after which we came suddenly upon a company of twenty armed men dressed in citizen's clothes. As we were not posted in regard to the state of affairs in that part of the State, we were utterly at a loss to know to which side they belonged in this war.

We were first seen by a tall, awkward looking specimen of humanity, who stepped out in front of us and questioned us about who we were and what we were doing.

He held in his hand a double-barreled gun large enough to have killed all eight of us at one fire. Without answering his questions, as we wished to take items before committing ourselves, I asked "where is your Captain?" He replied that he was going to serve as captain himself, and immediately made a remark that led us to understand that they were merely a party starting out on a "bear hunt."

At night we stopped at the Round Pond, and ascertained that there was but little Union sentiment in that part of the State, and that we would meet with no trouble from the Federals until we got into the counties bordering on Arkansas River. We avoided a military camp at Clinton, not knowing to a certainty whether they were Rebels or not.

We had no source of information upon which we could explicitly rely. On arriving in Conway county we stayed all night with an old gentleman in Point Remove; but being fearful that our horses might be stolen, we concluded to sleep under a shed between the stable and the smokehouse.

About one o'clock in the night we saw two negroes approaching the smoke house very cautiously; after some little time they succeeded in removing a log, when one of them crawled in. We made an attempt to arrest the one on the outside, but he got away, followed by two shots, which, however missed him. A great consternation was produced in the house, and out the old man came with a light. On taking our prisoner out he made a clean breast of it; he confessed that he belonged to a band of eight negroes, who were camped on the bank of Arkansas River, between Point Remove and Gilmore's Landing; that they were led by a white man, and were in the habit of robbing white people, and making them tell where their money was concealed by burning their feet.

On the next morning he consented to pilot us to the place where they were camped; but instead of taking us directly to the place, he took us a mile around through the cane, and finally brought us back to within two hundred yards of where we had been before, and then pointed to their camp. Here it was, sure enough, but the birds had flown.

For this trick the body of a dead negro was soon discovered floating down the muddy river.

I was much mortified in thus failing to squelch the foot-burning scallawag who was leading the negroes on to such acts of cruelty; but he succeeded in getting away and is no doubt by this time in Congress.

After remaining in the woods a few miles from Lewisburg for several days without being able to do any good toward ferreting out the "foot-burners," we started back through Van Buren and Izard counties without molesting any one until we got near a little town called Mount Olive, where we captured a man whom we accidentally met in the road. Several of my men knew him, and stated that he had been run off from Bloomfield, Missouri, for professing loyalty during the second year of the war, and thus betraying the confidence his neighbors had hitherto placed in him. He was also accused of having had a man shot near Bloomfield, by reporting on him; this accusation he virtually acknowledged after we had captured him.

We took him a few hundred yards from the road, hung him to a limb, and proceeded on through Lawrence county to our old headquarters.

Chapter Thirty-three

Gloomy prospects for the South.—Takes a trip to Missouri with four men.—Saved from capture by a woman.—Visits his mother on Big River.—Robs the store of J. V. Tyler at Big River Mills.—Escapes to Arkansas.

I HAD A LONG conversation with Capt. Bolin, who had just returned from an expedition on the head waters of Current River concerning the probable termination of the war.[1]

He was a man of considerable intelligence, and I always noticed on his return from a raid his pockets were stuffed full of Yankee newspapers.

I found him sitting on a log deeply absorbed in examining his miscellaneous pile of news.

"Well, Captain! what's the news from the North? Are they ready to give it up yet?"

"Give it up, indeed! Sam, the war is very near to a close."

"I thought so! I knew they could not hold out much longer; I suppose we have killed nearly half of them; I hope they will grin and bear it until we get another swipe at them!"

"I rather think they will! but Sam, it is the South which is going under; her fate is already sealed."

"What makes you think so?"

"I think so because the great armies of the Confederacy are crippled and almost annihilated; their whole country is overrun and impoverished by immense Northern armies; I fear that our great chieftains will be compelled to yield, and when they go under, our little fighting here must also stop."

"Ah, Captain, you get that from your Yankee papers; I can't believe anything that they contain."

I must acknowledge, however, that I was somewhat staggered by Capt. Bolin's candid remarks, I immediately selected four men, being determined to make another trip to see whether the Federals had literally swallowed up the whole country or not.

We made our way up Black River, thinking that we would be very likely to make the trip on that route without ever seeing a Federal.

One evening, on the first day of March, 1865, after remaining in a thicket nearly all day, we concluded to approach the house of a friend with whom we had stopped on a previous trip.[2] A terrible rain storm was coming up, and we thought we could leave our horses where they were and repair to the house for shelter until the rain should cease.

Our friend was from home; he had gone toward Springfield to look after his son whom he feared had been murdered by some of the roving bands of Federals. We learned from the good woman that none of the enemy had passed that road for a long time; so feeling perfectly safe we repaired to the barn intending to get a little sleep, but took the precaution to crawl up into the loft and over the hay into a low place near the wall.

Directly after dark we were awakened by the noise of a large empty wagon that was driven up to the barn, just under our window; on peeping out the truth flashed across our minds in an instant that not less than fifty Federal soldiers were in the barn yard all around us; but on watching their maneuvers a few minutes, we became satisfied that they knew nothing of our presence.

The barn floor below us was soon full of them and in a few minutes eight or ten of them crawled up through the window on the hay and rolled up in their blankets, between us and the window. Our escape seemed impossible; we could not slip out the window without stepping on the soldiers; we might indeed lay still and escape detection for a while, but we knew full well that as soon as it was light enough they would load their wagon with the hay and be sure to discover us. For once I was at my wit's end.

In this predicament we lay for two long hours, when all at once we heard the alarm of fire; our good woman was calling lustily for help. In the corner of the yard about fifty feet from the house there stood a little cabin that had once been her dwelling house but which was now used as a kind of receptacle for old boxes and barrels.

This house was in flames, and we learned afterwards that she set it on fire herself to draw the soldiers from the barn so that we might effect our escape. In this she succeeded admirably; every one broke for the fire and prevented it from catching the main building, while we made our escape without any trouble whatever. We took a long breath of relief, mounted our horses and made one good night's travel. Passing near the town of Buford then west of Fredericktown, we arrived in the vicinity of Flat Woods and remained concealed in a thick forest during the day. In the evening, two of my men who were dressed in Federal uniform, wandered off from the camp and were discovered by a citizen named John Myers, who mistook them for Union soldiers and immediately commenced telling them how, thus far, he had succeeded in deceiving the Rebels. He handed them a sheet of paper on which he had written out a full report of his success in ferreting out the friends of Sam Hildebrand in that neighborhood. He stated that he was in the habit of reporting to the Rebels also, and to prove the matter he drew from his pocket a half worn paper purporting to be an account of the Federal movements in that section of country. He manifested a great desire for my capture, and when they told him that I had actually been captured and was a prisoner at their camp near by, he waved his hat and shouted like an Indian. They brought him into camp to satisfy his curiosity; but on discovering that I was not tied he started to retreat, but was stopped by my men. As soon as night began to approach we shot him and proceeded on toward Big River, but stopped in the pinery northwest from Farmington, where we remained two days.[3] On leaving there we took supper with a friend near Big River Mills and proceeded down the river to the old Hildebrand homestead.

During Price's raid into that section of country I left word for my enemies that they should build my mother another house at the old homestead in lieu of the one they had burned, otherwise, I would burn the last one of them out. Some of my friends, however, seeing that they were slow about commencing it, and wishing perhaps to screen them, met together and in a very short time built her a cabin, which answered her purpose very well for a temporary abode. Into this cabin she removed, and there I found her on the night of March 6th, 1865.[4] I left my men and horses in a secure place near by, and quietly approached the premises where once had been the happy home of my childhood. It was late at night when I called at the door, but my mother had not yet retired; knowing my voice she laid her spectacles upon her open Bible where she had been reading, and softly opened the door. Her motherly arms entwined around my neck, the same arms that had so often lulled me to sleep in my innocent childhood, that had so often clasped me to her bosom and made me feel secure from all the dangers and storms of life. My heart beat strangely as all those dear scenes and all the events of my life in one short minute crowded through my memory. I could not help contrasting her own condition at the happy period with the cheerless present. As she took her seat I could not help noticing the calm serenity of her countenance; a quiet resignation seemed to pervade her nature. Considering the terrible loss that her kind heart had sustained in the cruel death of her three boys, and in the utter uprooting of all her cherished hopes in this world, I was at a loss to account for it, and was about to express my wonder when she seemed to divine my thoughts before my question was formed, and with a slight motion of her hand toward the Bible, she said in a faltering tone: "My dear boy! you are more unhappy than I am!" The remark was so true, that I wished I had the power to obliterate the past, and to commence life again as a little frolicsome boy around my mother's chair.

I remained with her most of the time during the next day. It was her impression that the war was near its close; that the triumph of the Union cause was almost complete, and she insisted strongly that when the Southern soldiers should lay down their arms, that I with the rest would yield obedience to the government and claim its protection.

I was so softened by this interview with my mother, that I almost forgot my enemies; and I made up my mind to return to Arkansas without killing any one if I could do so with safety to myself.

But it was necessary that I and my men should take some goods with us, for our families, at this time, were rather needy; and believing that friends as well as foes should bear a part of the burden of our suffering families, inasmuch as all our energies had been directed to the accomplishment of an object which they so strenuously contemplated was right, we concluded to make a small raid into the town of Big River Mills, that my friends might still know we were on the war path. We started late in the evening and kept along the main road, arriving in town between sundown and dark. We went to the store of J. V. Tyler, and helped ourselves to such articles as we actually needed. After mounting our horses we did not remain long to see the balance of our friends, but hurried on all that night to get as far beyond the gravel road at night as possible.

We lay up to rest ourselves during the day; but about two o'clock in the evening, we discovered a considerable force of Federals on our track; they came to the place where our trail commenced winding around the hill, and there they began to move very cautiously.

I plainly saw from their movements that they had learned my trick of making a circuit before camping; this being the case I determined to escape by the same knowledge. We started very cautiously down the hill in an opposite direction, rode about three miles, made another circuit and went on in a great hurry. Every few miles we made a similar curve, but continued on, and by the time they had crept cautiously up to the last place we were far beyond their reach.

We had no further trouble with the Federals and reached Arkansas with all our goods.

Chapter Thirty-four

Started to Missouri with four men.—Surrounded at night near Fredericktown.—Narrow escape by a cunning device.—Retired to Simms Mountain.—Swapped horses with Robert Hill and captured some more.—Killed Free Jim and kidnapped a negro boy.

ABOUT THE FIRST of April, 1865, I started to Missouri with four men, one of whom was Tom Haile. We passed west of Bloomfield, and made an attempt to take in a German living on the edge of Wayne county, whose name I never could pronounce. He had rendered himself rather obnoxious to us in his officiousness in carrying news to the Federal authorities.

On going up to his house about sunrise, thinking to find him asleep, we made no attempt at concealment, but marched directly up toward the front of his house; when we got within a hundred and fifty yards of the house he ran out and struck across a little field; we fired our guns at him, shooting one at a time; everytime we fired he squalled like a panther, which tickled Tom Haile so well he could not shoot, but laughed about as loud as the Dutchman yelled. We made no attempt to pursue him, as we cared very little about him any way. We marched on toward Fredericktown, reaching that place one morning about daybreak, and secreted ourselves for the day, during which time Haile went into Fredericktown.

After tying up an old coat in a dirty cotton handkerchief, and swinging it on a stick which he carried on his shoulder, he walked into town, passing himself off for a lame Irishman who wanted a job for a few days; he found some soldiers there but did not learn their number.

While in town he met several acquaintances who kindly passed him without recognition.

It appears, however, that in the morning as we were passing Mr. Blake's farm we were discovered by some one and reported to the soldiers.

A company was ordered out to guard a gap where we were in the habit of passing, and we distinctly heard their horses' feet on the gravel road as they passed our retreat where we lay concealed in the thick forest awaiting the approach of night.

Immediately after dark we started, but on crossing the gravel road two shots were fired at us from a short distance; we dashed through the thick brush, but my horse soon got tangled in a grapevine, and the boys all left me, vainly endeavoring to get him along.

The firing became very rapid. In riding through the thick tangled brush I made too much noise, and the first thing I knew I was completely surrounded, though their lines as yet were at some distance.

Having no time to lose I quickly dismounted, dropped the bridle rein over a snag, and ran back about one hundred yards; I stepped behind a bush and remained very quiet, knowing if I fired they would see the flash of my pistol.

They were closing up in regular order toward the point where my horse stood. I waited until they were within ten steps of me, then facing toward the horse which now gave a snort, I gave a few steps, then in a low but commanding tone I cried out: "Advance with more caution! they can hear you a mile!" By this time I was in their line, and under the pretense of correcting some irregularity in their movements, I stepped behind them and got away without creating the least suspicion.

Being next discovered by the guards who were holding the horses, I told them that we had the bushwhackers all surrounded, and that to make a sure thing we must have more men.

Mounting the best looking horse I could find by the dim light of the moon, I started toward Fredericktown in a great hurry; but when out of danger I changed my course for Simms mountain in St. Francois county the place designated for our meeting in case of trouble.

The Federals probably captured my horse, but that was no loss to me, for I had obtained a much better one.

I rode all night and part of the next day by myself before I reached our place of rendezvous. My men were not there, and as the day wore away I began to fear that some misfortune had befallen them; but they made their appearance after dark, and reported that the Federals had given them a severe chase; immediately after which they met a squad of Federals who chased them the other way.[1]

Simms Mountain is a very high elevation of land scarcely ever visited except by hunters at certain seasons of the year. It looms up above the other hills, affording a fine view of the whole surrounding country. While we lay here Tom Haile took a trip to Iron Mountain to learn the news at the military camp, and get some provisions. After getting near the place he left his horse and his arms in the woods, stopped at an old coal pit to smut his face and hands, and then went into town disguised as a collier, of whom there were many in the neighborhood. While purchasing some provisions at a store he learned that "five hundred soldiers had Sam Hildebrand surrounded in a thicket from which it was impossible for him to escape."[2]

This was good news, for it would enable us to make a raid on Big River in broad daylight with perfect impunity. We passed down Flat River during the latter part of the night, crossed Big River at Haile Ford and rode into town just as the sun was rising. Finding no goods there that suited us we continued along the main road until we got to the residence of our good Union friend, Robert Hill. We wished to make him a friendly visit and swap off some of our horses, for Tom Haile dissuaded me from doing him any personal injury.[3]

I took two of his best horses and left two in their place; we charged him some boot, but had to take it in clothing and such articles from the house as we could make use of.

On leaving there we turned south and passed along the most public road four or five miles until we came to Nesbit Orton's. We took a fancy to a couple of mares that some neighbors had there, one belonging to Tom Highley and the other to Tom Crunkleton.[4] The mare, however, which we took from the latter did not like Rebels, for on getting a few miles I concluded that she would make a splendid war horse; but she threw all my men, one at a time, and when I was about to try my luck she gave a snort, broke away from us and made her escape.

Tom Haile had remained behind to visit some of his friends on Big River, and did not overtake us until we got to Cook settlement.

I and my other men continued to travel along the road until we reached the shanty belonging to an old free negro by the name of Jim. He had made himself the dread of Southern sympathizers in his neighborhood by frequently visiting the different military posts with various charges against them, such as feeding bushwhackers, etc.

To satisfy myself in regard to his complicity in the matter, we rode up to his cabin, each one being dressed in Federal uniform.

On calling him out I gave him a hearty shake of the hand, and inquired if he had learned anything more about that man Madkins he was telling me about at the Knob; at this the old negro imagined that he recognized me as Col. ——, and asked me what I had done with my shoulder-straps; to which I replied that I wanted to find out a few things for myself, and enjoined secrecy on him in regard to my disguised appearance.

He made charges against several of the best men in the neighborhood, which was calculated to consign them to summary punishment according to Federal usage.

After making his statements, he asked me if I was still willing to take his son for a waiting boy; I told him that I was, and that I designed taking him along with me this time, having brought a horse for that purpose. He called the boy out and told him to mount the horse, which he at first refused to do; but after I had got the old negro to mount another horse for the purpose of going with us a few miles, the boy consented and seemed very reconciled.

After going about two miles I shot old Jim, but took the boy on with us.[5]

We stopped near the residence of Francis Clark, in Cook settlement, to get our dinners; and while there some Federals came along, but seeing us they turned off the road and went around without molesting us. We proceeded on without any further trouble, but traveled altogether in the night.

On reaching the St. Francis we found it still out of its banks; we, however, succeeded in swimming it by resting our horses on an island about half way.[6] From there we arrived safely at home, and for the first time in my life I owned a negro. I was to all intents and purposes a genuine slaveholder.[7]

When the war first broke out in Missouri, and after the persecutions against the Hildebrand family had become so intolerable that I was compelled to flee the country, I owed a small debt to D. W. Taylor, a merchant living at Valley's Mines, in Jefferson county.

After the mob had destroyed my property and driven me into the Southern army for protection, it was impossible for me to pay the debt during the struggle.

In all communities there are "land sharks" who are willing to befriend an intended victim to a certain extent, but who are ready at the first approach of an unforeseen disaster to gobble up his lands.

In this instance Taylor attached my interest in the Hildebrand homestead, and while the country was in the ebullition of civil war, had sold it at public venue, bidding it in himself for a mere nominal sum.

For this little piece of ingenuity I now determined to award him with a clear title to another small tract of land, four feet by six, to have and to hold, as his own individual possession, until Gabriel should blow his horn.

With this intention, on the 28th day of April, 1865, I started with four men for another raid into Missouri.[8] We made our way quietly and cautiously through the southern counties of Missouri, all of which were now held by Federal soldiers, for the protection of the citizens—the protection, however, being the same kind that the vulture gave the lamb.[9]

Immediately after I left Big River on my last raid, Robert Hill became satisfied that, as I took his horses, he could no longer pass himself off for a Rebel and a Union man at the same time. He was a member both of the "Knights of the Golden Circle" and the "Union League." A few days after I "*swapped* horses" with him, he went before the provost marshal, at Potosi, and represented that in consequence of his Union sentiments he could not live at home on Big River without a band of soldiers for his protection.

Failing, however, in his purpose, he went to Ironton and made a similar statement to the provost marshal at that place. Certain Union men, however, who knew all the facts in the case, represented the whole matter as arising from personal enmity against Dr. A. W. Keith and others.[10]

Thwarted again in his designs, he was left a few days to muse over his misfortunes; but a bright idea finally came to his relief. He would expose the "Knights of the Golden Circle," and consign his brother members to an indiscriminate butchery!

The war was nearly at an end; the Union cause was about to triumph; and one string was enough to play on during the balance of the struggle. He would startle the world by his disclosures; the earth should be dumbfounded, and mankind should stand aghast at the magnitude of his revelations! He sought and obtained a private interview with the provost marshal. At this time, the sun was serenely smiling upon the earth; spring had just made her advent, and was strewing garlands of flowers along the meadows and sunny hillsides, as if nothing was about to happen; and men throughout the world, unmindful of what was about to take place, were plodding on in their daily pursuits.

All things now being ready, he told the marshal that he was a member of the Union League. This announcement was satisfactory proof of his loyalty, for this Northern Ku Klux League was instituted to save the National Union secretly.

He then stated that, for the good of his country, he had also joined the Knights of the Golden Circle; that the Circle met at the house of Joseph

Herrod, on Big River, and that many of the leading men in that neighborhood were members.[11]

The patriotic motives of Robert Hill will be very apparent to the reader, when I state that at the outbreak of the rebellion, when he joined the Golden Circle, he was a slaveholder, and utterly pro-slavery in sentiment.

How pure, then, must have been his motives when, for the good of his country, even at that early day, he bound himself with oaths like adamant for the purpose of finally exposing the Circle, as soon as it should have run its race and become defunct!

If the Southern Confederacy had won, his patriotism would have prompted him to expose the Union League; and when the last expiring beacon of Federal hope was about to be extinguished, he probably would have called for troops to crush the members of the Union League to which he belonged!

The representations he made to the provost marshal had the desired effect; a telegram was sent to Col. Beverage, at Cape Girardeau, who sent Lieutenant Brown of Perry County, with forty men, to Big River Mills.[12]

The statement made by Hill, however, needed confirmation. It was desirable to prove the charges by some one whose word, on account of the color of his skin, could never for a moment be doubted.

A negro man by the name of Buck Poston lived in the neighborhood; his skin was black enough for him to be perpetually under oath, so they repaired immediately to his domicile, for the purpose of implicating certain persons as belonging to the Golden Circle.

Brown and his men put a rope around his neck, and tried to frighten him into a belief that he would be hung unless he confirmed Hill's statements. But Buck was a brave man, and answered "no" to each one of Hill's accusations against his neighbors.

Finally they told him that he was now about to be hung, and appealed to him to know if he did not love his wife and children, and urged him just to say "yes," and live; but the old man replied: "Well, Massa, I does know some little things; but I's gwine to take it all to t'other world with me!" Neither persuasions, threats, the glittering of bayonets, nor the prospect of death, could make him divulge anything.

The color of his skin, however, saved his life, and his tormentors had nothing to do but return to camp. During the night following he gave warning to those whom he knew to be in danger.

On the next day, May 16, 1865, Lieut. Brown took four men, rode up to the house of Mr. Joseph Herrod, and found him at home. They ordered him to get his horse and go with them to Farmington. He did so, but on getting half a mile from the house, they took him twenty or thirty steps from the road and shot him through the back of his head. There they left him, where he was found the next day.

Thus perished a young man who, for kindness of heart, strict integrity, and moral honesty had no superiors, and but few equals.

Before proceeding any further with the slaughter, Lieut. Brown went and consulted with Franklin Murphy, who told him that the whole matter was the result of a neighborhood difficulty, which did not warrant Federal interference in any manner what ever.[13]

Chapter Thirty-five

Trip to Missouri with four men.—Fight with Lieut. Brown and his soldiers.—Killed Miller and Johnson at Flat Woods.—Return home from his last raid.—The war is pronounced to be at an end.—Reflections on the termination of the war—Mrs. Hildebrand's advice.—The Parole at Jacksonport.

REACHING BIG RIVER late one night, we repaired to the Pike Run hills and slept until morning. Knowing that we would be more apt to catch Taylor in daytime, we started in the morning and rode over to Taylor's store, which was distant only about six miles. He was not at home, and having no time to lose, we went into his store and commenced selecting such goods as we wanted, when we were suddenly run on to by some Federal soldiers, under Lieut. Brown, who was at that time stationed at Big River Mills, with forty men, one-half of whom he had with him on the present occasion.

They came up within two hundred yards of the store, and commenced firing and yelling at a terrible rate. We ran out to our horses, which were tied to the brush not more than forty yards off, but on the opposite side from the soldiers. One of my men was killed by an accidental shot, and another one who happened to be a new recruit left his horse and ran off through the woods, leaving me with an army of only two men, besides myself, to repel the attack of twenty regulars.[1] The Federals, however, after their first fire, took refuge behind some old houses about one hundred and fifty yards off, and from there showed us a very harmless and cowardly fight. After I gained my horse, I used him for a fortification and shot several rounds at them; occasionally I could see one's head bob around a corner, but they were out of range, and my shots fell harmless to the ground. My other two men now left me alone, and for several minutes I remained, trying to get a dead shot at one of the Federals; but having no chance to do so, without charging them myself, I mounted my horse and retreated, leaving my dead man upon the ground, whom they charged and shot several times after I left. I went on to an adjoining hill, but failing to find my men, I rattled my cow bell, which I had with me for emergencies of this kind, and in half an hour my three men were with me.[2]

Brown and his men, during their stay on Big River, were engaged in a wholesale robbery and plunder of the citizens, taking their property without even a promise to pay. Their depredations were even more intolerable than the same number of hostile Indians would have been; but after Brown had been better informed as to the true nature of affairs he became half civilized, and on taking property he gave government vouchers. These debts against the government, however, were finally rejected, the people having been reported as disloyal.[3] Even the widow Baker lost over one hundred dollars by some one reporting her as a Southern sympathizer.

After feasting off the neighborhood for about two months, Brown and his infamous band of vandals took their departure. The conspiracy founded on the marvelous revelation of a broken oath, and emanating from the fertile brain of base malignity, suddenly collapsed.[4]

Having made a complete failure, it is not unreasonable to suppose that we felt very much chagrined at our ill luck, and knowing that if we started south then, we would be annoyed by Federals on our trail, we repaired again to the Pike Run hills for safety, where we could easily have whipped all the forces within the three surrounding counties. My comrade who was on foot went about four miles to the house of an old acquaintance and obtained a horse, by promising to return him again in six weeks; which promise, I will here state, he afterwards faithfully performed.

We were anxious to be on our way back; so we started one night and went as far as Flat Woods.

Before McIlvaine and the soldiers had driven me from there, I became acquainted with two men, George Miller and Joseph Johnson, who professed great friendship for me; but some time after my expulsion from that neighborhood, they visited my house and used abusive language to my wife, making threats what they intended to do with me. Johnson had the impudence to remark that he intended to kill me and bring my head to her swinging to the horn of his saddle.

These were not vain threats, for they watched for me for a long time; but after they learned a little more about me, they were very shy, and up to the present time I never got my eyes upon either of them.

Late in the evening, on the next day after our arrival in the neighborhood, as I was passing a house I saw a lady dressing some butter, and wishing for a good drink of buttermilk, I alighted a moment and went in the house. As I was dressed in Federal uniform, the good woman asked me if I was hunting for Sam Hildebrand; on telling her that I was, she went on to give me the particulars of our affray at Taylor's store, ascribing to the Federal arms the most brilliant victory, by stating that "Lieut. Brown, with only twenty men, ran upon Hildebrand's Bushwhackers and completely routed them, killing fourteen and wounding several more; a great many soldiers are now after him, and have him surrounded in a place where he can never get back here to bother us again!" I asked her if she would please give Sam Hildebrand a drink of buttermilk? She looked at me a moment and then replied: "Yes sir; you can have all in the churn if you want it."

Not long after leaving there, I found Mr. Miller in his field, and shot him. After night I found Mr. Johnson at home, took him out of the house, and cut off his head with my bowie knife.

The reader will perceive that the threats of Johnson would have been completely reversed if I had carried his head to his wife swinging to the horn of my saddle; but instead of imitating his designs any further, I leisurely pursued my way home to our headquarters in Green County, Arkansas.

On the next day after my arrival at home, Capt. Bolin called on me and stated that he wished us all to meet him at headquarters that evening at three o'clock. At the time appointed I was there, and so were about forty more of the boys, most of whom had just returned from their various scouts.

The Captain seemed a little agitated, and for several minutes after we were all assembled he did not say a word. Presently he began, and these are about his words:

"GENTLEMEN: It is my wish that we remain quietly at headquarters a few days until my other scouting parties return.

"I wish to say to you now that, in my opinion, this war has virtually closed. General Lee, the great head and front of all our hopes, as you are already aware, was compelled to succumb to superior numbers, and surrendered on the 12th day of April. General Johnston surrendered on the 18th of the same month. The hopes held out by General Kirby Smith in his general order issued at Shreveport can never be realized.

"The Southern Confederacy is at an end; our course must be governed by circumstances over which we have no control.

"The course we have pursued during the struggle is only justified by the fact that a great war existed. While the eyes of the world have been riveted on great actors and on events of an astounding magnitude, the minor details of the struggle have been overlooked. That condition of affairs now no longer exists; the war has ceased, and our operations must cease also.

"Finally, it is my request that each and every one of you submit manfully to the same terms that have been forced upon our great chieftains; that is: Lay down your arms, surrender on parole, and return to the pursuits of peace."

This little speech fell like a wet blanket on most of the men, and I must confess that I was one of that number; but we held Capt. Bolin in such high esteem that not a murmur of dissent was suffered to drop from the lips of any of his men.

On the next day, however, the matter was fully discussed in every camp. Nine-tenths of the men fully endorsed the statements made by our noble captain, and I could not but acknowledge that his reasoning seemed plausible; yet I was annoyed beyond all measure by the reflection that the war had suddenly ceased before I was done fighting.

I cared not so much about the general result. I knew but little, and cared still less, about the great political problem that the war was supposed to have solved, nor to the technical question discussed by old fossil statesmen, whether the States formed the Union or the Union formed the States, whether the South had inherent rights or whether inherent rights had the South, whether the General Government was a restricted agent of the people, or whether the people were the restricted agents of the General Government.

These questions probably originated with the ante-diluvians, and they ought to have been left to a committee of twelve Egyptian mummies, with the "man in the moon" for chairman.

The practical question with me was, whether all the scoundrels in the nation were yet killed off or not. As far as my knowledge extended, the war had only gobbled up about one-tenth of them.

Most of those men who had composed the Vigilance mob on Big River were yet alive. They were in the center of military camps, crawling around the feet of Federal officers, and whining for protection against my vengeance.

To reach them it would be necessary to overthrow the Federal power; just that far my heart was in the National war.

My mind was troubled by the reflection that as soon as the war should be ended, all those cowardly miscreants would crawl out from their hiding places, boast of their loyalty, make a grand rush for office, swing their hats, and cry out: "Well, didn't we whip them?"

I made up my mind that, for my part, I would take as many of the boys as were determined never to surrender, escape to Texas if possible, fight under Gen. Kirby Smith until he should surrender, and then make our way into Mexico—there to annoy the Federal Government all I could until I could get another "whack" at my old enemies.

I thought, however, that I would consult my wife for once, and see what she thought about it. She looked serious for a minute, and then burst out into a laugh.

"I once heard about some little boys," she said, "who were left at home by their parents, who had gone to church. One of them discovered a rat which had taken refuge under a pile of lumber in the yard; but the boys tore away the lumber, splitting about half the boards. The rat then ran under the ash-hopper, and when that was torn down it took refuge under the barn floor. One of the boys ran to the house for matches, in order to burn out the rat; but his little sister, the youngest one in the crowd, cried out: 'If you burn the rat we will have no barn!' The boys saw the force of her reasoning, and made peace with the rat. So I would advise you to make no further efforts toward destroying the Federal barn for such a purpose."

I must confess that this little speech from my wife, given in such good humor, contained a little more good sense than anything I had heard for a long time.

It sounded a little like a Union speech, and seemed strange on that account; but, although I had not at first the least idea of ever swerving from my purpose, yet I now determined to follow her advice, for I concluded that as she had waded through the hardships of war with a devotion to me that has but few parallels in the history of mankind, I ought to respect her comfort as well as my own.

On the next day I told Capt. Bolin that I consented to his arrangement. He started on to Jacksonport to give in the list of his men, and I started a few days afterwards to the same place, and received my parole on the 26th day of May, 1865, the very day on which General Kirby Smith surrendered at Shreveport.[5]

The war now being over, I tried to banish the subject from my mind as much as possible, and soon went to work on the place I still occupied, for no owner had yet returned to claim it. Most of our men were afraid to return to their homes in Missouri while a remembrance of our depredations were still fresh in the minds of the people, and went to farming in different parts of Green County.

With what I captured during the war I did not have more than half as much property as I had lost by the hands of the Vigilance mob in Missouri.

One might suppose that, from the name my enemies gave me, I might have grown rich by my depredations during the war; but such was not the fact; plunder was only a secondary consideration with me; I resorted to it merely to sustain myself while I pursued my main leading object—that of killing my enemies.

We sustained ourselves during the whole war off of our enemies. If objections are made to that kind of warfare, I can point to the example of Sherman, in Georgia, and to a host of other Federal commanders, both great and small, even down to that pigmy lump of insignificance—the Big River Militia. But, unlike those illustrious examples, we did not charge our government with anything we captured; neither was I a burden to the Confederacy to the amount of one dollar; neither did I ever stoop so low as to become an incendiary, and burn out my enemies. I left that for the Indians to do, and for those who saw proper to imitate them.

So, at the close of the war, and in fact during its whole continuance I was poor, and my family were in straitened circumstances; but I went to work and raised a good crop of corn and everything else that we needed. In the spring of 1866 I rented another place in a better locality, and farmed on a larger scale. This I also did on the year following, and at the close of 1867 I had succeeded in rendering myself and family as comfortable as could be expected.

The negro boy I had taken from Free Jim in St. Francois county still remained with me; he was free, I suppose, but he seemed to prefer good living and light work to "free starvation."

Chapter Thirty-Six

Imprisoned in Jacksonport jail.—Mrs. Hildebrand returns to Missouri.—Escape from prison.—Final settlement in Ste. Genevieve county.—St. Louis detectives make their first trip.—The Governor's reward.—Wounded by Peterson.—Removed to his uncle's.—Fight at John Williams'.—Kills James McLaine.—Hides in a cave.

EARLY IN THE SPRING of 1868 I put in a good crop of corn, and devoted much of my time to gardening; my prospects looked flattering indeed, and I fancied that I was getting along as well as any of my neighbors, and better than most of them. My negro man worked cheerfully, and I put in much of my time in "overseeing." I claim that I was the last slaveholder in the United States.

A circumstance now took place that destroyed my future prospect, and cast a shadow over the happiness of my family. It is a circumstance that I deeply deplore, and one, too, that I could easily have avoided, at the expense, perhaps, of losing one friend.

Early in the month of April one of my old war associates, with whom I had passed many a hardship, came to my house and stated that he had received bad news from home; that his sister had been deserted by her husband without any cause, and that the fellow had taken up with a negro woman, and was living with her not more than ten miles off. He requested that I should aid him in taking the couple out and giving them a good flogging.

The matter was talked over, and one of us might have made the remark that they deserved to be tied together. This conversation was heard by the wife of my friend; two or three days after which the guilty pair were taken from a mill pond, drowned, and still tied together. After the first excitement was over, nothing more was heard about the matter for nearly six weeks. My friend's wife told all about the conversation, and suspicion rested upon us.

Finally Major Surge, with three men, arrested us, and took us before the authorities; the preliminary examination was had, and we were both lodged in the jail at Jacksonport.[1]

We were secured by handcuffs and by ball and chain. In this condition it soon became apparent to us that our escape was impossible. Negroes frequently passed our prison, and told us that we would be hung by a mob.

We were loaded with chains, and so strongly guarded that I began to doubt the ability of our friends to release us, even if they should attempt it; in fact I began very strongly to doubt the probability of their ever coming at all.

In June, my brother William, who had served during the war in the Union army, came down to Arkansas, where my family was, for the purpose of taking them back to Big River, in Missouri; for the probabilities were that my wife would soon be left a widow. She sold the crop as it stood on the ground for what she could get, and hired a teamster to haul the family to Big River.

She made the trip in safety; arriving at the old homestead, she lived with my mother and brother William.[2] My prison life every day became more intolerable. I had been in jail for four months, and had almost abandoned all hopes of being released.

HILDEBRAND'S LAST BATTLE.

On the last day of August, as I lay brooding over my helpless condition, some one, about dark, whispered in through the grates, telling me to be of good cheer for that on the following night his friends were going to make an attempt to release me.

Fortunately for us, as our friends lay in wait on the next night, a boat landed at the wharf, which attracted the attention of all those who were yet up, and we were let out without any disturbance whatever.[3]

I was so overjoyed at the idea of being free once more, that I leaped off the platform in the dark and sprained my ankle. I was in a bad fix for traveling, but we were soon out of danger. I rode until daylight; then we all scattered and each one took his own course. I hobbled on this way, living on nothing but May-apples until I made about thirty-five miles, to the house of an old friend, where I remained until I recruited up, and then I started to where my family was, in Missouri. I found them at my mother's residence, on Big River; but after remaining a few weeks, finding that my presence was anything but pleasing to my old enemies, I removed to Illinois and settled on the Mississippi, about forty miles below St. Louis.[4] Here I went to chopping cordwood for a livelihood, not intending to molest any one, as the war was over, and fully determined to withhold my hand from the commission of any act that would indicate anything else than that I was a peaceable and law-abiding citizen.[5]

In January, 1869, I moved across the river on to the Missouri side, at a place called Rush Tower, and continued cutting wood until the first of April, at which time I rented a small farm of Samuel B. Herrod, on the Three Rivers, in Ste. Genevieve county, near the county line of St. Francois and about four miles from Big River Mills.[6] To this place I moved my family. My oldest boy was twelve years old, and on him devolved most of the labor on the farm.

My arrival seemed to create a panic among those who had robbed me, killed my brothers, and persecuted my family. They still had a fear of retributive justice, and though I had no such designs, they secretly went to work to effect my destruction.[7]

Joe McGahan, as I am informed, took several trips to influence the Governor of Missouri to crush me out of existence. Gov. McClurg instructed Col. Myers, Police Commissioner of St. Louis, to send out men for my arrest. In May, 1869, he sent McQueen and Col. Bowen, who were met at Irondale by Joe McGahan, to pilot them to the scene of operations. On going about ten miles, however, daylight overtook them, and McGahan, after informing them that to be seen there in daylight would be death to him, went on home and never returned. At the approach of night the detectives were obliged to proceed without a guide, on foot, and in a strange neighborhood. After wandering around all night, wading Big River at a deep ford, they were obliged to pass another day in the woods. As they could not find my house without some further information, one of them, disguised as a rude countryman in search of employment, got all the information he wanted. It appears that those two detectives watched around my house for eight days and nights. Their provisions then gave out, and not being able to get away from my enemies, they started back to Irondale at ten o'clock at night and from there took cars for St. Louis. While this was going on I was working at the mouth of Isle Bois on the Mississippi.[8]

It appears that some time during the war Governor Fletcher had offered a reward of three hundred dollars for my capture.

This and other rewards which were offered was the price of blood—an inducement held out for assassination! Men can be found, who, for a certain reward, will shoot any man down whom a Governor may designate.[9]

Thank God, I have never come to that yet! I have killed many men, but it has always been either in self-defense, or for the purpose of redressing some terrible wrong.[10]

Some persons wrote to Governor McClurg to ascertain whether the reward was still valid; on being answered in the affirmative, they determined, even for that paltry sum, to attempt my assassination. James McLaine, as he afterwards boasted, prowled around my house for one whole month for that purpose.

On the night of June 6th, 1869, I ventured up to my house at a late hour to see my family, and remained with them all night. In the morning I stepped out into the yard, when I heard the report of a gun from a cluster of hazel brush about eighty yards off. I went into the house for my gun, and discovered that I had been shot through the fleshy part of my thigh.[11]

On going out I could discover no one, the person having left as soon as he fired, so I went into Mr. Pratt's stable, a short distance off. Presently McLaine passed by with his gun; after going up to my house, he came back and passed along the road not far from the stable. Believing him to be the assassin, I would have shot him, but was prevented by Mr. Pratt.

I was hauled to the house of William M. Highley, who went after a physician to have my wound dressed.[12] The wound proved to be a very serious one, and disabled me for a long time in such a manner that I was unable to walk. I was next hauled to Samuel Gossom's, and then to the residence of my uncle, John Williams. As this became the scene of a furious battle a few days afterwards, I shall be a little minute in my description. My uncle's family consisted of himself, Aunt Mary and a granddaughter about six years of age. His house is among the hills in the western part of St. Francois county, five miles from Big River Mills, and one mile due south from the stone house formerly occupied by Dick Berryman. My uncle's premises consisted of one log house, one story high, and containing but one room. In the yard west of the house stood an old dilapidated cabin with the chimney torn down, near which stood the smoke-house and a cluster of young cherry trees. Opposite the south end of the house, at a distance of about eighty yards was the spring house.

I suffered much from my wound; and as my well known crippled condition emboldened parties afterwards to attempt my arrest, under the assumption that I was just about dead, I attribute all my sufferings and privations during the three months that followed to the attempted assassination. For many months afterwards I believed that it was James McLaine who did the deed, but I will here state that the man who shot me, as I am informed, was Cyrus A. Peterson, Fredericktown, and that Walter E. Evans was along with him.

Neither of those two men did I ever harm; Peterson I did not know, and Evans I had met a few weeks before, and shook hands with him.[13]

The Evans family resided on Big River, and we were raised up within a few miles of each other. The widow and her daughter remained at home in perfect safety during the whole war, although the family was known to be Union (with one or two exceptions), and two of her boys, Ellis G. and William C. Evans, were known to be two of the most uncompromising Unionists in the State. I heard Dick Berryman once tell his men, after calling them all up in a line, that he would not suffer them to interfere with the widow Evans, or with any property that she possessed. This order I sanctioned, and governed myself accordingly.

While I still lay at my uncle's confined to my bed, Sheriff Breckinridge and a party of about six men concluded that they would secure the reward offered by the Governor without any personal danger, as it was thought by some that I had died of my wounds.

During the night he went with his party to Mr. Highley's and got near the house by keeping behind a gate-post. Mr. Highley was called out, and when he assured them that I was not there they made a valiant charge upon the house, and entered it just as Mrs. Highley was endeavoring to put on her dress. The gallant Breckinridge thrust his gun against her dress and threw it to the other side of the room, denoting thereby that cowardice and ruffianism are blended together. From here they went on the balance of the night in search of "Sam Hildebrand"—*and they found him*![14]

They reached Uncle William's about daylight. Finding him at the crib they made a breastwork of him, by making the old man walk in front, while they marched on behind with their guns presented. I fastened the front door and refused to open it. The back door, however, was only latched, and a child could have opened it. I pulled a little rag out of a crack near the jamb, and as they attempted to pass I fired four shots at them before they fired at all; one tumbled up behind the ash-hopper, and others dashed back around the corner to the front side of the house. They fired several shots through the door, which struck the wall at the back of the house a few inches over the bed where the little girl lay. She raised a terrible yell; Aunt Mary ran to her, supposing that she had been shot. "Come away with her," said I, "and both of you stand in yon corner; break her a piece of pie to stop her crying, so that I can hear what is going on." I got two more shots through the crack near the chimney, one of which was at Noah Williams; he got in the chimney corner, and was hunting for a crack, but I found it first, and sent a shot after him that raked across his breast, and tore his clothes in such a manner that he left in disgust. They kept firing through the door; the beds were literally riddled; aunt got a shot on her chin; a whole volley was now fired through the door; one little shot struck her on the head, and five holes were shot through her dress.

They now marched the old man in front of them to the door; he stood with his right hand against the door-facing, and cried out: "Sam, open the door or they will kill me!"

"Hold on, Uncle," I replied, "and step out of the way."

Just then I opened the door, and crossing my arms I fired to the right and left with my pistols. Uncle's hand being in the way, I could only shoot Breckinridge through the groin, and another man through the shoulder.[15]

Andy Bean broke to run, and jumped the fence by a walnut tree just as a shot passed through his fiery red whiskers, grazing his face sufficiently to saturate them, and to make him believe that they were one huge stream of blood. The whole party now broke, and on leaping the fence fired off their guns, some of their shots piercing the door, one passed through my uncle's wrist, some struck the house, and some missed creation.

The man wounded in the shoulder was taken to the spring to have water poured on his wound, Breckinridge to Frank Simms to have his life written, and Andy Bean to Irondale to have the arteries of his whiskers taken up.

Aunt Mary now brought me a bucket of water and left, after telling me that there were provisions enough in the house to last a week.[16]

Telegraphic dispatches were sent to St. Louis, Potosi and Farmington for more men. James McLaine and Dennis O'Leary came from Farmington, and Captain Todd Hunter with eight or ten men came from Potosi and Irondale, and from a hill two hundred yards off, kept up an occasional fire at the house during the balance of the day.[17] The party behind the spring house were compelled to remain there on account of my shots; they, however, kept up a random fire, to show to their anxious companions that they were not yet dead. They once held a hat around the corner of the spring house, and instantly got a hole shot through it.[18]

While the firing still continued, I tried my hand at cooking my dinner. After eating a hearty meal and resting myself a little, I went on duty again.

About sunset McLaine climbed upon the old cabin near the house, but as there were three walls between us, the cracks did not range right for me to shoot him. After he had kindled a fire on the roof he came down and stood near the door on the far side of the cabin.[19] I got a glimpse of his body, and by a lucky chance I shot him dead.[20]

This created such an excitement that, as they crowded around his body, which they carried a short distance, I opened the back door, and unperceived by any of them, crawled out through the weeds and through the fence. Here I had to leave my gun, as I could not carry it, for I could not walk a step on

Sam Hildebrand's notorious cave on Big River near Bonne Terre.

account of my wounded leg. I crawled through the woods about two miles, for darkness now favored my escape, and arriving at the house of a friend, I obtained a horse and rode to my sister's (Mrs. Adams), living near the old homestead of the Hildebrand family.[21]

It was necessary that I should keep in a cool place on account of my wound, so I went into my cave in the Big River bluff, half a mile north from the residence of G. W. Murphy, and near the Pike Run hills, where I remained some time, my provisions being brought to me every day by my sister. My wife and children still remained on the Herrod place, where they were watched so closely that they could not come to my assistance.

Chapter Thirty-seven

Military operations for his capture.—Col. Bowen captures the Cave.—Progress of the campaign.—Advent of Gov. McClurg.—The militia called out.—Don Quixote affair at the Brick Church.—The campaign ended.—Mrs. Hildebrand escapes to Illinois.—"Sam" leaves Missouri.—His final proclamation.

MY NARRATIVE WOULD not be complete without a history of the military operations carried on by authority of the State government for my capture or destruction; yet I must depend almost exclusively upon what my friends told me from time to time as those events were transpiring.[1]

A few days after the fight at Williams', a detective with a dirty face and hair uncombed, riding an old mule, with a pack saddle and blind bridle, went to Big River Mills, and inquired of Dr. Keith and Samuel B. Herrod where "Sam Hildebrand" was, as he was an old "war chum" whom he wanted to assist. His ragged coat and old hat condemned him at once as a detective, for we were in the habit of dressing well during the war, as our *credit* was always good while we were well armed. He failed to elicit any information from them; in fact at this time I was nursing my wounds in the cave, and the dismal scene of my suffering was only visited by the angel of mercy, a kind sister.

It appears that the Police Commissioner of St. Louis sent Col. Bowen, McQueen, Schuster and Wadkins on a second expedition against me. They were joined at Irondale by Hughes, King, Fatchet and Zoleman; and on Big River by Joe McGahan and Dennis O'Leary.[2]

Col. Bowen, with his men, went to the house of my sister on the 21st day of June, just before daylight, and questioned her about where I was. My sister of course refused to answer any of their questions, but on threatening to hang two of her youngest boys, one of them divulged all that he knew.[3]

On the evening of the 22nd, the party arrested William Harris, my brother-in-law, also Mr. Cash and Mr. Dunham, and hung them up by the neck until they extorted from them the fact that I lived in a cave in a certain bluff which they described.[4] This bluff rises perpendicularly nearly three hundred feet above the waters of Big River, which runs at its base. A skirt of high timber on the margin of the river in a great measure hides the bold front of this towering mass of rock from view.

The cave can be seen neither from the top nor bottom, for it is about two hundred feet from the bottom, and is hid by a projecting rock in front. From the cave in one direction along the seam in the rock there is a narrow and very difficult causeway running several hundred yards where it can be approached from above and below. This narrow turnpike can easily be defended by one man against five hundred. I regret that I was not in my castle when Col. Bowen and his posse were prowling around in front of the cave on the morning of the 23rd, I would have had more fun than I did at Williams' house, where they had so much the advantage of me.

I retired from the cave during the night, and was absent when the party came to see my castle. They remained near the cave all day, but did not think it prudent to peep in to see whether I was at home or not. On the following night they built a large fire on the projection in front of the cavern, and kept it supplied with wood which they threw from the top of the bluff.[5]

On the next morning they learned from Mr. Nash, whom they hung by the neck awhile, that I was not in the cave.

On receiving this welcome information the party scaled the bluff and took the whole place by storm. The next move to capture me was through a confession made by a son of Mr. Nash, that he was to meet me at a certain point at night with a quart of whiskey.[6]

Col. Bowen determined to capture me and the "quart," so he and his party reconnoitered the place for several hours, but I kept two hundred yards from them. They were welcome to the whiskey, for I considered it my treat; and after taking a hearty drink from the branch I went away perfectly satisfied.[7]

After the capture of my cave, Col. Bowen made his headquarters at G. W. Murphy's. There of course he lived well; the boys were all happy, drawing good wages and incurring no danger,[8] for I solemnly promised my friends that I would not kill a single one of them unless they should indeed discover me.[9] The first time I saw Col. Bowen after his removal to Murphy's was three or four days after he had captured the bluff. I was aiming to cross the road two or three hundred yards east of Murphy's house, when on getting in a small glade fifteen steps from the road I heard horses' feet coming from the direction of Big River Mills. I stood behind a cedar bush with a cocked pistol in each hand. Col. Bowen rode by me with two of his men, but none of them turned their heads, and I moved around the bush as they passed.

I did not wish to hurt them; I had a high regard for the Colonel, and respected him for his magnanimity in not burning my cave after he had captured it, for I must say that he was the first man who ever drove me out of a place without setting it on fire.

A few days after this I concluded to hobble over to where my family was, for the purpose of paying them a short visit; but on passing through a wheat field I was discovered by a certain man who reported me. Col. Bowen took a squad of men to watch around my house at night. Before arriving there it was dark and raining; and as I heard the tramp of their horses I stepped out of the road until they had passed. I followed them on until they got near the house and commenced placing out their pickets.[10]

After the campaign had continued several weeks, it became apparent that the forces already in the field were insufficient for my capture; the disloyalty of the people of St. Francois county had been greatly magnified. Certain evil men in the neighborhood desired nothing so much as a pretext for martial law; some of them had rioted in murder and pillage during the war, and they knew that in all civil commotions the dregs arise to the top.

Governor McClurg is a good man; I can say that much for him, but in the goodness of his nature he is slow in detecting the evil designs of some of his party friends who live in the under current of cunning rascality.[11] To show the tardiness and disloyalty of the civil authorities in St. Francois County, Sheriff Murphy was ordered, just as the farmers had whetted their scythes and were preparing to enter their harvest fields, to call out the militia throughout the county to aid in scouring the woods.[12] To the mortification of the plotters, he responded and the people turned out.

Then the report was started that I was concealed in a deep mineral shaft among the Pike Run Hills. Murphy and his party scrambled over that terrible country until every snake was crushed by their feet.[13]

This severe ordeal continued for two or three weeks until fortunately the Governor made his advent on Big River, and was welcomely received by all parties.[14] To my regret I was out of the ring; however, I was anxious to see

Governor McClurg, for I had never yet seen a Governor; and having been informed by my friends that he would make a speech in Farmington on the following day, I posted myself in the corner of a fence at the end of a lane on the Green place about five miles from Farmington and watched for him to come along, knowing that he would pass on that road.

I did not intend to molest him, or even to speak an unkind word; but I was anxious that he might be alone so that I could step out, shake him by the hand, give him a drink out of my bottle, and have a social chat.

When he passed me he was riding by the side of a Methodist preacher from Caledonia, named Williams; he was followed by a train of about forty men, the saints being in front and the sinners in the rear. Not liking the rear-guard very well, I did not join in the procession, but retired further back in the woods.

Under the impression that the Governor would deliver a speech at the court house that night, I concluded that I would go and hear what he had to say about me. After dark I made my way to town and secreted myself opposite the courthouse door among some good boxes near Fleming's store.

I saw no indications, however, of a public meeting; I made a motion to adjourn, which was seconded by a large woolly dog that found me occupying his sleeping apartment.

I ascertained afterwards that McClurg did make a speech during the day, and that it was anything but flattering to me.[15] To avoid the necessity of a resort to martial law, the citizens were very clamorous in their protestations of holy horror at the very name of Hildebrand. They passed a long string of resolutions; the first declaring the "Sam Hildebrand ought to be arrested;" the second that "it would be proper to arrest Sam Hildebrand;" the third "that to arrest Sam Hildebrand would be a good idea;" the other sixteen resolutions not differing materially from the first three, I need not repeat.

The resolutions being read to me a few days afterwards, I fully sanctioned them, and cruised around several days myself, in search of desperadoes.

Governor McClurg appointed six deputy sheriffs for St. Francois county; their number was afterwards increased to ten, each one of whom were allowed a posse of ten men, by which arrangement one hundred men would be in active service.

In order to create the impression that he was performing some prodigious deeds of valor, Col. Bowen pretended to have fought a terrible battle single handed with "Sam Hildebrand and his men" at the Brick Church on Big River.

I have heard the battle at the Brick Church frequently mentioned, and I have a word to say in regard to that matter. I was not there myself, neither was any of my friends at the time the firing took place.

The whole tragedy was concocted by the cunning of Col. Bowen himself, in order to cut a figure and stamp himself a hero.

I could easily have killed him at any time previous to this, but as he had done me no harm, and was not likely to do any, I took the advice of my friends and let him peaceably pursue his brilliant campaigns for the sake of eclipsing the renown of Don Quixote.

It seems that two of his men had stationed themselves in the brush near the Brick Church by the road leading from his headquarters at G. W. Murphy's to Big River Mills. On a certain evening between sunset and dark, when Sheriff Murphy and himself were riding by the church on their way from Big River Mills, those two men in ambush fired off their guns. The valiant Colonel drew out his pistol and commenced firing; but to prevent the sheriff from taking a pop at the two men, he cried out to him to dash on to Big River Mills for more men, which he did and soon returned.

The Colonel remained on the ground and was master of the field, but his horse was slightly wounded by a shot nearly perpendicular, which might have been made by himself. The horse, however, not understanding the matter thoroughly, threw his master high in the air; but luckily the Colonel came down head foremost, and striking on a rock he received no injury except a ringing in his head like the rattling of a cow-bell.

He dispatched one of his men to Irondale to telegraph to the authorities at St. Louis the astounding intelligence that at the Brick Church, Col. Bowen had encountered the irrepressible "Sam Hildebrand" and his band of outlaws; that his horse had been shot from under him, but that single-handed he had driven the enemy from the field, and only received a slight wound. This Don Quixote campaign against me terminated in a spree, and the Colonel returned to St. Louis.[16]

Previous to this, however, by Col. Bowen's orders, my wife and children were removed, first to Irondale and then to Farmington; they remained at the latter place under the supervision of the sheriff for a month. They were kindly treated, but my wife was anxious to escape from the ceaseless annoyance of Bowen's military operations.

On a certain night a friend of mine from Illinois, named Crittenden, proceeded into Farmington with a light wagon, and before the break of day my wife and family were in Ste. Genevieve county, on their way to Illinois.

They stopped for breakfast at a house by the roadside, and by a strange coincidence it proved to be the house of the late James McLaine. The widow not knowing the party, made them very welcome, and in apologizing for her straitened circumstances, observed: "I am now left a destitute widow, and all these poor children of mine are left orphans, by the hand of Sam Hildebrand."[17]

Mrs. McLaine's father, George Shumate, was present, and while the good woman was preparing breakfast, he addressed himself to Crittenden, and gave a terrible account of my desperate deeds.

After breakfast the party arose to continue their journey; the widow would have nothing for her trouble. My wife, taking Mrs. McLaine kindly by the hand said:

"Mrs. McLaine, I am sorry for you—truly sorry for you and your dear little children; sorry for the many hardships you have had to encounter. I know how to sympathize with you, for I am a widow myself."

"You a widow?"

"Yes, Mrs. McLaine; I am worse than a widow; I am the wife of Sam Hildebrand!"

The good woman stood amazed and said nothing; but the look that Mr. Shumate gave Crittenden was truly comical; he drew up his neck, threw his head a little back, and exclaimed:

"Well—my—God! and you are not Sam Hildebrand—are you?"

"Oh, no sir! I am not; but his wife here is my cousin."[18]

They continued on to Illinois, and as soon as all military operations against me in Missouri had subsided, I left the State; and since that time I have been wandering through the Southern States as a peaceable citizen.[19]

The Governor's reward against me, of course, is still unrepealed; and I hope that it will be chiseled into one of the pillars of the State Capitol, that it may be handed down to posterity in the same category with two rewards offered during the last generation—one for a feasible northwest passage, and the other for the invention of perpetual motion.

Let the legend pass down the corridors of time to the latest generation, that the strange flickering light sometimes seen at night in the dreary lowlands of the South is none other than "Jack with his lantern" trying to get the reward by finding Sam Hildebrand.[20]

If the strange hallucination should ever enter the mind of a man that I could be captured, let him immediately send for a physician, have his head emptied and filled up with clabber to give him a better set of brains.[21]

All fighting between "Uncle Sam" and myself has ceased long ago. He came out of the war unconquered—and so did I.

It will be a long time, however, before he gets entirely over the effects of our fight. I am hale, and have the free use of my limbs; but his southern arm is paralyzed, he is terribly in debt, can only see out of one eye, and his constitution is broken; he has the KuKlux nightmare, the Salt Lake cancer, the African leprosy, the Fenian rickets, the bondholder's cramp, and the Congressional blind staggers. The war left me out of debt, with a good horse and forty dollars in cash.

As several proclamations have been issued against me, without ever eliciting one in return, I shall now swing my hat and proclaim:

"Peace and good will to all men; a general amnesty toward the United States, and to 'Uncle Sam'—so long as the said Uncle Sam shall behave himself."[22]

Notes

CHAPTER ONE

1. While his characterization is vastly overstated, Hildebrand's underlying thesis is essentially correct: although he generally operated either by himself or with just a few men, at times whole battalions of Federal troops were detailed to hunt him down.

2. Law-enforcement officers killed Hildebrand not long after these words were first published. See chap. 37, footnote 21.

3. One such dime novel, *Hildebrand, The Outlaw*, was written in 1869 and was marketed by DeWitt's Ten Cent Romances along with other pulp-fiction works with titles such as *Six Shooter Jim* and *Prairie Pete*.

4. Hildebrand's own memoir is considered by some historians to fit into this very category. However, it does have a measure of use as a historical document when his claims can be verified through other primary source materials.

5. Regarding his mother's "sorrow," it was reported in the press that "his mother died of grief after the massacre of her family" (*St. Louis Republican*, 15 June 1869).

CHAPTER TWO

1. Also part of the Hildebrand family household, at least by 1850, were two slaves, a mother and daughter, age thirty-five and age two. See the 1850 Slave Census for St. Francois County, Mo., George Hildebrand Household.

2. Hildebrand shows up on the 1860 census as having just one hundred dollars in assets. See the 1860 Census for Liberty Township, St. Francois County, Dwelling 695.

3. Regarding his neighbors' opinions that the Hildebrands "needed watching," two different newspaper articles touched upon the family's reputation: "It was well enough to state that Hildebrand always bore the reputation of being a bad man" (*Farmington News*, 23 Jan. 1914); "His father was a farmer in rather bad repute" (*St. Louis Republican*, 15 June 1869).

CHAPTER THREE

1. In the spring of 1861 St. Francois County was a hotbed of support for the secessionist movement in the area, as is related in a nineteenth-century regional history:

> After the National flag had been fired upon at Fort Sumter, and President Lincoln had issued his first call for troops, the sympathy in favor of the South grew stronger, and a call was made for a public meeting to be held at De Soto, on the 16th day of May following. A pole was raised, and on that day the flag, with a single star, emblematic of State sovereignty, was to be suspended thereon. It was understood that this meeting was to be composed of those who were in deep sympathy with the southern cause. Accordingly, on the morning of the day appointed, the citizens began to assemble at De Soto, and a company of seventy-five mounted men, from St. Francois County, were on hand. At this juncture a railroad train, with a company of Union troops, under command of Capt. Nelson Cole, arrived from St. Louis. When these soldiers began to emerge from the cars the men from St. Francois County mounted their steeds and quietly retired, and thus avoided a collision. (*History of Franklin, Jefferson, Washington, Crawford and Gasconade Counties,* 415)

2. The political and military situation in Missouri was indeed quite complicated at this time. In early 1861 the Missouri General Assembly, split between Unionists and secessionists, granted authority for a convention to be convened on the issue of secession, after which the voters of the state elected an overwhelmingly pro-Union slate of delegates. At the same time the U.S. government was raising localized Union-supporting military units in the state to counter militia forces controlled by the southern-leaning governor, resulting in a clash of arms in St. Louis on 10 May. Matters continued to deteriorate over the following weeks, culminating in the governor and legislature evacuating the state capital on 13 June. With the governor and legislature having earlier granted a sweeping carte blanche for the convention "to adopt such measures for vindicating the sovereignty of the State and the protection of its institutions as shall appear to them to be demanded," that express authority was aggressively used to fill the power vacuum resulting from the government's absence. Appointing a Unionist governor, the convention thereafter began operating as a legislative body. With two governors and two legislatures claiming the right to lead, matters were further complicated as the Unionists split into two sometimes violently opposing factions, with the Radicals seeking the immediate abolition of slavery and desiring the prosecution of the war in the state to be managed by the national government and the Conservatives seeking gradual emancipation, as well as state control of military forces within the borders of Missouri. See Parrish, *A History of Missouri,* 3–23; Rader, *The Civil Government of the United States,* 346–47; *Journal of the Missouri State Convention, July 1861,* 5, 9–10; Ross, "James O. Broadhead."

3. In Sept. 1861, a month after the killing of Ringer, a Thomas Cooper and William Hildebrand (Sam had a brother by that name) were tried by a military commission and convicted of treason at Ironton, Mo., a Union stronghold five

miles south of the St. Francois County line. Both men were sentenced to hard labor during the existence of the war, the punishment to be carried out at Ironton through working on the fort that was being built there. See *The War of the Rebellion: A Compilation of the Official Records of the Union and Confederate Armies,* ser. 2, vol. 1, p. 284 (hereafter *O.R.*).

4. Hildebrand's narrative fails to place into context the events that were transpiring in the area. Ringer's assassination, six miles east of Potosi, in Washington County, on 9 Aug., was prominent enough to be reported in the St. Louis press, occurring at the forefront of a relatively large Confederate foray that included a sharp skirmish against the Home Guard in Potosi the following night. Afterward, the attackers reportedly retreated into Liberty Township in St. Francois County—which was, coincidentally or not, the location of Sam Hildebrand's home. Said one newspaper report relating to this Rebel offensive, "all accounts represent that a perfect reign of terror has prevailed for some time from the threats and murders committed by the gang under charge of these men" (*St. Louis Democrat,* 12 Aug. 1861). See also *Annual Report of the Adjutant General . . . 1863,* 116–17.

5. Hildebrand's assertion that he was innocently sitting out the war at this time rings hollow: reports mentioning him by name have him moving his operations to Jefferson County in the aftermath of the Potosi raid. The Rebellion was erupting quite violently in Missouri at this moment, and while U.S. troop strength was wanting, the Union command felt compelled to marshal their overstretched resources to use several hundred soldiers to specifically target Hildebrand during these same early days when he claimed to be sitting at home, attending to his own business. There are two related Federal accounts:

> Pacific [Mo.] September 3, 1861—Sir: Major [Samuel A.] Holmes [Tenth Missouri Infantry], with a detachment of 320 men, returned from Jefferson County on the 1st instant. He did not succeed in finding the enemy in force, but found a camp which had recently been deserted, and saw squads of mounted men at a distance too great for pursuit by infantry. Several flying rebels were fired upon. . . . I desired very much to arrest two of the more notorious leaders of the rebels, one Hildebrand and a Dr. Smith. . . . Having heard that the secessionists had assembled again after Major Holmes left, I sent another party to attempt to surprise them last night. As they probably supposed our men to be wearied out, and as the night was dark and stormy, the attempt may be successful. I shall not hear from them before the evening train leaves. (Col. Chester Harding, Tenth Missouri Infantry [U.S.], *O.R.,* ser. 1, vol. 3, pp. 160–61)

> On September 4, in the afternoon, received orders to be ready to march at a moment's notice, in order to disperse or capture about four hundred

> rebels reported to be in possession Big River Bridge, about eighteen miles south of Franklin [Pacific]. Just before sundown, [Co. I, Tenth Missouri Infantry] in company with A and C, were ordered to fall in and make a forced march during the night, so as to surprise the rebels before daylight next morning. But shortly after fording the Merrimac River a dreadful rain storm came up, and the night became so dark that our guides lost their way. A halt was ordered until the storm passed, when the march was resumed, but the delay caused by the storm was the means of the rebels escaping. On arriving almost within sight of the bridge just before sunrise, a young lady seeing the advance of our column from where she stood in the road, ran to the bridge and gave the alarm in time for the main body to escape, but we captured fourteen prisoners who were on picket. (Frost, *Regimental History,* 271–72)

An account from Ink's Pacific Battalion, which participated in this hunt but was disbanded on 17 Sept., specifically refers to pursuing "the notorious bushwhacker Sam Hilderbrandt." See Rombauer, *The Union Cause in St. Louis,* 475. Further evidence that Hildebrand was not sitting idly by at this time exists in sworn affidavits detailing how his brothers-in-law Firmin Hampton and Joseph Shannon drove him from the farm of his wife's father, Henry Hampton, in the fall of 1861 because of his activities. Included are statements that Shannon was afraid of Hildebrand, thinking him dangerous, and that Firmin Hampton threatened to shoot him if he ever came back onto the farm. See the Joseph Shannon File, Affidavits of John B. Coffman, Henry Fry, John H. Headle, Beverly S. Kenner, Christopher Walton, and Daniel Coffman, 1862, File of Papers Relating to Individual Civilians, Sew–Sha, Provost Marshal Papers, Missouri State Archives, Jefferson City.

6. The Missouri Home Guard, existing for only a few months in 1861 and serving only inside the state, was directly led by the U.S. national military command. See *Organization and Status of Missouri Troops,* 146–64; Ross, "Federal Militia in Missouri."

In mid-1861 ten thousand firearms were distributed by the Federal government to the Missouri Home Guard, with the stated intention of "enabling them to protect their own homes and neighborhoods." While most of these units were created under the official authority of the Union command (including Ink's Pacific Battalion, the Potosi Home Guard, and the De Soto Home Guard, in Hildebrand's area), many others were more informally organized, such as the so-called Vigilance Committee. See the *Adjutant General's Report of Missouri State Militia . . . 1861,* 7–8; *Annual Report of the Adjutant General . . . 1863,* 116–17.

7. John House was related by marriage to Abraham Ringer. See Murdock, *Sam Hildebrand's Footprints,* 11.

CHAPTER FOUR

1. Capt. Thomas Castleman led Co. E, Washington County Battalion, Six Month Militia. He was commissioned on 19 Sept. 1861 and mustered out on 8 Jan. 1862. See the *Annual Report of the Adjutant General . . . 1863*, 166–67. After a U.S.-supporting state government took control of Missouri, the Home Guard was dismantled, with the state-controlled Six Month Militia taking its place. For more on the Six Month Militia, see *Organization and Status of Missouri Troops*, 18–20; Ross, "Federal Militia in Missouri."

2. Franklin Murphy had officiated at Sam Hildebrand's marriage in 1854, so his decision not to handle the case may have been influenced by friendship. See Samuel Helterbran and Margaret Hampton, 30 Oct. 1854, *St. Francois County Marriages, 1818–1903*, vol. 2, p. 37, St. Francois County Clerk. Later serving as sheriff, Murphy was reluctant to join in manhunts for Hildebrand; see chap. 37.

3. A legal inquest investigating the death of James Frank Hildebrand was held on 14 Apr. 1862. A report filed the next month stated: "We the Jury agree that Frank Hederbrand came to his death by hanging he had two ropes round his neck his neck was broken his skull was broken his jawbone was also broken. He had the appearance of been lying some two or three months, it appears that he had been hung over a limb and thrown into a sinkhole and was found by Henry Jones on 13th of April 1862." See Coroner's Inquest, James Frank Helderbrand, filed 22 May 1862, St. Francois County Office of the Coroner, Inquests 1850–1932, reel C31546, Missouri State Archives.

4. Firmin McIlvaine was indeed rich. According to census records, the family household in which he resided in 1860 had a total valuation of thirty-seven thousand dollars in real estate and seventy-three thousand dollars in personal property—huge amounts in comparison to most other Missouri residents. See the 1860 Census for Liberty Township, St. Francois County, Dwelling 32.

5. Hildebrand refers to Co. C, Thirty-second Enrolled Missouri Militia Regiment, but gets his timing wrong: it was not brought into service until Aug. 1862, around nine months after the time period he suggests. Capt. James Craig and 1st Lt. Joseph B. McGahan mustered into this regiment at Big River Mills in St. Francois County on 15 Aug. Also mustering in at Big River that same day was 1st Sgt. John House, whom Hildebrand earlier names as a member of the Vigilance Committee, and who was also a kinsman of Abraham Ringer, whose murder was blamed on Hildebrand. See the *Annual Report of the Adjutant General . . . 1863*, 328; James Craig, Record of Service Card, Office of Missouri Adjutant General, Civil War, 1861–65, box 18, reel S781, Missouri State Archives; Joseph B. McGahan, Record of Service Card, box 56, reel S781; John House, Record of Service Card, box 41, reel S781.

When the Six Month Militia was dismantled for economic reasons, the state-controlled Enrolled Missouri Militia was soon afterward created to fill its role. The Enrolled Missouri Militia, or EMM, was a part-time civilian reserve force whose troops were called to duty only in time of need and served only within the confines of the state. For more on the Enrolled Missouri Militia, see *Organization and Status of Missouri Troops*, 48–81; Ross, "Federal Militia in Missouri."

CHAPTER FIVE

1. It is uncertain which Bolin brother, John or Nathan, Sam Hildebrand knew as "Captain Bolin." Some southeast Missouri historians claim he was John F. Bolin. However, while it is known that John was killed in Feb. 1864, Hildebrand makes reference to Captain Bolin from 1862 through mid-1865, and there is no hint he is speaking of two different people. Further, Nathan Bolin is referred to in at least one Federal report as being a "guerrilla chief" and received a formal commission as captain in the Confederate Army in 1864. Given these facts, for the purposes of this book, it is assumed that the person to whom Hildebrand refers was in fact Nathan. For a similar conclusion, see Nichols, *Guerrilla Warfare in Civil War Missouri,* 71.

Nathan Bolin (a.k.a. Bowlin, Bolen, Boland) was twenty-six years old in 1862 and resided in Stoddard and Cape Girardeau Counties prior to the war. Early in the conflict his brothers Thomas J. Bolin and John F. Bolin served with him as privates under Capt. Solomon G. Kitchen in Co. B of the Confederate Second (McCulloch's) Missouri Cavalry (a regiment that figures very prominently as Hildebrand's story continues to unfold). After leaving that unit, Nathan belonged to the independent, unsanctioned company of partisans referred to as "the Bolin Boys," or "the Bolin Gang," which was noted for its participation in the so-called Round Pond Massacre, as well as the plundering and burning of Hamburg, Mo. By 1864 this group had become legitimized as Co. H, Ninth (Elliott's) Missouri Cavalry, with Nathan as captain and Thomas as first lieutenant. See *O.R.*, ser. 1, vol. 34, pt. 3, p. 690; Ingenthron, *Borderland Rebellion,* 289–90; 1850 Census for Castor Township, Stoddard County, Mo., Dwellings 572, 575; 1860 Census for Hickory Ridge, Cape Girardeau County, Mo., Dwellings 97, 101; Nathan Bolin, John F. Bolin, and Thomas J. Bolin, all in Index to Compiled Service Records of Confederate Soldiers Who Served in Organizations from the State of Missouri, M380 roll 2, National Archives and Records Administration, Washington, D.C.

2. The route of travel described would have taken Hildebrand through Wayne County, the home county of Thomas McGee. McGee, who is documented as having closely supported Hildebrand (including personally dressing his wounds on at least one occasion), was ultimately killed by Federal troops, as were all three of his sons. Thomas was a patriarch of the McGee/Cato clan and father of Confederate guerrilla chieftain Daniel McGee, who served in the

Second (Hunter's) Missouri Cavalry Battalion, First Division, Missouri State Guard, and the Second (McCulloch's) Missouri Cavalry Regiment (CSA) before organizing his own independent band of irregulars, known as the McGee Gang. See Rhody Holsell, interview, 14 July 1937, WPA Slave Narrative Project, vol. 10, pp. 195–96, 200, 201, Federal Writer's Project, U.S. Works Project Administration, Manuscript Division, Library of Congress; Daniel McGee, Record of Service Card, box 107, reel S735.

3. Brig. Gen. M. Jeff Thompson of the Confederate-supporting Missouri State Guard was a legend in southeast Missouri. Commonly referred to as the "Swamp Fox," Thompson received nationwide attention for his colorful response to a Union general's threat to execute Confederate prisoners in Missouri, claiming that he would "hang, draw and quarter" Union prisoners he held in retaliation. See *O.R.*, ser. 2, vol. 1, pp. 181, 221.

Up until 5 Mar. Thompson had been fighting around New Madrid, Mo. He then proceeded to Memphis, Tenn., his command disbanding, making it possible that some were arriving in the Hildebrand camp near the Stoddard County/Butler County line west of Bloomfield in Apr. 1862. See Stanton, Berquist, and Bowers, *Jeff Thompson,* 147–59.

4. This acquaintanceship likely preceded the war, since Thomas Haile, like Hildebrand, was a native of Liberty Township in St. Francois County. He went on to join the Second (McCulloch's) Missouri Cavalry but was dropped from its rolls after he took leave and never returned. It was probably through Haile that Hildebrand became so closely associated with a number of other veterans of this unit in days to come. Notably, Haile had also fought at Big River Bridge in a skirmish with the Union Tenth Missouri Infantry on 3–4 Sept. 1861 (at a time when Hildebrand states he was sitting out the war, although he was reportedly leading secessionist forces—see chap. 3). See Thomas J. Haile, Record of Service Card, box 102, reel S731; 1850 Census for Liberty Township, St. Francois County, Dwelling 182.

There is an overarching theme regarding most of the men Hildebrand mentions having personal alliances with in his memoir; it relates to the McGee/Cato clan and its members' service first in the Confederate Second (Hunter's) Missouri Cavalry Battalion, then in the Second (McCulloch's) Missouri Cavalry, and finally in the Fifteenth (Reeves's) Missouri Cavalry. David Reed was a commanding officer of these men in all three units, and Daniel McGee was an officer in two of them. (He was dead by the time the third was formed.) After Hunter's Battalion was disbanded in early 1862, many of its members moved en masse into Co. C/K, Second (McCulloch's) Missouri Cavalry. As that regiment was ordered out of Missouri and east of the Mississippi River in 1862, most of the company deserted so they might continue fighting in their home area in the small unit sometimes referred to as the McGee Gang. (David Reed was one of the few who stayed with Co. C/K, but he soon left to join his absent comrades.) No longer belonging to a properly constituted Confederate unit for a period of time, these men began operating as illegal combatants—sometimes referred to as "bushwhackers" by Union forces—and consequently were not subject to the protections of war afforded regular combatants. Ultimately, a number of these men who survived a concerted and successful Federal extermination campaign against them ended up in the Fifteenth (Reeves's) Missouri Cavalry. See the Index to Compiled Service Records of Confederate Soldiers, M380 rolls 1–16.

Daniel McGee, the leader of the McGee Gang, was a scion of Wayne County's most prominent slaveholding family. Out of twenty-three slaves listed in the 1860 census, the McGees owned eighteen of them. One, Rhody Holsell, confirmed the family's close ties to Sam Hildebrand during the war (her vernacular quoted directly from the interviewer's original transcription): "Once during de war de soldiers was around me very thick. I was coming back from carryin' de dinner out in de woods to Sam Hildebrand. I took him a table cloth, napkins and everything first class. . . . While Sam et his meal I would stand 'round and watch in de woods. I was de oldest one on de place and I was de only one what had to carry his meals to him. . . . I was seventeen years old when de war was over. My boss was Thos. McGee in Wayne County. . . . I took Sam Hildebrand's dinner to him many times." See Holsell, interview, vol. 10, pp. 195, 196, 200, 201; 1860 Slave Census for Wayne County, Mo., Thomas McGee Household.

There was never actually a "Co. C/K" in the Second Missouri Cavalry; the reference to such is made in order to differentiate the McGee/Cato unit from others in the regiment. Daniel McGee's Co. C literally ceased to exist upon the desertion of most of the men who were serving in it. Afterward a new, unrelated Co. C was created in its place, with the few remaining troops from the original Co. C being detailed to form the basis of a new Co. K. (Some of these men thereafter also deserted, joining the others in Missouri.) Further complicating matters, during the course of its existence the Second Missouri Cavalry had three separate, unrelated units that were designated Co. K. Consequently, the only way to readily identify the company in which McGee and his compatriots served is to refer to it as Co. C/K.

CHAPTER SIX

1. Hildebrand's claim of receiving a commission from Thompson is quite problematic. According to the timeline presented by Hildebrand, this meeting would have transpired around 15 Apr. 1862. Thompson's memoir, however, has Thompson leaving the vicinity of New Madrid, Mo., on 5 Mar. and arriving in Tennessee on 24 Mar. From there, Thompson says, he proceeded down the Mississippi River—away from Missouri—arriving at Helena, Ark., by 15 Apr. Afterward returning to Tennessee, he then spent several weeks manning cotton-

clad gunboats in that vicinity. Nowhere in his memoir does General Thompson mention returning to Missouri during the time in question, traveling cross-country to the swamps east of the St. Francis River, going into camp there, or meeting with Sam Hildebrand and handing him a major's commission. To the contrary, the facts as related by Thompson make it impossible for him to have met Hildebrand at the time and place Hildebrand alleges. Notably, neither is there any verifying primary-source documentation of any such commission in Missouri State Guard or Confederate archives. See Stanton, Berquist, and Bowers, *Jeff Thompson*, 147–59.

In a war where combatants operating without official sanction were often subject to summary execution when captured, claiming to have a military commission tended to be an act of self-preservation. For summary execution practices relating to unsanctioned troops, see *O.R.*, ser. 1, vol. 22, pt. 2, pp. 237–44; ser. 2, vol. 1, pp. 247–49; Gerteis, *Civil War St. Louis,* 132. In *Inside War* Michael Fellman makes note of Hildebrand's declaration of receiving a major's commission from General Thompson: "In this fashion, he claimed to have been a legitimate Confederate" (252–53).

2. Not only was he answering to the orders of Captain Bolin, but "Major" Hildebrand was engaging in this type of subordinating behavior on a fairly regular basis. In 1915 former Confederate Jesse Ellison asserted that Hildebrand was a member of his company in early 1863, at a time when Ellison was just a captain. In chap. 23 of his own memoir, Hildebrand acknowledges accompanying Capt. David Reed's men on a mission in late 1863, after they "insisted." In chap. 26 Hildebrand "yield[s]" to a request from a Captain Bowman in June 1864. See Jesse Ellison to Richard Jackson, 17 Mar. 1915, Jesse Ellison Letters, William L. Skaggs Collection, Arkansas History Commission, Little Rock.

CHAPTER SEVEN

1. Scatterville and the surrounding area in Greene County, Ark., were headquarters to some of the most prominent and feared irregulars operating in southeast Missouri during the war, including Hildebrand, the Bolins, and Timothy Reeves. Scatterville was located two miles northwest of present-day Rector, in an area that was part of Greene County until 1873. For information on the location and early history of Scatterville, see Webb, *History and Traditions of Clay County.*

2. While Hildebrand was in Arkansas at this time, his wife remained in Missouri, a neighbor of her family asserting in a sworn statement that she sought refuge at her sister's home in the spring of 1862 but was turned away. See the Shannon File, Affidavit of Henry Fry, 18 Sept. 1862.

3. George *Canisius* was a twenty-eight-year-old Prussian-born blacksmith residing in Fredericktown, Mo., at the time of his death. Tradition passed down through his family holds that he happened upon Hildebrand and then was killed

because he did not speak English. See Murdock, *Sam Hildebrand's Footprints*, 147–48; 1860 Census for Fredericktown, Madison County, Mo., Dwelling 229.

4. On 2 July the following statement was issued from the headquarters of the military district: "A Cowardly murder has been committed in St. Francois County, in the killing of John F. McIlvaine, while quietly working on his farm, for nothing else than because he used the best of his endeavors as a good citizen should, to prevent a party of horse thieves, calling themselves Confederate State soldiers, from stealing the property of his neighbors and himself" (Col. Lewis Merrill, Headquarters St. Louis District). As punishment, an assessment of five thousand dollars was imposed upon the area's Southern sympathizers. See *O.R.*, ser. 1, vol. 13, p. 459.

5. McIlvaine was around twenty years old. See the 1860 Census for Liberty Township, St. Francois County, Dwelling 32.

6. Both McGahan and House enrolled in the Thirty-second EMM within weeks of these events. See the *Annual Report of the Adjutant General . . . 1863*, 328.

CHAPTER EIGHT

1. As discussed in chap. 3, William Hildebrand was convicted of treason at Ironton in Sept. 1861 in the midst of a major Union offensive that was targeting Sam Hildebrand and the "Hildebrand gang." While this would seemingly have placed William in confinement for the duration of the war, it was not uncommon to release Confederate prisoners if they posted a bond and took the Oath of Allegiance to the United States. (Having done so, as a now "loyal" citizen, Hildebrand would have been required to enroll in the EMM.)

In Aug. 1862 William Hildebrand enrolled in Co. C, Eightieth Enrolled Missouri Militia, in Jefferson County, where his mother had just moved to live with her brother. Forebears in both his maternal and paternal lines had settled in that county in the very early 1800s, so William had an extended family network there within which he could dwell in relative safety—at least much more so than in St. Francois County. (Sam Hildebrand took refuge in Jefferson County for a time after the war—see chap. 36.)

Note that William did not enroll in the Eightieth EMM until 9 Aug. 1862—nearly a year and a half into the war. Significantly, his enrollment appears to have been an act of self-preservation, having occurred in the immediate aftermath of Firmin McIlvaine's death, as well as the retaliatory deaths of William's brothers Henry and Washington (see below). William had earlier served a very brief stint in the Federal three-month First Missouri Infantry, marred by his conviction for treason in Sept. 1861. Some who have studied the Hildebrand story assert that the Hildebrand brothers, including Sam, would have followed William's example and joined the Union Army had Federal authorities not targeted them. However, these arguments suffer given William's treason conviction, the date of that conviction, and the coinciding documented timeline of Sam's active support for the South. The Hildebrands began being killed after these events, not before. See William Helterbrand, Record of Service Card, box 38, reel 812.

For a wartime comment by a provost marshal asserting that Confederate sympathizers and ex-Confederate soldiers who took the Oath of Allegiance were subject to the Federal draft and required to enroll in the militia, see the Charles Burks File, Statement of Captain/Assistant Provost Marshal Gustavus St. Gem, 14 Oct. 1864, File of Papers Relating to Individual Civilians, Bul–Burk. There is some dispute within the Missouri historical community on this point; however, the actual taking of the oath was the key. Those who did not take it were barred from Federal military service, and those who did take it and then violated it were subject to execution or imprisonment.

2. "Mr. Landusky" was Stanislaus "Targh" Landusky. See the *St. Louis Democrat*, 15 July 1862.

3. "The party . . . captured Washington Hildebrand and a man named Landusky, and, taking them out into a lane about a hundred yards from the shaft where they had been at work, shot them. Washington fell at the first fire, but Landusky was fired at nine times before he fell" (*St. Louis Republican*, 15 July 1869).

4. The Union response just days after Hildebrand's murder of Firmin McIlvaine was indeed severe. While a detailed report relating to the Federal actions has disappeared, very obscure entries in very obscure military files shed light on events. "Flanche" was William Flentge, a prewar neighbor of Hildebrand allies Richard D. Cowan, James Cato, and Daniel McGee in Wayne County. During the Rebellion he was captain of Co. D, Twelfth Missouri State Militia (MSM) Cavalry, which was stationed at Pilot Knob at the time Landusky and Washington Hildebrand were executed. An understated entry in Flentge's company records for 9 July reports that sixty-eight men of Cos. D, C, and H "proceeded to St. Francois Co. to route a gang of guerrillas who made disturbance among the loyal citizens. Scouting in the neighborhood of Big River when we discovered some of the gang." Another entry, this one on the regimental level, is more specific and outlines the result of this foray: "Co. C. On July 5 went on scout in conjunction with Comp's D & H, commanded by Capt. [William T.] Hunter, to Taylor's Settlement about 20 miles N.W. from Ironton & returned to camp July 7 with 2 prisoners. Co. D. On July 9 left camp on a scout to St. Francis Co. discovered a guerrilla Band. Killed two men, returned to camp July 12." See the Record of Events, July 1862, "Scouts Marches Changes of Stations &c.," Twelfth MSM Cavalry Regiment, Microfilm Reel, State Historical Society of Missouri, Columbia; Record of Events, July–Aug. 1862, Co. D, Twelfth MSM Cavalry Regiment, State Historical Society of Missouri; 1860 Census for Cowan Township, Wayne County, Dwelling 21; *Annual Report of the Adjutant General . . . 1863*, 88; Douglass, *History of Southeast Missouri*, 607.

The Missouri State Militia was a unique hybridized organization that was both state controlled and Federally controlled. Its activities were restricted to Missouri, except in the immediate defense of the state. For more on the Missouri State Militia, see *Organization and Status of Missouri Troops*, 21–47; Ross, "Federal Militia in Missouri."

5. "Esroger" was Bernhard Essroger, captain of Co. C of the Union Fifth Missouri Infantry Volunteers. Co. G records indicate that it was also detailed to his command at this time (although regimental records fail to confirm this). Essroger was mustered into service on 19 June 1862 and assigned to guard bridges along the Iron Mountain Railroad. See Bernhard Essroger, Military File, State Historical Society of Missouri; Record of Events, July–Aug. 1862, Co. G, Fifth Missouri Infantry Regiment, Microfilm Reel, State Historical Society of Missouri.

The Missouri Volunteers were state-raised troops under the command of the national government and served as needed in any theater of operations in the country. For more on the Missouri Volunteers, see *Organization and Status of Missouri Troops*, 122–32, 133–40, 141–45.

6. Essroger explained his actions by stating his victim was "a Rebel secessionist who did boast himself several times that he had killed allready three union men." This is the same number of men Hildebrand and his allies were accused of killing in the area at this point in time—Abraham Ringer on 9 Aug. 1861, George Canisius on 14 June 1862, and Firmin McIlvaine on 23 June 1862. See Essroger, Military File.

7. On 16 Jan. 1862 John Roan Jr. joined the command of Hildebrand nemesis Capt. William T. Leeper in Co. B, Twelfth MSM Cavalry, and Co. L, Third MSM Cavalry. His service in that organization was troubled, and he was court-martialed in late 1863 for desertion of his post at Pilot Knob and for threatening to kill an officer. On 1 Sept. 1864 he deserted again, this time just prior to a major Confederate raid into Missouri.

There is no record of Allen Roan having served in the Confederate Army, but he does show up on the rolls of Co. F, Sixth Missouri Cavalry, of the Union Army, having enlisted at Ironton on 10 Nov. 1861, in the aftermath of the treason trial of William Hildebrand at that same place. Within weeks he deserted, taking his government horse and equipment with him. See Allen Roan, Military File, State Historical Society of Missouri; Record of Service Card for Allen Roan, box 70, reel S827; Military File of John Roan, State Historical Society of Missouri; John Roan, Record of Service Card, box 70, reels S837 and S844; John Rowan, Court-martial File, Record Group 153, file nn649, folder 1, National Archives and Records Administration; 1860 Census for Liberty Township, St. Francois County, Dwelling 8.

8. The *St. Louis Democrat,* a Radical newspaper (unlike the Conservative *St. Louis Republican*), carried the following account:

> A LIVE COLONEL. Col. A. H. Poten, commanding 5th Regiment Infantry [Missouri Volunteers], stationed along the Iron Mountain Railroad, has succeeded in producing a lively impression in the counties of Jefferson, Washington and St. Francis, that it is dangerous to be a rebel, and that it is the business of the militia to fight the rebellion with powder, lead and bayonet, instead of oaths and conciliatory speeches. He has effectually broken up the band of bush-whackers and horse thieves in St. Francis county, who have been killing Union men in their fields. He has given an example which other militia commanders may imitate with honor to themselves and profit to the country. On Saturday a detachment of his men found John L. Rohan, Wash. Hildebrand and Targh Landowsky, three of a notorious band of outlaws, *and killed them.* When Col. Poten's men find such fellows there is no further trouble with them. Somebody, or something else finds them soon afterwards. The union men of those counties are unanimous in his praise. Of course secessionists will write many bitter complaints of outrages committed by his command and publish them in the *Missouri Republican.* This has been done, and will be done in all cases where secesh are treated as enemies and traitors. We only want a few more Colonels in Missouri like Col. Poten, who will pull off their gloves and handle secesh a little roughly, to give the Union men confidence and bring the rebels to submission. (*St. Louis Democrat*, 15 July 1862)

The following also appeared in the *Democrat* that day: "BUSHWHACKERS KILLED.—Col. [August H.] Poten [Fifth Missouri Infantry], from Camp Merrill, reports to the Provost Marshal that John L. Roan, Wash. Hildebrand and Targh Blandowski, notorious rebels and bushwhackers, were last week killed by National scouts in the vicinity of the Camp named, near the Iron Mountain Railroad."

Entries into Co. G's books state that it had two platoons stationed on railroad bridges above Mineral Point. On 26 June—three days after McIlvaine's death—a scout was sent to Big River Mills, where a prisoner was taken and subsequently "shot trying to escape." An undated entry for July and Aug. discusses a subsequent mission in which scouting parties were sent out to Big River Mills and Old Mines with a plan "to suffuse bushwhacking and marauding bands and to exterminate bands of horse thieves and assassins who infested the country and murdered several prominent men." Specifics are lacking as to what actions were taken in furtherance of this plan.

Providing a clue, Essroger, in a written response to a "reproach" directed at him during this time, on 30 July, denied committing any "abuses" and asked for a full investigation, including a court of inquiry, regarding accusations being made against him. Shortly afterward he was placed in confinement "on having given order to kill a certain man." Essroger's response was to state that he was "able to justify his conduct." There is no record in the file as to how this matter was concluded. See Essroger, Military File; Record of Events, July–Aug. 1862, Co. G.

9. Philip Adolph, captain of Co. D, Fifth Missouri Infantry, was stationed with his company at the Big River Bridge on the Iron Mountain Railroad. See Philip Adolph, Military File, State Historical Society of Missouri.

10. Unlike those documenting the actions of Flentge and Essroger, no company-level notes regarding Adolph's actions are known to survive, but what does exist indicates the possibility of a cover-up. In Adolph's personnel file, a cover jacket dated 31 July 1862, from his commanding officer, Col. A. H. Poten, states that a report of Adolph's recent scouts is enclosed, but no such report was found in the file reviewed or in the original at the National Archives. (Note that Hildebrand states Adolph's raid occurred on 23 July.) Colonel Poten's own military file contains a letter from him dated 15 Oct. in which he apologizes for the conduct of his men but denies they were "unmanageable." In conclusion, he tenders his resignation in order "to preserve my honor. " The "conduct" for which he apologizes goes unstated. The entire regiment was disbanded en masse a month later, Essroger and Adolph both receiving honorable discharges. See Adolph, Military File; August H. Poten, Military File, State Historical Society of Missouri; *Annual Report of the Adjutant General . . . 1865*, 110.

CHAPTER NINE

1. James Cato was a first cousin of Daniel McGee, as well as a veteran of the Second (Hunter's) Missouri Cavalry Battalion and Co. C/K, Second (McCulloch's) Missouri Cavalry Regiment. Like the male members of Hildebrand's family, the McGee/Cato men were beginning to be targeted for extermination by Federal troops. See Cato, Palmer, and Cato, "Research on the Name Cato," 30 Nov. 2000; Adruain Cato to Kirby Ross, 19 Nov. 2000, 21 Jan. 2001, 26 Mar. 2001; James Cato, Index to Compiled Service Records of Confederate Soldiers, M380 roll 3.

CHAPTER TEN

1. The Hildebrand Cave is discussed in much greater detail in chaps. 27 and 37.

2. According to southeast Missouri writer Gene Murdock, in Sept. 1862 William Hildebrand, charged with murder, horse stealing, and desertion, was being pursued in St. Louis by Lt. Joseph McGahan, the Hildebrand family's personal nemesis. Murdock claims William Hildebrand was captured by law-enforcement authorities on 12 Sept. but escaped the night before McGahan was to take personal custody of him. As his source Murdock cites an order from the "Washington County Regiment E.M.M." (the Thirty-second EMM) but fails to

provide its provenance or archival repository (*Sam Hildebrand's Footprints*, 30–31).

A personal communication with Murdock did not uncover an archival source for the order, and independent research has proven inconclusive. In the communication Murdock asserts that William Hildebrand served in the Federal First Missouri Infantry for three months early in the war (which independent research confirms) and further notes William's Sept. 1861 treason trial at Ironton. Gene Murdock to Kirby Ross, 6 Nov. 2004; William Hildebrand, Index to Compiled Service Records of Union Soldiers Who Served in Organizations from the State of Missouri, M390 roll 22.

CHAPTER TWELVE

1. William Clarke Quantrill (1837–65) was the most prominent Confederate guerrilla leader in Missouri during the Civil War. Operating primarily along the Kansas/Missouri border, Quantrill gained lasting notoriety on 21 Aug. 1863 for leading several hundred raiders in the sacking of Lawrence, Kans., and the killing of around 183 men and boys there. See Castel, *William Clarke Quantrill*; Leslie, *The Devil Knows How to Ride.*

2. The specific individual Hildebrand hunted is impossible to determine, but the Scaggs/Skaggs family in and around Madison County staunchly supported the Union—no fewer than seventeen members served in Federal units, most particularly the Sixty-eighth EMM. See the 1860 Census for Scaggs and Skaggs in Madison and adjoining counties. Also see the Record of Service Cards for the following, all in the Missouri State Archives—"Scaggs": Abraham, Francis, *James* (2), *James Jr.*, Wesley; "Skaggs": *Alfred, Cyrus, Edward, Erastus, Isom, Israel, Jefferson, John, Stephen*, Thomas, *William* (italics denote service in the Sixty-eighth EMM Regiment).

3. Throughout his memoir Sam Hildebrand repeatedly refers to "Leeper's men." Given the context of the statements, he seems to be indicating a broad collection of troops who had any type of association with Radical Unionist William T. Leeper. This group included troops of Co. B, Twelfth MSM Cavalry; Co. L, Third MSM Cavalry; Co. K, Sixty-eighth EMM; and Co. H, Forty-seventh Missouri Infantry (a successor unit to Co. K, Sixty-eighth EMM), as well as men who did not actually serve under Leeper but belonged to other companies in those regiments—which goes beyond the few dozen men who served in Leeper's immediate command and encompasses several thousand other soldiers.

Leeper was one of the more controversial southeast Missouri Unionists. It was once written of him by a close associate, "notwithstanding Capt. Leeper's shortcomings and all of that, I have to say of him, and for him, that his firm stand early in '61 for the Union done great things for the cause of the Union in Wayne and adjoining counties." Leeper, this associate remarked, was held in "high esteem for [his] firmness, and good work for the Union." In 1861 he was elected to be one of ninety-nine members of the State Convention, which rejected secession and became the acting legislative body when the southern-supporting General Assembly fled the state. Contemporaneous with his duty as a convention delegate, Leeper, early in the war, joined the Wayne County Cavalry, Six Month Militia (a.k.a. the Haw Eater Scouts), serving for a few months in that unit as a private. In 1862 Leeper became captain of Co. B, Twelfth MSM Cavalry (soon after redesignated Co. L, Third MSM Cavalry). As the senior officer at Patterson, Mo., Leeper also on occasion had under his command a Wayne County company of the Sixty-eighth EMM (Co. K) that served out of that base. Despite his company-grade rank in the Missouri State Militia, Leeper operated autonomously and outside the normal military chain of command, receiving orders directly from the Union hierarchy in St. Louis. Described by the aforementioned friend who complimented him for his steadfast Unionism as also being "a little shaky in his boots" during a fight, and as having "showed the white feather" too often in the "shock of battle," Leeper was dismissed from the service for incompetence in 1864 but was soon afterward rehabilitated by his Radical allies (see chap. 29). See the *Proceedings of the Missouri State Convention,* 101–4; "Roster of the Haw Eaters—Wayne County Cavalry," Cyrus A. Peterson Papers, box 1, folder 22, Missouri Historical Society, St. Louis; *Perryville Union,* 2 Oct. 1863; H. C. Wilkinson to Cyrus A. Peterson, 18 Mar. 1907, Peterson Papers, box 8, folder 2; H. C. Wilkinson, "Biographical Sketch of Captain Pinkney L. Powers, Commander of Companies as Follows: 'Haw Eaters' Scouts Missouri State Militia, Co. K, 68th Regiment Enrolled Missouri Militia, Co. M, 8th Provisional Regiment Enrolled Missouri Militia, and Co. H, 47th Missouri Infantry Volunteers, or Four Different Companies," Peterson Papers, box 5, folder 5; *Annual Report of the Adjutant General . . . 1863*, 87, 89–90; *Annual Report of the Adjutant General . . . 1865*, 463, 465, 599; *Official Army Register of the Volunteer Force,* vol. 7, 14, 42; William T. Leeper, Record of Service Cards, box 50, reels S837, S844, S898.

For evidence of Captain Leeper's autonomy and a sampling of his ongoing, direct contacts with Brig. Gen. Clinton B. Fisk, see *O.R.*, ser. 1, vol. 22, pt. 2, pp. 600, 676, 715, 724, 740–41; ser. 1, vol. 34, pt. 2, pp. 20, 108, 213, 388, 506, 650. For direct, late-war military contacts between *Private* Leeper and Brig. Gen. Thomas Ewing, as well as Maj. Gen. Grenville M. Dodge, see *O.R.*, ser. 1, vol. 41, pt. 3, pp. 189–90; vol. 48, pt. 1, pp. 1054, 1095. (Leeper was still being referred to by his higher rank of captain in Mar. 1865, although he had long since lost this rank upon his dismissal from the MSM in Apr. 1864.)

4. This skirmish appears to have transpired early on 27 July 1862, during the timeframe of Hildebrand's earlier visit to his mother (see chap. 9) and a month prior to the date he recalled when his memoir was first published eight years later. According to a Federal account of this July skirmish, the two sides fought on the farm of Hildebrand ally/McGee kinsman William Cato, the skirmish

involving elements of Leeper's regiment, the Twelfth MSM Cavalry (but not Leeper or his company). After leaving Greenville, three companies of the Twelfth MSM converged on the Castor River and then went into camp on Cato's farm: "Greenville, Mo. July 29, 1862— . . . Early in the morning our pickets were fired on by the enemy. The firing lasted some twenty minutes, . . . the enemy [then] disappearing" (Capt. Levi E. Whybark, Co. F, Twelfth MSM Cavalry, *O.R.*, ser. 1, vol. 13, p. 181).

Another account, this one by a first sergeant in the Twelfth MSM, published in a regional newspaper a few days after the fight, mentions the killing of a Union man who may have been Scaggs:

> Fredericktown, Mo. July 30, 1862— . . . I have just returned from a five days scout to the Mingo Swamps. Capt. [Peter] Hagan and myself, accompanied by thirty men [Co. E, Twelfth MSM] . . . started for the flat woods, nine miles west of Dallas, and on the road we got information that a Union man had been murdered by a party of rebels that day. On the third day we fell in with Capt. Whybark and twenty-six men, and Lieuts. [Erich] Pape and [George W.] Humble [Hummel] of [Capt. Lindsay] Murdock's company [Co. A, Twelfth MSM] at Bollinger's mill, on Castor river. We camped that night at a good old secesh, Billy Cato's, on the Bloomfield road. About 3 o'clock the next morning our pickets commenced firing, when all rose in a minute and formed into line of battle, expecting the enemy every minute. The pickets kept up the firing for half an hour, and succeeded in driving 40 of the ragtails back. (1st Sgt. Charles W. Noell, Twelfth MSM Cavalry, *Perryville Union*, 9 Aug. 1862)

For a skirmish involving Leeper's company and occurring closer to the date outlined by Hildebrand, but bearing no resemblance to the action described by him, see *O.R.*, ser. 1, vol. 13, pp. 258–59.

5. Co. C of the Thirty-second EMM went into service two weeks after the fight at William Cato's farm. See the *Annual Report of the Adjutant General . . . 1863*, 431.

6. Wright Bean mustered into Co. D, Thirty-second EMM, at Irondale on 19 Aug. An Andy Bean in the same company later played a very prominent role in the hunt for Hildebrand and had his whiskers shot off by him (see chap. 36). See Wright Bean and Andy Bean, Record of Service Cards, both box 5, reel S781; 1860 Census for Liberty Township, St. Francois County, Dwelling 631.

CHAPTER THIRTEEN

1. No Federal or independent Confederate military report has been located that corresponds with the date of this claim (Nov. 1862). However, the Bolin

Gang was involved in a well-documented action at Round Pond in Aug. 1863 during which a number of Federal wagons were captured and burned. This incident was very similar, with the exception of the number of casualties alleged, to that which Hildebrand has described here. Given Hildebrand's and/or his biographers' occasional penchant for confusing dates, it is possible he was involved in the Aug. 1863 action, which has been referred to as a massacre. For details on that affair, see chap. 20.

CHAPTER FOURTEEN

1. Hildebrand is correct in his assertion that it was the policy of the Union Army to "arrest, burn out, shoot and destroy" neutral civilians in southeast Missouri. So too was it the policy of the Confederate Army. Confederate general Joseph Shelby, whose command encompassed the region, once proclaimed, "It is time that every man should determine whether he is for or against us; if he is for us let him take his musket; if against us let him take the consequences or leave our country." The property of those choosing to leave was "subject to confiscation." As for the neutrals who did not leave the area, "you will use all the force in your power, and when necessary shoot them down." He also specifically authorized Timothy Reeves, one of Hildebrand's close allies, to "resort to any means you deem best" in dealing with neutrals. See *O.R.*, ser. 1, vol. 34, pt. 3, p. 835; ser. 1, vol. 34, pt. 4, pp. 652, 653, 683.

2. William Tecumseh Sherman (1820–91) was a Union general who conducted a march through Georgia and the Carolinas late in the war that he claimed was designed to "make its inhabitants feel that war and ruin are synonymous terms." See Fellman, *Citizen Sherman.*

3. Denying the burning of houses is strange for Hildebrand, since by his own admission he burned one that was sheltering enemies (see chap. 20) and was party to the burning of another that belonged to a person he thought to be a Union supporter (see chap. 30).

As for making war on women, the following reports appeared in the Missouri press identifying a specific woman, Louise McLane, the wife of a veteran of the Union Tenth Missouri Cavalry: "Sam. Hildebrand, cruelly and wantonly outraged his [McLane's] wife, and within the same hour held her hands to allow Bob Hiley to accomplish the same diabolical purpose" (*St. Louis Democrat,* 16 July 1869); "In 1863 Hilderbrand made a raid on McLean's farm, and besides assaulting his wife, took away his stock, valued at between $5,000 and $6,000" (*St. Louis Republican,* 14 June 1869).

For a report generally contradicting Hildebrand on the issue of both homes and women, see the *St. Louis Democrat,* 30 June 1869: "It has been asserted that he suffered injury at the hands of a Union officer—having his house burned down and his family driven forth homeless and shelterless.

Whatever of truth or falsehood may be in these stories, it is certain that Hildebrand became a desperate and unscrupulous man. He wreaked a terrible vengeance upon those who had been his enemies, shooting men down in their fields and by the wayside, burning houses and outraging women." For an article, probably exaggerated at least in part, that refers to a child, an aged person, and a woman, see the *St. Louis Republican*, 16 July 1869: "Hilderbrand is charged with the burning out of the eyes, with gunpowder, of a boy, the son of one of his enemies. In 1863, it is told that in Callaway county he killed and quartered an old man, and threw the remains down before the door of his victim's house. In the same year he made a raid on the farm of a man named James McLean, in St. Francois county, insulted Mrs. McLean and drove off about $6,000 worth of cattle and horses." For more on Louise McLane and James McLane (whom Hildebrand later killed), see chap. 36.

For a more specific account of the alleged Callaway County incident, see the *St. Louis Republican*, 14 June 1869: "[Hildebrand] was famous during the war as a daring bushwhacker, and his name became as notorious as those of Quantrel and Bill Anderson. It is alleged that in 1863 he, with a squad of men, shot an old man in Callaway county, and quartering the body in the presence of the wife of his victim, threw the mutilated remains down the doorsteps. One of the accomplices in the above tragedy, named Jordan, was subsequently captured; tried by a drum-head court martial, composed of Col. Bruns, 8th Missouri Volunteers, on the banks of the Missouri, at St. Aubert, and was led out and shot by eight volunteers."

4. Resinger and Lasiter are listed on the rolls of the company of Capt. Jesse Ellison, a former member of the Second (McCulloch's) Missouri Cavalry and soon to be commanding officer of Co. D, Seventh Missouri Cavalry. (He would ultimately be lieutenant colonel of that regiment.) While Hildebrand's name does not appear on the rolls, after the war Ellison claimed Hildebrand was with his company during this time. See Henry Resinger, Index to Compiled Service Records of Confederate Soldiers, M380 roll 12; Ellison to Jackson, 17 Mar. 1915.

Prior to joining Ellison's command, Lasiter had served in Co. C/K, Second (McCulloch's) Missouri Cavalry. Still earlier he had fought in the skirmish at Big River Bridge in Sept. 1861 (when Hildebrand claimed he was sitting out the war but was reported by other sources to be leading the Rebel forces in the skirmish—see chap. 3). Later in the war Lasiter went on to serve as first lieutenant under David Reed in the Fifteenth (Reeves's) Missouri Cavalry. See G. W. Lasatur/Laster, Index to Compiled Service Records of Confederate Soldiers, M380 roll 9; G. W. Lasater, Record of Service Cards, box 106, reel S734/box 50, reel S902.

5. William L. Jeffers of Cape Girardeau County was there forming the Eighth Missouri Cavalry (CSA). See McGhee, *Campaigning with Marmaduke;* Ross, "The Fight at Jackson Fairground," introduction.

6. Addison Cunningham was an enlisted man home on leave from Co. H, Sixty-eighth EMM. The muster roll for the unit records him as being "killed by guerrillas near Farmington." See Muster Roll, Co. H, Sixty-eighth Enrolled Missouri Militia, box 16, folder 90, Missouri State Archives; Wilkinson, "Biographical Sketch."

A sworn statement that differs from Hildebrand's version of events holds that Hildebrand shot Cunningham after Cunningham surrendered his revolver to Lasiter, a deed for which the two guerrillas were indicted for murder in St. Francois County on 15 May 1863. According to the legal statement of William F. Miller:

> On the 15th of December five men [came to] . . . the stable. They [asked] me if Ad Cunningham was there. I told them no. They would not believe it and searched the stable. I told them he was not there. Then they told me to get his bridle and catch his horse. They then told me to lead him out of the stable and give him to them and to lead out my horse. Then they told me to get on my horse and go and show them where Ad Cunningham lived. They then told me if I told them a lie, they would burn our property up. They came along in site of the house and asked me if that was the house. I told them yes. Then they told me to stay behind and I done so. Then I heard the guns fire and they hollowed, "boys come in and help lay him on the bed."

Cunningham's son John also provided his testimony (the spelling and grammar again remaining as in the original document):

> Five men came galloping down the road when they came to the house. George Laserter jumped of his horse, drew his pistol, and came in to the porch to shoot and hollowed for pap to come out there and pap asked him what he wanted and he said surrender and give up his arms. Pap reached out the gun to him and he snatched it out of his hands, and then there was a man came running from the fence and shot pap. He fell. I was standing right behind him when he fell and he reached out his hands to Mother and asked her to help him up. He was so heavy she could not raise him up and had lay him back on the floor and I asked them to help him up and they [said] certainly we will. They helped me lay him on the bed and George Laserter came to him and shook hands with him and said farewell and then searched his pocket and started to pull of his boots. I told they had done enough by killing him not to take off his boots. They took a blanket and a short musket and a French revolver and a rifle from me and a horse and a saddle and bridle that belonged to my father. Saddle and bridle was government property. They took my father's pocket book and knife after he was

dead. (Court Inquisition Taken in Regard to the Death of Addison Cunningham, 16 Dec. 1862, St. Francois County Office of the Coroner, Inquests 1850–1932, reel C31546; *State of Missouri vs. George Lasiter and Saml Helderbrand*, St. Francois County Circuit Court, 28 May 1863, St. Francois Circuit Court Records, reel C15693, Missouri State Archives)

Hildebrand barely escaped capture after this event during a general manhunt for supporters of his ally Daniel McGee, in the course of which the short musket was recovered:

> Then there was old man Cobb and Columbus Bailey who had taken a horse from a medicine man. Old Cobb was brought in because they found Bailey harboring at his house. Just right along them close by, Bailey slipped out of the guard house one awful dark night. . . . Bailey slipped off, and made tracks. He some where down Castor [River] got the medicine man's buggy horse, and rode away. Jack Aker, and some one or two more rode into camp whistling to give notice that he was slipping in. He reported rebs gone down Castor. A good scout was instantly made, but I was sick and was not called. They come into contact with the traveling medicine man and hastily gathered a few facts, and they cut a bee line for Old man Cobb's. At daylight they closed in around the house, and had a fine lot of fun as they found several there. One was a Gibbs, one was Sam Hildebrand, but he got away. And one was Columbus Bailey! . . . In this drive they got 8 or 9 prisoners—I think, as I know when they got back to the mill, we then had 12 prisoners in the guard house. . . . The boys had just come in a day or so before that Sunday, having been down to Dan McGhee's. They got his horse and saddle, but he somehow passed poor old sleeping Wash Sitze, and got on his old U.S. horse and what a race they had! [Capt. Pinkney] Powers [Co. K, Sixty-eighth EMM] wounded his horse in that loose flesh on the outside of the upper end of his left fore leg. Wash could have then killed Dan as easily as not, but you know him anyhow. (H. C. Wilkinson to C. A. Peterson, 12 Dec. 1902, Peterson Papers, box 7, folder 1)

Note that a Malcolm M. Gibbs served with McGee in the Second (Hunter's) Missouri Cavalry and then in Co. C/K, Second (McCulloch's) Missouri Cavalry, having deserted that company in Sept. 1862. See Malcolm M. Gibbs, Record of Service Card, box 31, reel S906.

According to a different, related account of this same action:

> Other "game" being plenty not miles away, Capt. Powers began scouting the country near him, and soon had twelve prisoners in his "Guard

> House" at Bollinger's Mill [now Zalma]. One of the prisoners was "Old Man Cobb" who lived down some miles below the mill, on Castor River. He was not a Confederate soldier, but was found feeding and harboring them at his house, so he must suffer imprisonment for his dis-loyalty to the U.S. Government. It was at his house on Capt. Power's second visit there that the famous Sam Hildebrand narrowly escaped capture or death. He escaped however, by fast running as Jack Aker emptied his carbine at him as he ran. Had it been known that Sam Hildebrand was there, all possible efforts would have been made for his capture. Capt. Powers' men found a [Enfield] carbine or "musketoon" there in Cobb's house, brought there by Hildebrand from Madison or Ste. Francois County, taken from Ad Cunningham of Capt. Finley's company of the 68th EMM. Cunningham had gone home from Capt. Finley's camp to visit his family and had his arms with him, but he was surprised and murdered by Hildebrand, and his arms and acoutrements taken by Hildebrand. (Wilkinson, "Biographical Sketch")

Hildebrand appears to provide his version of this fight at Old Man Cobb's in the first few paragraphs of chap. 18.

7. Capt. Thomas B. Walker's Co. C, Twelfth MSM Cavalry, had been a part of Capt. William Flentge's three-company battalion, which had killed Sam Hildebrand's brother Washington at the St. Joseph Lead Mines six months earlier (see chap. 8). While it is not known whether Walker was present at this murder, it is known that he resigned his commission in the immediate aftermath of that affair after having been in constant conflict with his former commanding officer, who was of the opinion that Walker was a Rebel sympathizer. Where his brother's death was involved, this fact appears to have had no relevance for a revenge-consumed Sam Hildebrand. See Record of Events, July–Aug. 1862, Co. D; *Annual Report of the Adjutant General . . . 1863*, 88. For Walker's suspected southern sympathies, see "Narrative of the Service of Lindsay W. Murdoch in the War of the Rebellion," *Echo* 1 (Oct: 1979): 147–48; Lindsay Murdoch, Pension Record, Record Group 704 293, National Archives.

Before the war Reuben Barnes resided in Liberty Township near Hildebrand. Notably, Barnes had very recently been a sergeant in the company of Solomon G. Kitchen of the Second (McCulloch's) Missouri Cavalry. Indicative of Hildebrand and Barnes's single-minded purpose to kill Walker was their apparent willingness to incur the ire of Kitchen. Kitchen, who soon after this event became colonel and commanding officer of the Seventh Missouri Cavalry, was not only the recent superior officer of Barnes but also the uncle of Thomas Walker, the man slain by Barnes and Hildebrand, and the uncle of Walker's wife (husband and wife were cousins). See the 1860 Census for Liberty Township, St. Francois County, Dwelling 210; Cletis Ellinghouse to Kirby Ross,

6 Sept. 2002. Ellinghouse is a newspaperman, author, historian, and genealogist who focuses on southeast Missouri.

In regard to the gunfight, Walker, now a civilian, had been trying to negotiate an arrangement with local Confederates that would allow him to remain in the area unmolested. Rebuffing these efforts, Reuben Barnes assembled a squad of men reportedly numbering from twelve to fifteen (not just four, as suggested by Hildebrand) and began hunting Walker, locating him at his father's cabin and demanding his surrender.

Probably realizing that Hildebrand's presence meant certain death and preferring to go down fighting, Walker burst from the house shooting two revolvers, mortally wounding Barnes as a barrage of return gunfire brought him to his own end. (Hildebrand's suggestion that he alone killed Walker is an exaggeration.) According to the sworn testimony of Walker's wife, "when I got to Mr. Walker his face was bleeding, the blood was running from out his mouth and nose and his brains was running out on the ground. I seen but one bullet hole that was in his forehead there was eleven bullet holes in his coat. There was one hundred or more shots fired." This event was dissected in detail in a postwar criminal trial, *State of Missouri vs. Erastus W. Hill*, Stoddard County Circuit Court, filed 1866. See also Ross, "The Fight at Jackson Fairground," chap. 1, nn. 8, 11.

8. Some southeast Missouri historians have expressed doubt at Hildebrand's participation in the Walker/Barnes shootout. However, as noted, Walker's company and perhaps Walker himself had been party to the murder of Washington Hildebrand, and Reuben Barnes lived near to the Hildebrand family before the war. Furthermore, the two men Hildebrand claims to have taken along with him to help out Barnes—Resinger and Lasiter—were documented members of the company of Jesse Ellison; like Barnes, now-Captain Ellison had recently been an enlisted man in Kitchen's company of the Second (McCulloch's) Missouri Cavalry. Finally, after the war, Ellison stated that Hildebrand had also been a member of his newly formed company around this time. These Ellison connections are important because Ellison and his company were stationed at Bloomfield during "the forepart of Jan."—the exact time of the killing of Walker. Given the fact that Hildebrand and Reuben Barnes resided near one another before the war, coupled with the evidence that Hildebrand was in the Bloomfield area at the time of the gunfight, there is little reason to doubt the assertion that Hildebrand was present at the killing of a man who had a connection to the death of his brother. See Wilkinson, "Biographical Sketch." For Ellison's presence in Bloomfield as late as 27 Jan. 1863, see the *Perryville Union*, 6 Feb. 1863.

CHAPTER FIFTEEN

1. Hildebrand's return to the region would have coincided with a major Confederate setback there: on 27 Jan. the Rebels were routed at Bloomfield. See

the *Annual Report of the Adjutant General . . . 1863*, 25–26; *O.R.*, ser. 1, vol. 22, pt. 1, pp. 221–22; "Lindsay, James, Col., 68th EMM, Report of the March and Attack on Bloomfield, Missouri," Adjutant General Papers: Oaths, Orders, etc., Record Group 133, Missouri State Archives; *St. Louis Democrat*, 6 Feb. 1863; Wilkinson, "Biographical Sketch."

According to one report of the "Bloomfield Scout" and the quick Confederate exit:

> Ironton, Mo. February 3, 1863— . . . Here they were in sight of Bloomfield. The preliminaries for the battle had been made, all the commands had been given. The Colonel gave the order, *charge the town*, and away they went, Capt. [Pinkney] Powers leading the column. . . . On they went under spur, the inner pickets of the enemy taken back aghast, poking up their guns, crying "Halt! Who are you?" No one regarded them, and terror-stricken, they broke for timber. The artillery was run up to a commanding position, unlimbered, and made ready by the time the boys were in the town charging and yelling like hyenas, when the Colonel ordered the cannon to fire. They did, and the scamps fled like rats from their porthole building, running helter-skelter through back-ways, and hiding in gullies, while some, who were fortunate enough to get farther off, were shooting back at their pursuers. . . . A large number of prisoners were in the meantime collected and stored away under guard . . . fifty-three prisoners, about sixty or seventy horses were captured. . . . Not one of the Colonel's command was hurt, and probably not over three of the enemy. . . . Every officer and every man behaved like a *hero* and a "dare devil." (*St. Louis Democrat*, 6 Feb. 1863)

Also see Lindsay, "Report of the March and Attack."

2. This claim of a Confederate victory at Bollinger's Mill on the night of 4 Feb. has confounded local historians and helped further the aura of Hildebrand being a serial liar. This is because a widely reported contact between Confederate and Federal forces occurred at Bollinger's Mill on the *afternoon* of 4 Feb., one in which the Federals emerged as victors. However, a recently identified account of the day's events written by a Union veteran confirms Hildebrand's claim. The skirmish Hildebrand speaks of was actually the first of *two* there that day, occurring at 12:20 A.M. on the *morning* of 4 Feb. and thereafter going unreported by the combatants on either side. After Hildebrand, Jesse Ellison, and their allies were forced out of Bloomfield on 27 Jan. by the Sixty-eighth EMM, they made their way to Bollinger's Mill and were moving into position at 11:00 on the night of 3 Feb. to engage in the short but vicious skirmish that then took place just after midnight on 4 Feb.

According to the Union account of this fight:

> While resting up from the "Bloomfield Scout," at about 12:20 o'clock A.M., Feb. 4th 1863 Captain [Jesse] Ellison and Dan McGhee coming from Bloomfield stole a march on Co. K [Sixty-eighth EMM] coming up in a bright moonlight and light snow behind the mill and charged Co. K's camp. . . . The first they knew of the presence of the Rebels—some 100 men, was the crack of their guns and revolvers and the whine of their bullets, followed by the cries and groans of the wounded. For the moment, all was lost, but as it happened [nine Federals] were quartered in a saw mill house about 75 yards or more from the row of tents. This little handful at once armed and charged the Rebel line, or rather mass, as it closed around the large center tent, and at once staggered them. The Rebels never recovered from the shock, but at once beat a glorious retreat by running as scared men can and do, for timber. They [the Rebels] succeeded in mortally wounding one man and . . . wounding [nine others]. . . . It was never ascertained just how many Rebels were wounded in the fight of about 5 minutes, but one Rebel was left dead on the ground and the remains of another was afterward found not far away on a hill. . . . Following this night fight, on the next day, Dan McGhee and his band of 30 men or more, were wiped from the face of the earth by the MSM boys. (Sgt. H. C. Wilkinson, Sixty-eighth EMM, in Wilkinson, "Biographical Sketch")

Confederate Jesse Ellison later confirmed his own presence at this fight, along with that of Sam Hildebrand: "Made raids and battles in various parts of Mo. Went as far as Fredericktown in Madison Co., Mo. Had a battle at Bollinger's Mill in Bollinger co. . . . Broke up Capt. Powers company [Co. K, Sixty-eighth EMM] in Bollinger Co. The noted Sam Hildebrand was a member of my co." (Ellison to Jackson, 17 Mar. 1915).

3. Later in the day on 4 Feb., a battalion of the Twelfth Missouri State Militia commanded by Maj. Frederick Reeder came upon Bollinger's Mill, capturing a few Rebel stragglers who had remained behind (thus leading to the present-day confusion as to which force it was that prevailed at Bollinger's Mill). Reeder's report of his actions that day speaks of learning from these "outlaws" that McGee was nearby and that he had "four Union citizens as prisoners." (Note that this is consistent with Hildebrand's assertion that the Confederates had captured four prisoners. Also note that the EMM troops were citizen-soldiers, not full-time troops.) See *Organization and Status of Missouri Troops*, 48–81.

4. The "MSM boys" thereafter trailed Daniel McGee through the Mingo Swamp and to the farm of his uncle, Simeon Cato. The ensuing skirmish, sometimes referred to locally as the McGee Massacre, resulted in the wholesale slaughter of the McGee/Cato partisans: "We dashed upon them before a single

one had the chance to escape. They were at once recognized as McGee's band, and as our approach was as sudden as it was unexpected, they fled in confusion across the large corn-field in the center of which the house of Cato stood. My men now were in their element, and whilst others quickly tore down the fence of the corn-field, the rest surrounded it, and within fifteen minutes we had exterminated the whole band. We took no prisoners from amongst them, as I had previously given the order not to do so. We counted 9 killed, amongst them McGee; 20 mortally wounded, and 3 slightly" (Maj. F. W. Reeder, Twelfth MSM Cavalry, *O.R.*, ser. 1, vol. 22, pt. 1, pp. 225–27). See also the *St. Louis Democrat*, 16 Feb. 1863; Moore, *The Rebellion Record*, vol. 6, 415–16; Cato, Palmer, and Cato, "Research on the Name Cato"; Cato to Ross, 19 Nov. 2000.

The sweep through the region by the Twelfth MSM continued for the next ten days, after which five more men belonging to "the band of General McGee" were reported killed and wounded. At the conclusion of the offensive it was said that "there are not more than three of the notorious ones of the gang left—Hetterbrand, Cowan, and Dixon." Richard Cowan and a Thomas E. Dixon were veterans of Co. C/K, Second (McCulloch's) Missouri Cavalry. In addition, Cowan was Daniel McGee's brother-in-law (Hildebrand refers to Cowan as being "one of my men" in chap. 23). See *O.R.*, ser. 1, vol. 22, pt. 1, pp. 224–25; Hahn, *Bollinger County 1851–1976*, 676; Richard D. Cowan, Index to Compiled Service Records of Confederate Soldiers, M380 roll 3; Thomas Dixon, Record of Service Card, box 22, reel S907.

Civilian members of the Cato family were also dying in Federal custody. Nathan Cato died at Alton prison across the Mississippi River from St. Louis the day after the McGee Massacre, as Chapman Cato and Wilson Cato Sr. had the previous 3 Jan. and 9 Nov., respectively. See the Register of Confederate Soldiers, Alton, Ill., Register of Confederate Soldiers, Sailors, and Citizens Who Died in Federal Prisons and Military Hospitals in the North, 1861–1865, 6–7, National Archives and Records Administration; Cato, Palmer, and Cato, "Research on the Name Cato."

5. William Cato, whose farm had been the site of a skirmish between Hildebrand and the Twelfth MSM Cavalry in July, was a first cousin of Daniel McGee. Like Daniel McGee and Dick Cowan, Cato was a veteran of the Second (Hunter's) Missouri Cavalry Battalion in the Missouri State Guard, as well as a deserter from Reed's Co. C/K, Second (McCulloch's) Missouri Cavalry. After these events both he and Cowan joined Reed's Co. C in the Fifteenth Missouri Cavalry of Tim Reeves, another ally of Hildebrand. See Cato, Palmer, and Cato, "Research on the Name Cato"; William Cato, Record of Service Card, box 15, reel S902.

6. Hildebrand has merged two series of events into one. The skirmish at Bollinger's Mill occurred in early Feb. 1863, while the pursuit Hildebrand describes and the deaths of his seven comrades are quite consistent with actions

taken by Leeper's company the following Sept. and Oct., during the course of which Hildebrand's name was raised twice in Union dispatches (see chap. 21).

Adding further credence to an Oct. timeframe instead of a Feb. one is the fact that William Cato was still with the Second (McCulloch's) Missouri Cavalry east of the Mississippi River at the time of the Bollinger's Mill skirmish and did not desert and rejoin his kinsmen in southeast Missouri until later that year. See William Cato, Record of Service Card.

7. This is not possible. What they may have "afterwards learned" is that the man who executed their comrades the following Oct. was Captain Leeper, not that Leeper commanded the Federals at Bollinger's Mill in Feb. The officer in command of the Federals whom Hildebrand, Ellison, and McGee engaged at Bollinger's Mill on 4 Feb. was 1st Lt. James T. Sutton, Co. K, Sixty-eighth EMM. Capt. William T. Leeper of Co. B, Twelfth Missouri State Militia Cavalry, was eighty-five miles away at Van Buren in Carter County on 4 Feb. *O.R.*, ser. 1, vol. 22, pt. 1, p. 227; Wilkinson, "Biographical Sketch."

Note should be made that a Sutton encampment was attacked later that year, and in the aftermath of that affair Captain Leeper did engage in the pursuit and killings of a similar number of Confederate guerrillas (see chap. 21). *O.R.*, ser. 1, vol. 22, pt. 2, pp. 574, 600, 679.

8. In the immediate aftermath of the capture of Bloomfield and the defeat of Daniel McGee, the atmosphere in which Hildebrand's wife would have been stranded would have been very inhospitable, as the intense Federal campaign against the remnants of the McGee/Cato clan continued unabated:

> One of the most notorious of these bushwhackers was a desperado known as Jack Cato, who boasted that he had made at least eighty Union men bite the dust. Some forty rods down the hill, east of the old jail [in Bloomfield], was a piece of timber land, and at the point of the timber was a tree, a large limb or branch spreading over the ploughed ground, on the upper side of which the bark was worn off, and Cato boasted that it was done by the rope, hanging Union men thereon. Three Union men were caught and made to dig three graves under that tree. The first was hung and thrown into the first grave, the second was hung and put into the second grave, the third was hung up and then let down and ordered to go and report to the Yanks, and his grave left open. Just as the first ray of light could be seen in the east on a beautiful April morning Jack was taken from jail, marched down to that grave where a rough coffin was placed, required to about face and kneel upon the coffin when the unerring bullet from the gun of one of the guards, selected for the purpose, sped to his heart. He fell upon his coffin with a terrible oath on his lips and soon filled a felon's grave. On the night before the execution of the wretched man, some of the boys were on guard at the jail and when they informed him of his fate, he swore that

> he did not care; he had had his satisfaction in killing Union men; at least eighty "Yanks" had died from the shot of his rifle when they didn't know he had the drop on them. Chaplain Wood called to see him, but was only met by defiant sneers and curses. (Scott, *Story of the Thirty Second Iowa Infantry Volunteers,* 45–46)

CHAPTER SIXTEEN

1. Brig. Gen. John McNeil (1813–91) was headquartered out of Cape Girardeau and commanded Federal troops who were en route to Bloomfield on 16 Feb. to permanently garrison that town. During the early months of the war he served as colonel in a series of regiments, ultimately leading the Second Missouri State Militia Cavalry in northeast Missouri. At this position McNeil received notoriety for his execution of Confederate prisoners of war at Palmyra, Mo., in retaliation for the kidnapping and murder of a local Union supporter. After a successful campaign against Confederate irregulars during the summer and fall of 1862, he was promoted to brigadier general and was transferred to southeast Missouri along with the Second MSM. See *The Union Army,* vol. 8, 170–71; Col. James Lindsay to Capt. H. H. Finley and Lt. James T. Sutton, 16 Feb. 1863, Peterson Papers, box 2, folder 9.

2. Casualty reports for the Second MSM Cavalry fail to support this claim. See the Muster Roll, Second MSM Cavalry, Missouri State Archives.

3. Hildebrand has misremembered the name of either the man or the town: it was now just Mar. of 1863, and Capt. Hiram Rice of Co. I, Third Missouri State Militia Cavalry, was based at Pilot Knob and did not garrison Fredericktown until Aug. of that year. See the Record of Events, Co. I, Third Missouri State Militia Cavalry, State Historical Society of Missouri.

4. As noted in chap. 9, James Cato was the first cousin of Daniel McGee. Cato and William Washington Neighbors had served under Dan McGee in the Second (Hunter's) Missouri Cavalry Battalion and more recently in McGee and David Reed's Co. C/K, Second (McCulloch's) Missouri Cavalry Regiment. (Cato and Neighbors deserted that unit together on 1 Apr. 1862.) Both men were also close neighbors of McGee before the war—in 1860 James Cato lived next door to him, while Neighbors was two houses away. After the McGee Gang was eradicated, Neighbors appeared on the rolls of Williams's Missouri Cavalry, which was headquartered in Greene County, Ark., near Hildebrand, the Bolin Boys, and Tim Reeves. Neighbors's close association with Hildebrand is documented as continuing into 1865 (see chaps. 21 and 23). *O.R.*, ser. 1, vol. 48, pt. 1, p. 1070; Cato, Palmer, and Cato, "Research on the Name Cato"; 1860 Census for Jefferson Township, Wayne County, Dwellings 59, 60, 62; W. W. Neighbors, Record of Service Card, box 61, reel S902.

5. This alleged battle of three men against an entire regiment (around one thousand men) would have constituted the greatest defeat of U.S. forces in the

history of the war in southeast Missouri, as well as the second-largest number of Federals killed there in a single engagement, and serves to illustrate why Hildebrand's memoir is derisively received by many mainstream Missouri historians. There is no record in Union or Confederate annals of such an encounter having occurred.

6. "Captain Hicks" is later identified as being Nathaniel Hicks (see chap. 29). There is no record of him in the command of General McNeil, in either a Volunteer unit, a State Militia unit, or an Enrolled Militia unit. Early in the war he does show up on the rolls of Co. E, Tenth Missouri Cavalry, but he deserted from that regiment on 29 Dec. 1862 and never returned. See Nathaniel Hicks/Higgs, Military File, Tenth Missouri Cavalry, State Historical Society of Missouri.

It is possible that Hicks was not operating under U.S. authority and was intent on robbing the Hildebrands of his own accord or that Hildebrand was mistaken as to the identity of the man who was following him. Nathaniel Hicks had sons who were of military age during the Civil War, and there were also two other Hicks households located on either side of his home, both of which had a number of males of military age. One of them may have been in the Union Army and leading the pursuit. See the 1860 Census for Castor Township, Stoddard County, Dwellings 584, 585, 586.

CHAPTER SEVENTEEN

1. Given Hildebrand's shoulder wound and the geographic locale described, the "old Rebel" was almost certainly Thomas McGee: "I told dem dat [Hildebrand] had a mark behind his shoulder dat dey could see. I 'member once when Sam Hildebrand was shot and came to our place to have his sore washed out. I held de wash pan for old Tom McGee to wash his wound" (Holsell, interview, vol. 10, p. 201).

2. "Helterbrand—This not very noted nor very agreeable rebel has been roaming through Madison county and counties adjoining for many months, enacting all kinds of devilment. We are informed that he has murdered a number of peaceable Union citizens in the past few months. The Militia in that section are endeavoring to hunt the murderer up, and we hope they may get him" (*Perryville Union*, 12 June 1863).

CHAPTER EIGHTEEN

1. Hildebrand (or his biographer) is again in the process of combining two separate engagements into one. The event described up to this point appears to have occurred several months earlier than Hildebrand places it and has close similarities to the one described in chap. 14, n. 6 (involving the fight with Co. K, Sixty-eighth EMM, during which Addison Cunningham's musketoon was

recaptured from Hildebrand, which took place at the "unoccupied house" of "Old Man Cobb," who was being held in a Federal guardhouse at Bollinger's Mill).

As Hildebrand continues telling his anecdote, he merges that first event into yet another one that is readily identifiable and actually involved many more Confederates than just his own band.

2. Given the Black River locale described, the involvement of Federal troops from Patterson and Greenville, the description of the Union officer being shot, and the Federal loss of horses being a significant part of the story, Hildebrand is describing the Battle of Horseshoe Bend, a.k.a. the Battle of Brushy Creek (which is an arm of the Black River), which occurred near the Carter/Wayne County line, north-northeast of present-day Ellsinore, on 1 June 1863. However, in chap. 17 Hildebrand claims to have been in St. Francois County on 31 May and to have left directly for Arkansas. If in fact he happened to get his dates confused, this part of his story, as he describes it, is right on the mark as having occurred at Horseshoe Bend, if one adds around a hundred or more Confederates under Hildebrand ally Timothy Reeves to fight with him.

According to a Federal account of the Horseshoe Bend skirmish, upon receiving word that a Rebel force was gathering on the Little Black River halfway between Poplar Bluff and Doniphan, Maj. Lothar Lippert of the Thirteenth Illinois Cavalry sent out two patrols on 30 May from Patterson, Mo., in a pincer movement. Taking personal command of the flanking force, Lippert led thirty-three men from his own regiment and another forty from Leeper's company of the Third MSM Cavalry, reaching a farm twenty-five miles southwest of Patterson, where he went into camp for the night.

Around 10:00 P.M. word was brought in from his outlying pickets that a large force of men had been seen moving into position around the Federal encampment. As the Federals spent most of the night waiting and preparing, skirmishing finally commenced around 3:45 A.M. In the course of heated fighting, Major Lippert was severely injured by a shotgun blast, with six of his enlisted men also being wounded. The Confederates, led by Reeves, pressed forward until they overran the Union position, scattering most of the Third MSM, as well as twenty-seven of their horses. The troopers of the Thirteenth Illinois Cavalry, still mounted, rallied, drew sabers, and forced their way through the Rebel line with their dismounted militia comrades following in their wake. Reforming at a more defensible point, the Federals waited out the Confederates, ultimately making their way back to Patterson the next day. *O.R.*, ser. 1, vol. 22, pt. 1, pp. 344–45; ser. 1, vol. 22, pt. 1, pp. 345–47; *St. Louis Republican*, 2 June 1863; *Louisiana (Mo.) Journal*, 6 June 1863; Eddy, *The Patriotism of Illinois*, vol. 2, 632; Field, *Three Years in the Saddle*, 29–31.

In an official Confederate account that partially corresponds with both the Federal and the Hildebrand versions, it was reported that Captain Reeves, in command of his own independent company of Missouri Scouts (a precursor to the Fifteenth Missouri Cavalry Regiment), as well as an eighty-man detachment from Burbridge's Brigade (perhaps Ellison's company of the Seventh Missouri Cavalry, which was part of the brigade at the time), had undertaken a three-day march from Powhatan, Ark., to Big Brush Creek in Wayne County, Mo., where his men "attacked the enemy and routed them. Captured thirty horses and rigging, arms, etc." See the Record of Events, 1 May–30 Aug. 1863, Co. A, Fifteenth Missouri Cavalry Regiment (CSA), Hewett, *Supplement to the Official Records,* ser. 1, vol. 38.

CHAPTER NINETEEN

1. On this trip it appears Hildebrand may have initially been somewhat active a bit further north than he indicates: "HELTERBRAND AGAIN.—This notorious scoundrel is still running at large in Madison county. We are informed that while two soldiers were on the road from Fredericktown to Ironton, they were captured by Helterbrand, and taken, no one knows where. It would be an exceedingly good thing if this rascal could be caught and hung. No man deserves it more" (*Perryville Union,* 17 July 1863).

2. In May 1863 the Sixty-eighth EMM combined with other southeast Missouri EMM units to form the Eighth Provisional Enrolled Missouri Militia. Pinkney Powers was given command of Co. M in this new regiment, which was the force that Hildebrand acknowledged "somewhat worsted" him on the Castor near Bollinger's Mill. According to one account of this fight that provides a more thorough description than Hildebrand's version:

> Very soon after arming of Co. M at Mineral Point, somehow Capt. Powers "scented game" above. Sam Hildebrand and his band was somewhere up country and Capt. Powers, true to his instinct as a scout, obtained permit to take with him picked men, and by night marches, reached his home in Wayne County and steal over onto Castor River in the night to watch for Hildebrand to come along on his way south. Co. M armed with the Enfield Carbine, and several revolvers, they left camp at Mineral Point in Washington County late P.M. The 3rd night out found them posted on the Bloomfield and Fredericktown Road on Castor River, in the barn shed on the farm of Solomon Whitener [in Fillmore Township in Bollinger County] and some 3 miles south[east] of Gravelton. They had hardly settled to business when the guard in obedience to orders stole in, and reported horsemen approaching. Soon they came along side and one made a pass to shoot Capt. Powers' guard, but, all at once 3 out of the 4 Rebels lay in the road dead men, one of the 4 escaped but cut all over by bullets. Capt. Powers had 17 trusty men with him and their fire proved it. Daylight revealed the fact that

> Sam Hildebrand was about a hundred yards or more to the rear with some 8 or 10 men with him, but at the fire of Capt. Powers and his men on his advance guard they took to the hills leaving the road. This affair put an end to guerrilla bands traveling that road for a long time. (Wilkinson, "Biographical Sketch")

Dr. Cyrus A. Peterson also added a few details to the fight:

> Were you in the squad with Capt. Powers which killed the three bushwhackers at old Soloman Whitener's corn crib in the summer of '63 or '64? The three killed were Bayless, Boyce & some other fellow whose name began with "B" but I have forgotten it. There were 12 in the bunch and the 4 men in the advance got the fire of Powers' squad and 3 of them went down—only one escaping. The 8 men behind changed their course to the brush and avoided a conflict. We lived two miles north of old Soloman's place and this gang earlier in the evening in passing our place surrounded a very spry little mule of ours, in the horse lot, and tried to bridle her, but she kicked her way through the cordon of horse thieves and got away from them. She had sport with them for half an hour, in the dark, and finally we heard them say: "G-d d—n the mule, let it go!" and they rode away defeated. (Cyrus A. Peterson to H. C. Wilkinson, 22 Jan. 1903, Peterson Papers, box 7, folder 1)

The Provisional Enrolled Missouri Militia (PEMM), to which Captain Powers belonged at this time, was a full-time offshoot of the part-time Enrolled Missouri Militia and had been created in the spring of 1863 to deal with deficiencies involving that original organization. For more on the PEMM, see *Organization and Status of Missouri Troops*, 82–86; Ross, "Federal Militia in Missouri"; *Report of the Committee of the House of Representatives*, 231–32. Also see the 1860 Census for Fillmore Township, Bollinger County, Mo., Dwelling 1243.

3. Hildebrand represents that he was by himself and that this killing occurred during the summer of 1863. However, in the course of filing first-degree murder charges after the war, a grand jury determined: "On the 10th day of January, 1864, Samuel Helderbrand with a gun held in his right hand did shoot Nathaniel Hicks in the head and the back of the body giving him a mortal wound one inch wide and five inches deep, and was aided by Bud Hinkle, instantly killing Hicks" (*State of Missouri vs. Samuel Helderbrandt*, Stoddard County Circuit Court, 21 Oct. 1865, Stoddard County Circuit Court Records, reel C13359, Missouri State Archives).

The codefendant may have been William B. Hinkle, who was married to David Reed's sister and had been a corporal under him and Daniel McGee in

Co. C/K, Second (McCulloch's) Missouri Cavalry. In addition, William B. Hinkle and a number of other Hinkles had served under Reed and McGee in the Second (Hunter's) Missouri Cavalry Battalion. See Hahn, *Bollinger County,* 109; William B. Hinkle, Index to Compiled Service Records of Confederate Soldiers, M380 roll 7; Cletis Ellinghouse to Kirby Ross, 24 Jan. 2004.

CHAPTER TWENTY

1. It was within days of this timeframe that the so-called Round Pond Massacre was perpetrated (see chap. 13). According to a report by Hildebrand ally Jesse Ellison, now lieutenant colonel of the Seventh (Kitchen's) Missouri Cavalry, nine men reporting to his command conducted the attack on the Union supply train while the camp was sleeping, killing and wounding thirty men, destroying thirty wagons by fire, and capturing nineteen horses. Federal reports, which state that the dead men belonged to the Union Sixth Missouri Cavalry and the Second MSM Cavalry, generally correspond with Hildebrand's own account, which states that the Rebels were able to move in close prior to the attack due to the heavy foliage surrounding the encampment.

Members of the Bolin Gang were said to be part of the raiding party, which put a torch to the wagons as "the Captain said to the prisoners, 'this is the way I burn houses,' referring to the burning of his own house by the Union troops." Six months later John F. Bolin was captured by the Second MSM Cavalry, which promptly transported him to their nearby headquarters at Cape Girardeau and announced he would be tried for his alleged crimes. In undergoing an interrogation, he was said to have admitted, "I was at Round Pond; there were eight men killed, two by Nathan Bolin and one by John Wright. They were killed with handspikes. I emptied one revolver" (*St. Louis Republican,* 14 Aug. 1863). Note that John Wright was yet another veteran of Co. C/K, Second (McCulloch's) Missouri Cavalry, from which he deserted in Dec. 1862. He later joined David Reed's Co. C, Fifteenth (Reeves's) Missouri Cavalry.

One day after his capture, John Bolin was forcibly taken from his guard by a large number of soldiers and citizens and lynched. According to the commanding officer of the post, "no force could be used [against the mob], owing to the fact that no symptom of their intention was manifested until too late, and nearly all the available force was engaged in the act." See *O.R.*, ser. 1, vol. 22, pt. 1, pp. 466, 467–68; *St. Louis Republican*, 10 Aug. 1863; *St. Louis Republican*, 14 Aug. 1863; *St. Louis Republican*, 6 Feb. 1864; *St. Louis Republican*, 7 Feb. 1864; *Charleston (Mo.) Courier*, 19 Feb. 1864 (reprinting an article from the *Cape Girardeau Argus*); John Wright, Index to Compiled Service Records of Confederate Soldiers, M380 roll 16.

2. No such skirmish at Hamburg is found in military or regional records for the date claimed; however, on 19 May 1864 the Bolin Gang was reported to have

raided that hamlet (now New Hamburg), setting a house on fire, as well as the Catholic Church and other buildings. See the *St. Louis Republican*, 23 May 1864; *O.R.*, ser. 1, vol. 34, pt. 3, p. 690.

3. Hildebrand refers to Maj. Gen. Frederick Steele (1819–68), who had troops in southeast Missouri very briefly in the fall of 1862, but never during the time-frame established by Hildebrand. Assuming command of the Department of Arkansas in mid-1863, Steele was leading the assault on Little Rock at the time Hildebrand places his troops near Hamburg, Mo., in Aug. 1863. Taking into account the more likely May 1864 date for the Hamburg raid, however, also remains problematic since Steele had conducted a major southwest Arkansas offensive that spring and returned to Little Rock in May. At no time during the period in question did Steele have a command in Missouri. See Garraty and Carnes, *American National Biography*, vol. 20, 606–7.

4. "Fredericktown, Mo.—Sam. Helterbrand, a notorious bushwhacker, who has been roving Southeast Missouri with impunity, carrying terror to the hearts of Union men ever since the outbreak of the rebellion, passed through [Madison] county a few days since. He is cunning and enterprising, and with a small band of followers carries on a paying business of wholesale outrages under the nose of the military" (*St. Louis Republican*, 29 Aug. 1863).

5. Hildebrand's third raid on Bean's store in just over a year (see chaps. 12 and 17) was afterward described in detail in a newspaper report:

> Irondale, Mo.—Last evening our unusually quiet village was suddenly thrown into a state of great excitement by the appearance of a band of desperate and bold robbers, who robbed the well known firm of J. Bean & Son, of three or four hundred dollars in cash, besides clothing, pistols, &c.
>
> The circumstances of the robbery were about these: About 7 o'clock, P.M., Dr. Poston, a physician of the place, was making a professional call at Mr. Bean's, (Mr. Justus Bean, the junior member of the firm, being ill at the time, in a room adjacent to the storeroom,) when, on approaching the front door, he was suddenly confronted by five armed men, who, presenting their revolvers at his breast, demanded of him his arms, and ordered him to open the door, or call up the inmates. The Doctor told them, if they would permit him to go around to a rear door, he would arouse the inmates, and make known their request—thinking thereby he could escape from them, and alarm the inmates and the town. To this they would not consent, but compelled him to go with them to the rear of the building, where they rapped at the door, and, representing themselves as the Doctor, they were admitted, taking Mr. Justus Bean prisoner, and compelling him to give up money, arms, &c.

When they entered the room, they forced the Doctor to enter also, and placed one of their number with revolver in hand, to guard him, threatening his life if he gave any alarm, or aroused those sleeping above. Two of them compelled Mr. Justus Bean to enter the storeroom and unlock drawers, desks, &c.—in search of money and valuables. They got all the money in the house, except what was in the safe, which they fortunately overlooked in their hasty search.

The Doctor, finding the attention of his guard diverted to some object in the room, sprang out of the door and made his escape, and alarmed the town; but, before a sufficient number could be got together, who had arms, the ruffians had made their escape.

In their search of the house they encountered the elder Bean, who was sleeping in an upperchamber and who would have shot them with his pistol if not prevented by his family.

They also roughly dragged from his bed, another younger son of Mr. Bean, who was also sick, and robbed him of a small amount of money. Military orders, disarming the citizens along the line of the St. Louis and Iron Mountain railroad, have left the citizens at the mercy of thieves and assassins, and they roam over the country, robbing and murdering indiscriminately. (*St. Louis Republican*, 14 Sept. 1863)

CHAPTER TWENTY-ONE

1. No record—either Union or Confederate—exists for this skirmish at the time and place described. However, a Federal report of a skirmish near Osceola, not Springfield, occurring a few months earlier, is very similar to Hildebrand's account, including the somewhat unusual name of the creek, the total surprise suffered by the Confederates, the failure of the Confederates to engage the attackers, and the Confederates' abandonment of their horses in their rush to escape: "Germantown, Mo. May 24, 1863— . . . The next day [22 May] they [the First MSM Cavalry] came upon a band of rebels on Panther creek. Dismounted, unobserved by the rebels, they approached within 75 yards of them, and opened fire. Without returning the fire, the rebels sought safety by running. The creek being between the two parties, it became necessary for our men to remount, in order to pursue, and by the time they were over the creek, the rebels were out of sight. In the melee our men captured twenty horses" (Maj. Alex W. Mullins, First MSM Cavalry, *O.R.*, ser. 1, vol. 22, pt. 2, pp. 294–95).

2. The unspecified "privations" spoken of by Hildebrand at the time he describes—Oct. 1863—included being hunted down and nearly captured or killed by Captain Leeper of the Third MSM Cavalry. This particular Oct. pursuit involving Leeper appears to be the same as that mistakenly mentioned by Hildebrand as occurring in Feb. (see chap. 15). Hildebrand further asserts that William Cato was present at that affair, but note must be made of the fact that

Cato was east of the Mississippi River until Oct., at which time, deserting his unit, he returned to southeast Missouri, further bolstering the likelihood that Hildebrand was mistaken about when the executions occurred.

In Sept. and Oct. 1863 two events were converging in southeast Missouri, resulting in a Federal offensive being ordered by Brig. Gen. Clinton B. Fisk. The first was the gathering of large numbers of Confederate irregulars along the Arkansas border who appeared as if they might have designs on making a raid into Missouri; the second was the upcoming judicial election scheduled for 3 Nov. and Fisk's strong desire to secure his military district so that balloting could take place in every county contained therein. (Several of the counties were in a no-man's-land that was not held by either side.) See *O.R.*, ser. 1, vol. 22, pt. 2, pp. 580, 661, 668–67, 676, 678.

With these goals in mind, General Fisk had large numbers of cavalry out for the entire month of Oct., with instructions that "the mission of each detachment will be the extermination of bushwhackers, guerrillas, thieves, and murderers, and the restoration of good order and quiet. . . . Vigilance, determination, and perseverance will put an end to the reign of terror, jayhawking, and murder which has been supreme in the border counties." So that his troopers might have the proper mind-set for the task, he was also issuing—as was his personal style—very colorful secondary orders, such as "give them fits if you get a chance at them. Grant them furloughs for all time"; "kill every rascal they find bushwhacking or jayhawking"; and "give old Tim [Reeves] and his rascally gang such a hunt and extermination as they never yet had." One particular entreaty at this time even contained the promise of financial reward: "Do you hear anything more from Hildebrandt? I will give any of your boys [in the Third MSM Cavalry] 80 acres of land that will bring in his head either on or off his shoulders." See *O.R.*, ser. 1, vol. 22, pt. 1, p. 681; ser. 1, vol. 22, pt. 2, pp. 632, 665, 676.

Having the orders and inducements in hand, Captain Leeper, of the Third MSM, and Lieutenant Sutton, formerly of the Sixty-eighth EMM and now an officer in the Eighth PEMM, moved into Wayne, Butler, and Ripley Counties. (Note that Lieutenant Sutton was the officer in command of the Federal force at Bollinger's Mill in the early morning hours of 4 Feb. and Hildebrand had confused him with Leeper in that fight; see chap. 15.) Within a few days of the new Federal preelection offensive, in an assault similar to the one at Bollinger's Mill, Sutton's camp was attacked: "notorious Wash. Neighbors ran on his pickets at 3 o'clock this morning, [Sutton] fired on him, and captured a stolen horse he had, but failed to get him" (*O.R.*, ser. 1, vol. 22, pt. 2, p. 574).

In the immediate aftermath of this action, in a report that is reminiscent of Hildebrand's mistaken memories of the supposed action that took place right after the fight at Bollinger's Mill in Feb., Leeper reported, "we have 6 rebel soldiers prisoners, and have killed 7 more"—a number of dead similar to that spoken of by Hildebrand regarding Leeper's executions. Another unrelated dispatch issued later that month states: "Captain Leeper had started the gang from about Hog-Eye, from whence they made for the swamp. My boys pursued and found they had divided, six with Hildebrandt and seven with Neighbors." While this message states that these particular Confederates escaped, an official report would not necessarily include mention of executions. In addition, reports of this pursuit seem to have similarities to Hildebrand's own description of being chased after Bollinger's Mill and having his squad divided. See *O.R.*, ser. 1, vol. 22, pt. 1, p. 681; ser. 1, vol. 22, pt. 1, pp. 600, 679.

CHAPTER TWENTY-TWO

1. "Pilot Knob, Mo. November 25, 1863—Hildebrandt, with 20 men, plundered Farmington this afternoon, and left with their pillage on the Jackson road at about 4 o'clock. I think you can certainly catch him. Strike swiftly. Keep [Capt. George W.] Hummel [Co. K, Third MSM Cavalry]. Get horses for his men, if possible, and don't stop until you kill these rascals. Go at once. Kill them as you find them" (Brig. Gen. Clinton B. Fisk, *O.R.*, ser. 1, vol. 22, pt. 2, p. 715).

As a result of this raid, Capt. Henry B. Milks and Co. H, Third MSM Cavalry, were moved from Pilot Knob to Farmington, where they spent the next four months. See the Record of Events, Dec. 1863–Apr. 1864, Third MSM Cavalry (Second Organization), Compiled Records of Volunteer Union Soldiers, State Historical Society of Missouri.

2. The following account appeared in a St. Louis newspaper:

> Sam Hildebrand's Guerrillas—On Friday last a notorious bushwhacker and guerrilla, named Sam Hildebrand . . . at the head of sixteen men, made a dash on Farmington, St. Francois county, (sixteen miles northeast of Pilot Knob) and robbed several stores in the village of goods to the value of perhaps $300. No other damage or outrage was committed. Before the scoundrels got as much as they could carry off, however, they took fright at a report that "the Feds are coming!" and "they all skedaddled." The Federal forces have been searching diligently for these fellows since the depredation referred to; and, on Sunday, by a decoy movement, five of them were found lying in ambush, waiting for the very company of militia who found them. By a circumlocutory movement, the Federals came upon the rear of the bushwhackers, and shot and killed five of them, the rest escaping. (*St. Louis Republican*, 4 Dec. 1863)

An account by Sgt. William Nevin of Co. K, Third MSM Cavalry, very closely mirrors Hildebrand's own discussion of nearly being surrounded and losing four horses:

> Sometime in November about forty of the company were ordered out on a scout on foot armed with a musket apiece and a blanket; we were in two squads of twenty men each, and the captain had a squad of about eight men mounted and disguised as Rebels. . . . Of the infantry squads [Second] Lieutenant [William M.] Brawner [Co. K, Third MSM] commanded one, and I commanded the other, our orders were to march at night and not to go on any road, the object of the scout was to try and catch Sam Hildebrand who was committing depredations. . . . On this trip we killed three or four guerrillas but failed to get Hildebrand, so we returned to Arcadia. . . . The next morning fifty of the company started back on the same route that we had been over on the foot scout, mounted, scouting through the woods commanded by Hummel, and . . . found the Rebels camped in a swamp surrounded on three sides by sloughs and a log fort, we had them very nearly surrounded when they discovered us and opened fire on us, we returned the fire very lively, and then they left in a hurry. The fight lasted about thirty minutes; none of company K were hurt, but two of their men were reported killed and one or two wounded. They left two wagons loaded with goods of all description which we got, also taking four horses. (William Nevin, "History of Co. K, 3rd M.S.M. Cavalry Vols. From its Earliest Organization in 1861, to Final Muster Out On January 31, 1865," Peterson Papers, box 12, folder 9)

Co. K, Third MSM Cavalry, was originally designated Co. A, Twelfth MSM Cavalry, and was directly involved in the fight that destroyed the McGee Gang on 4 Feb. 1863. See *O.R.*, ser. 1, vol. 22, pt. 1, pp. 225–27; *St. Louis Democrat*, 16 Feb. 1863; Moore, *The Rebellion Record*, vol. 6, 415–16.

3. "Pilot Knob, Mo. November 25, 1863—Hildebrandt must have passed very near your post, as he moved up to Farmington. The people must have known he was in the country. Press every man, horse, and gun you can find, and let the hunt, pursuit, and extermination be sure and swift. A portion of his gang are in Federal uniform" (Brig. Gen. Clinton B. Fisk, *O.R.*, ser. 1, vol. 22, pt. 2, p. 715).

4. Franklin Murphy lived right next door to Hildebrand's hated enemy Joseph McGahan but was still able to stay in the good graces of the different armed factions in the area. Note should be made of the fact that G. W. "Wesley" Murphy, probably Franklin's brother or cousin, lived directly on the other side of McGahan. Not only did Franklin avoid antagonizing McGahan or Hildebrand to the point of having his own blood spilled, but he maintained a legitimacy and even popularity that came to see him elected county sheriff in 1866. See the 1860 Census for Liberty Township, St. Francois County, Dwelling 165; *Goodspeed's History of Southeast Missouri,* 351.

5. Orville McIlvaine was the father of Firmin McIlvaine, whom Hildebrand had killed from ambush eighteen months earlier. In 1860 seventy-one-year-old

Isaac Baker was living in the McIlvaine household and was probably an uncle or father-in-law of Orville (the relevance of which becomes evident in chap. 25). See the 1860 Census for Liberty Township, St. Francois County, Dwelling 32.

6. According to one Federal account, this locality was known as "The Black Spot" by Rebels due to its heavy Unionist sentiment. See Wilkinson, "Biographical Sketch."

7. "Patterson, Mo. December 11, 1863—The citizens of Cedar Creek, Wayne County, Missouri, discovered on the 9th instant 5 armed men, supposed to belong to the Hildebrandt gang. They killed 1, wounded 1, and captured 2. I have the two prisoners. One of them was along when I was bushwhacked. He is a regular guerrilla. I know he will get away, for our men are very careless about prisoners. They took $130 in Confederate money from the man who was killed, which I inclose to you" (Capt. William T. Leeper, Third MSM Cavalry, *O.R.*, ser. 1, vol. 22, pt. 2, pp. 740–41).

The citizens who engaged in the melee were recently discharged veterans of Pinkney Power's company of the Eighth PEMM. While a more detailed Federal account of this fight mirrors Hildebrand's in regard to time, date, and location, it differs a bit in regard to how the fighting unfolded. According to the Federal version, after being discharged from the Union militia a month earlier:

> Orderly Sergt. Jas. P. Ellis made up a school of common education for 3 months, and several of his company comrades became school scholars, but they even went to school with their "Colt Navys" as regularly as they did with their "dinner baskets." One day during the school, word came that armed men were at a neighboring farmhouse eating breakfast. School disbanded in a twinkle, and the boys at school buckled on their "Navys" and soon they were mounted, and with other citizens were in hot chase. The Rebels about a half dozen more or less, when they ate their breakfast "took to the hills" having Cedar Creek to their left, as they were going eastwards. About 4 miles east of Cold Water on Cedar Creek the Rebels were overhauled, one made his escape to the thickets, and it was then thought with a wound in the leg. Then, it was thought by the pursuers he returned fire, but none of Sergt.-Teacher Ellis' boys were hurt. Two surrendered, but one, a young fellow was pursued so closely by two of the boys, he took to a tree. The two pursuers ordered him to surrender, and he said he would think of it. One brave boy, John B. Willmore, undertook to change trees so as to expose the Rebel to either himself or his mate Dan M. Parker; but in making the change he tripped and fell and lucky was that fall as the Rebel's charge passed over him as he fell. The move of the Rebel was watched by Parker, and in shifting to shoot Willmore he exposed his side to Parker, and in the same instant his exposed side was filled with buck shot from Parker's gun. He was "mustered out" on the spot. (Wilkinson, "Biographical Sketch")

8. One of these "scouting excursions" was a 23 Dec. raid on Centreville, Mo., which was garrisoned by a detachment of Hildebrand's enemy, the Third MSM Cavalry. The Confederates, who were troops belonging to the command of Timothy Reeves, were led in this assault by former Daniel McGee compatriot David Reed. (Reed's first lieutenant was George Lasiter, who, along with Hildebrand, was currently under a murder indictment for the killing of Addison Cunningham; see chap. 14.) In chap. 23 Hildebrand acknowledges joining Reed's men sometime after 15 Dec.—which would have been around the time of the Centreville Raid and an ensuing disaster for Reeves's command.

CHAPTER TWENTY-THREE

1. No officers by these names have been identified as having served anywhere in Missouri during the war. It is possible Hildebrand was speaking of a Cahren, Cochran, or Rhodes.

2. Cowan was married to Daniel McGee's sister and served as second lieutenant under McGee in the Second (Hunter's) Missouri Cavalry Battalion in the early months of the war. He afterward served under McGee and David Reed in Co. C/K of the Second (McCulloch's) Missouri Cavalry Regiment, enlisting in that unit at Lowndes on 17 Feb. 1862, en masse with a large number of other members of the McGee/Cato clan. After the McGee Gang was destroyed, Cowan went with other surviving members and joined David Reed's Co. C of the Fifteenth (Reeves's) Missouri Cavalry. See Hahn, *Bollinger County*, 109; Richard D. Cowan, Index to Compiled Service Records of Confederate Soldiers, M380 roll 3.

3. That "Major" Hildebrand's acceded to the demands of Captain Reed's force is quite revealing in regard to Hildebrand's supposed Confederate commission. This passage is also further evidence of Hildebrand's initial ties to the McGee/Cato clan and his subsequent alliance with Tim Reeves's Fifteenth Missouri Cavalry. David Reed served as captain in two Confederate companies, both of which had deep McGee connections—the Second (Hunter's) Missouri Cavalry Battalion and the Second (McCulloch's) Cavalry Regiment. By the time of this meeting, with other McGee/Cato survivors, Reed was serving under Reeves. Reeves and his command were directly compared to William Clarke Quantrill and Bloody Bill Anderson in the St. Louis press, which noted "the mode of warfare carried on by such cutthroats as Bill Anderson and Tim Reeves" and the "scoundrelly and murderous operations of Anderson, Quantrell, Reeves and other guerrilla chieftains in this state." See David Reed, Index to Compiled Service Records of Confederate Soldiers, M380 roll 12; *St. Louis Republican*, 27 Oct. 1864. See also Ross, "The Burning of Doniphan," 80.

In addition, according to a regional history written just two decades after the end of the war, during the latter part of 1863, "from this time until the close of the war the military operations in Southeast Missouri, with the single exception of Price's raid, degenerated into a merciless guerrilla warfare in which many citizens lost their lives at the hands of such bands as were led by Timothy Reeves, Hilderbrandt and the Bowlins" (*Goodspeed's History of Southeast Missouri*, 502–3).

Note should be made of the fact that both Timothy Reeves and David Reed were commissioned in the Confederate Army and therefore were technically not guerrillas.

4. Hildebrand's mother was a McKee, apparently causing his biographers to confuse the spelling of the name of Tom *McGee*. McGee was the father of the Rebel guerrilla Daniel McGee and a patriarch of the extended McGee/Cato family. Tom McGee, an active supporter of Hildebrand, in fact did not die at the time Hildebrand states—he was killed eight months later (see chap. 29). See Holsell, interview, vol. 10, p. 200; Thomas McGee, gravestone, McGee Cemetery, McGee, Mo.

In his memoir's sometimes obfuscating manner, Hildebrand has substituted this passage in the place of one that instead would have told of a major defeat for the Hildebrand/Reed/Reeves faction at this very time—a defeat that eclipsed the series of other military defeats Hildebrand had recently been suffering.

On 23 Dec. 1863 Co. C of Hildebrand's nemesis, the Third MSM Cavalry, was surprised and captured en masse at Centreville. This Confederate victory was led by Captain Reed, who had with him two hundred men of Tim Reeves's command who were reported to be "a concentration of the various bands in the southeastern part of the State, including the routed remnant of Sam Hildebrand's gang." (This statement is buttressed by Hildebrand's own admission that he was brought into Reed's company after 15 Dec. In addition, verifiable accounts by multiple sources—including Hildebrand himself—state that Hildebrand had in recent weeks been routed by Leeper and the Third MSM Cavalry in Wayne and Ripley Counties, by the Third MSM Cavalry near Fredericktown in Madison County, and by former members of the Eighth PEMM on Cedar Creek in Wayne County.) See the *St. Louis Republican*, 25 Dec. 1863; *O.R.*, ser. 1, vol. 22, pt. 2, p. 750; ser. 1, vol. 34, pt. 2, pp. 5–6.

Transporting the Federal captives to Pulliam's Farm, near the Arkansas line in southwestern Ripley County, the Centreville raiders began preparing to put seven of them to death in retaliation for the recent killing of a similar number of their own men by Captain Leeper (see chap. 21). In a true-life scene that might make a 1950s B-movie Western producer blush, as the executions were about to commence on Christmas Day, a relief column of the U.S. Cavalry (Third MSM), led by Maj. James Wilson, arrived in the nick of time, charging the Confederate military outpost with drawn sabers, killing 33 Rebels, capturing 112, and rescuing the Union troops taken prisoner at Centreville. The action was referred to in a letter to Gov. Willard P. Hall as being "brilliant in the extreme." See *O.R.*, ser. 1, vol. 22, pt. 1, p. 784; ser. 1, vol. 22, pt. 2, p. 600; ser. 1, vol. 22, pt. 2, p. 750; ser. 1, vol. 34, pt. 2, p. 177; *Louisiana Journal*, 2 Jan. 1864; *Louisiana Journal*, 9 Jan. 1864; *St. Louis Republican*, 29 Dec. 1863; *St. Louis Republican*, 1 Jan. 1864.

According to one of the men who was to be a victim of the Confederate firing squad: "That Christmas Day turned out to be a very happy one to us who were prisoners in the hands of Col. Reeves. I understand that myself and six of my men were to be shot on account of some men who were killed by order of Capt. William T. Leeper" (1st Lt. John W. Hendrick, Third MSM Cavalry, John W. Hendrick to Cyrus A. Peterson, 23 Feb. 1903, Peterson Papers, box 4, folder 1).

In a major ongoing cause célèbre in southeast Missouri, writer Jerry Ponder, a Ripley County native, began releasing a series of self-published books in 1987 that included claims that over five dozen women and children were "massacred" in the fighting at Pulliam's Farm. However, no such incident shows up in the archival historical record, nor were any of the 430-plus Confederate and Federal troops who participated in the skirmish reported to have made any such claim during the course of their lives, nor has a single grave for the dozens of alleged victims been located.

Pointing out these inconsistencies after years of controversy following the initial 1987 allegation, in 2002 Ray Burson, Ripley County Historical Society member and editor of the *Ripley County Heritage* historical quarterly, requested that Ponder produce supporting documentation. In a written response attacking Burson for broaching the subject, Ponder asserted that while he had the documentation in his research files, he was not in a position to produce it. He went on to state that proof could be found in civil proceedings that were pursued in northeast Missouri during the war. According to Ponder, "see the court records for Lincoln County, where, in January, 1864, Mrs. James Wilson sued for divorce, citing the brutality of Major James Wilson and the deaths of civilians at Pulliam's Farm."

Unfortunately, an actual review of the court file wholly refutes this assertion and reveals quite the opposite. One finds the following points in examining the case (*James Wilson Plaintiff vs. Margaret C. Wilson Defendant, Petition for Divorce*, filed 6 July 1863, Lincoln County Circuit Court, book F, pp. 398, 438, Sept. 1859–Jan. 1864; book G, p. 87, Mar. 1864–Apr. 1869):

- James Wilson filed for the divorce, not Mrs. Wilson.
- The grounds cited for the divorce were related to actions by Mrs. Wilson that occurred prior to July 1861—her abandonment of the marital home—not actions by Major Wilson that occurred in Dec. 1863.
- The divorce was filed in mid-1863, not early-1864.
- When the divorce was filed in 1863, the Pulliam's Farm skirmish had not occurred; it would not occur until nearly six months later.
- Mrs. Wilson filed nothing at all, not even a simple response to Major

Wilson's claims, despite the fact that the case was continued twice over the course of 1863 and 1864, allowing her ample opportunity to respond.

- On 23 Sept. 1864 the divorce was granted, with James Wilson being expressly named "the innocent and aggrieved party," not Mrs. Wilson.
- No reference of any sort is made in the divorce paperwork regarding either the Pulliam's Farm skirmish or the war, nor is any negative comment made concerning James Wilson.

Ponder has also cited "Doniphan during the Civil War," an obscure work by his aunt, Jean Ponder, as supporting his assertion of a massacre of women and children at Pulliam's Farm. However, like the Wilson divorce paperwork, an actual review of this article by Jean Ponder fails to find reference to any such killings. The piece does mention the skirmish between the two military forces at Pulliam's Farm (which is not in dispute) but makes no suggestion of any involvement of women and children. See Jerry Ponder, *History of Ripley County*, 52, 186 n. 139; Jean Ponder, "Doniphan during the Civil War" (undated five-page typescript included with press clippings and other items of local historical interest bound into a book called *Doniphan and Ripley County History*, located in the Reference Department of the Doniphan/Ripley County Public Library).

CHAPTER TWENTY-FOUR

1. "Agreeably," indeed. Hildebrand's daughter Margaret Ann was born nine months and one day after he left his wife. The uneventful winter appears to have been the result of an astute and successful effort to convince the Federals that he was dead. In early Jan. 1864 a woman arriving in Bloomfield identified herself as Sam Hildebrand's wife, claiming he had been killed in recent fighting and requesting assistance in burying him: "According to her statement, he was severely wounded in the groin in the skirmish referred to above, since which time she has been attending him in a lone hut in the woods, having escaped and made his way there in female apparel. A party was sent to the cabin, some seven miles from Bloomfield, who buried the rebel" (*St. Louis Republican*, 11 Jan. 1864). Also see the death certificate of Margaret "Annie" Ann Williams, daughter of Sam Hildebrand and Margaret Hampton, Stokes Mortuary, Renton, Wash., showing a date of birth of 11 Oct. 1864 and a date of death of 24 Aug. 1950; Margaret Ann Williams, gravestone, Greenwood Memorial Park, Renton; Alice Rae Williams to Kirby Ross, 26 Oct. 2004, 3 Nov. 2004, 8 Nov. 2004 (Williams is the great-granddaughter of Margaret Ann Hildebrand Williams and the great-great-granddaughter of Sam Hildebrand); Darryl Lawson to Kirby Ross, 29 Oct. 2004 (Lawson is the great-great-grandson of Sam Hildebrand through Hildebrand's daughter Rebecca).

Around this same time the post commander at Cape Girardeau reported: "January 6, 1864— . . . have killed Hildebrand. He was shot about two weeks ago and died early in this week. He is sure enough dead" (Col. John B. Rogers, Second MSM Cavalry, *O.R.*, ser. 1, vol. 34, pt. 2, p. 34).

2. Casualty reports for the Second MSM Cavalry fail to confirm this claim by Hildebrand. See the Muster Rolls, Second MSM Cavalry.

3. Around this same time—on 6 Apr.—Capt. Henry B. Milks and eighteen of his men in the Third MSM Cavalry made a raid via Ste. Genevieve and across the Mississippi River into Prairie Du Rocher, Ill.:

> Farmington, Mo. April 9, 1864— . . . Immediately on landing I arrested Landon Green, a guerrilla, one of Hilderbrand's men. Proceeding 2 miles farther, at Carr's farm I arrested 3 other guerrillas. I then charged on Prairie Du Rocher, where I found the notorious John Hiley and his gang, who made for the bluffs in rear of the town, where they took a stand. After a short and spirited fight we drove them from the bluff, killing Hiley and 2 others. . . . On my way back to the river 1 of the prisoners attempting to escape was shot by the guard. (Capt. Henry B. Milks, *O.R.*, ser. 1, vol. 34, pt. 1, p. 875)

Military records indicate a John Highley served in the Second (Hunter's) Missouri Cavalry Battalion and then in the Second (McCulloch's) Missouri Cavalry, from which he deserted in Oct. 1862. Census records further indicate a John Highly resided two houses from Hildebrand compatriot Samuel G. Haile in Liberty Township, St. Francois County, and right next door to James Wall, whom Hildebrand tried to bushwhack a short time after John "Hiley" was killed (see chap. 24). See the 1860 Census for Liberty Township, St. Francois County, Dwellings 89, 90, 91; John Highley, Record of Service Card, box 103, reel S732.

See the *St. Louis Union*, 25 June 1863, for an account of a Bob "Hyley" stealing a horse from Hildebrand's old enemy Orville McIlvaine. Bob Highley was closely associated with Hildebrand, according to other reports (see chaps. 30 and 35).

A list of thirteen Union men marked for death in retaliation for John Hiley's killing was issued by his allies. On it were the names of three members of the Evans family—a family Hildebrand prominently mentions several times in his memoir. See the *St. Louis Union*, 23 Sept. 1864.

In a postscript to the Illinois raid, one of the Confederate prisoners named Buck Perkins was killed on 9 Apr. while in custody. Given that date, he may have been the prisoner who was reportedly shot "attempting to escape." A member of the Enrolled Missouri Militia committed this killing while Perkins was being interrogated in the provost marshal's office in St. Francois County. According to the sworn statement of Captain Milks, who was an eyewitness to the shooting:

> I arrested Buck Perkins in Randolph County Illinois April 6th 1864, charged with being a guerrilla and outlaw and brought him to Farmington, St. Francois County, Mo. April 7th 1864, turned him over to the Provost Marshal Lt. James W. Bradley [Co. D, Third MSM Cavalry].
>
> . . . On the 9th day of April 1864 I entered the office of the Provost Marshal in which the said Perkins and Ruben Lasiter were with the Provost Marshal Lt. James W. Bradley. Provost Marshal asked the prisoner if he had a pistol when he was arrested. The prisoner replied, [and] I said the question was asked him could he identify it by the Pro Mar. He said he could, then the pistol was produced by the Provost Marshal which Perkins said belonged to him. Same pistol was claimed by one Ruben Lasiter who said it was taken from his premises when he was robbed when the prisoner had stated the pistol had belonged to him. Ruben Lasiter said damn you stole that pistol, shook it in the face of my wife and made her tell where my money was, then [Lasiter] instantly fired two shot at the prisoner with a revolver.

Other documents in the investigation file state that Lasiter had a revolver hidden on his person, pulled it when Perkins continued claiming ownership of the other pistol, and shot Perkins to death. Lasiter was a member of Co. C, Thirty-second EMM, which had once been led by Hildebrand's enemy Joe McGahan. After the killing of Perkins, Lasiter joined the Forty-seventh Missouri Infantry, from which he was honorably discharged in 1865. See the Buck Perkins File, Statement of Capt. H. B. Milks, 9 Apr. 1864, File of Papers Relating to Individual Civilians; Ruben Lasater, Record of Service Cards, box 50, reels S781, S867.

CHAPTER TWENTY-FIVE

1. After the death of Hildebrand's wife, Margaret, on 21 Dec. 1871, he acted in an especially reckless manner: three months to the day after she passed away, he forced a confrontation with law-enforcement authorities that resulted in his own demise (see chap. 37). See the *Jefferson City (Mo.) People's Tribune*, 31 Jan. 1872; *St. Louis Republican*, 23 Mar. 1872.

2. Hildebrand has omitted reference to a Federal raid against his headquarters during the week of 17 May that was led by Capt. Abijah Johns of the Third MSM Cavalry. Hildebrand shot and seriously wounded Johns at this time, although he mistakenly recounts it as occurring in July (see chap. 28).

3. John Baker was probably related to Firmin McIlvaine (see chap. 22). While the McIlvaines had a seventy-one-year-old man named Isaac Baker living in their household in 1860, elsewhere in the same township John Baker was residing with fifty-year-old Isaac Baker Jr., just four houses away from

Hildebrand's hated enemy Joe McGahan. Hildebrand's informant regarding the movements of the men he desired to kill may have been Samuel G. Haile, who lived next door to James Wall and near John Highley, recently killed by the Third MSM. Samuel Haile, who fled to Illinois around this time, was the brother of Irvin M. Haile and the son of Judge Thomas Haile (not "Devilish" Tom Haile), both of whom would soon be murdered by Federal troops in the tit-for-tat warfare that was taking place in the hunt for Hildebrand (see chaps. 29 and 30). See the 1860 Census for Liberty Township, St. Francois County, Dwellings 32, 89, 90, 91, 160; *Goodspeed's History of Southeast Missouri*, 638.

4. Hildebrand is mistaken regarding the unit of these soldiers. According to the timeline Hildebrand provides, this event occurred in June 1864. Col. John L. Beveridge and his Seventeenth Illinois Cavalry did not garrison Cape Girardeau until Apr. 1865. See *O.R.*, ser. 1, vol. 48, pt. 1, p. 488; ser. 1, vol. 48, pt. 2, pp. 45, 71, 948; F. A. Carpenter, "History of the 17th Cavalry Volunteers," chap. 35 (account serialized in unidentified newspaper, ca. 1886, copy at the Illinois State Historical Library, Springfield); Dyer, *A Compendium of the War of the Rebellion*, 1032.

CHAPTER TWENTY-SIX

1. A legal inquisition took testimony that "Henry Voges, and John Zimmer . . . came to their deaths by being hung, and from all signs those remains of the young men before mentioned laid there from last summer when the boys were taken." Further testimony revealed that "John Wampler distinctly said to her [Jayne Tinkler] that Mr. Atchison left his house on Saturday morning 23 day of June 1864 and did return next Tuesday night about 10 o'clock on the 26 day of June 1864 and he believed he was in the gang of guerrillas known as Hildebrand's gang, which took and hung Henry Voges and John Zimmer." See the Coroner's Inquest, Henry Voges and John Zimmer, filed 22 Sept. 1865, St. Francois County Office of the Coroner, Inquests 1850–1932, reel C31546. John Zimmer had enrolled in Co. B, Sixty-eighth EMM, at Farmington just seven weeks earlier. See John Zimmer, Record of Service Card, box 93, reel S805.

2. Jelkyll was captain of Co. B, Sixty-eighth EMM, but resigned his commission on 24 Feb. 1863 upon the petition of his entire company. It was alleged that Jelkyll had admitted he "was with the South and for the South, and that he was willing to shoulder his gun and go South." See the *Annual Report of the Adjutant General . . . 1864*, 418; *Report of the Committee of the House of Representatives*, 169, 170.

3. Hildebrand's meeting with Jelkyll shortly before the deaths of Hart and Zimmer might be small cause for suspicion: before Jelkyll was forced out of the Enrolled Missouri Militia, he was the commanding officer of their company. See George Hart, Record of Service Card, box 36, reel S804.

On 22 May 1863 Hart was detailed to the Eighth Provisional Enrolled Missouri Militia, where he was a sergeant in Co. L. It was apparently in the service of either the Sixty-eighth EMM or the Eighth PEMM that he committed the deed that led to his torture and murder. See George Hart, Record of Service Card, box 36, reel S821.

The nature of Hildebrand's killing of Hart went much deeper than he admits, according to a newspaper report: "Infernal Atrocity—The spirit of demons seems to possess the rebel guerrillas that are now robbing and murdering in different parts of the State. Last week a young man by the name of Geo. Hart, living in the neighborhood of Farmington, St. Francois county, a member of the EMM, was taken from his home . . . his hands were tied behind him by inserting small withes under the tendons of each wrist; he was then suspended by another withe around his neck, and at the same time his flesh was scored with knives. He was found dead the next morning! What punishment is too severe to be meted out to these fiends in human shape" (*Perryville Union*, 22 July 1864, reprinting an article from the *St. Louis Union*).

A grand jury empanelled to consider the matter found that on 27 June 1864 Sam Hildebrand "did with . . . malice aforethought hang, shoot, stab, and kill the said George Hart." See the Grand Jury in the St. Francois County Circuit Court, May Term, 1865.

4. Hildebrand was correct regarding the response to his activities. A Federal report alludes to the murder of Hart and the hunt for his killers the day after he died: "June 28, 1864—In obedience to orders I started with 25 men from camp on the morning of the 27th instant, in the direction of Indian Ford, [west of Bloomfield] on the Saint Francis River, for the purpose of cutting off the party of bushwhackers who had committed the depredations the evening previous at Farmington. After traveling 10 miles on the Dallas road, took a southeasterly direction. . . . I thoroughly scouted the country, but could learn nothing of any bushwhackers having been in that vicinity"(Maj. Samuel Montgomery, Sixth Missouri Cavalry, *O.R.*, ser. 1, vol. 34, pt. 4, p. 583).

CHAPTER TWENTY-SEVEN

1. The Federal reports were slightly different:

> St. Louis July 18, 1864—Hildebrand's band of fifteen men are reported on what I regard as good authority, as prowling about Big River Mills and Lawson's Station. . . . Have [Capt. Henry B.] Milks [Co. H, Third MSM Cavalry] to go out to find and kill them, whether found in Illinois or in this State. Instruct commanding officer at Farmington to go to work and, if necessary, strengthen the force for that purpose. This band is reported as having been prowling about there for a week, to the

> great alarm and disquiet of the people. They must be routed out promptly, and if possible exterminated. (Brig. Gen. Thomas Ewing Jr., Headquarters St. Louis District, *O.R.*, ser. 1, vol. 41, pt. 2, p. 241)

> Pilot Knob July 19, 1864—Lieutenant [Hugh M.] Bradley [Co. I, Third MSM Cavalry] has just returned from a scout down through Saint Francois and Madison Counties. He ran three men out of Saint Francois County whom he thinks belong to the Hildebrand gang. His command killed 2 guerrillas beside the one reported the other day; captured 1 horse and 3 guns. (Col. J. F. Tyler, First MSM Infantry, *O.R.*, ser. 1, vol. 41, pt. 2, p. 267)

2. William F. Rucker was another deserter from the Second (McCulloch's) Missouri Cavalry. He had enlisted in Co. C/K on 17 Feb. 1862, simultaneously with a large number of members of the McGee/Cato family. After the destruction of the McGee Gang he followed Capt. David Reed into Co. C of Tim Reeves's Fifteenth Missouri Cavalry. See William F. Rucker, Record of Service Card, box 111, reel S738; William Rucker, Index to Compiled Service Records of Confederate Soldiers, M380 roll 12.

CHAPTER TWENTY-EIGHT

1. Yet again Hildebrand and/or his biographers merge two different stories into one and in doing so play up a fleeting victory over Federal forces and overlook an overwhelming defeat. These two events involved Federal raids upon Confederate guerrilla concentrations—"headquarters," according to Hildebrand—around Scatterville, in Greene County, Ark., which were undertaken in May and July 1864. The Ironton/Pilot Knob area was the headquarters of the Third MSM Cavalry. Captain "John" was Abijah Johns of that regiment, who on the first mission in question had with him his own Co. A (Swamp Scouts) and detachments of the Sixth Missouri Cavalry and First MSM Infantry. The Johns-led raid into Greene County during the week of 17 May targeted Hildebrand compatriot Timothy Reeves and culminated in a rout of that command and Johns's imbibing of a meal that had been prepared for Reeves. En route back into Missouri, Johns went into camp and was attacked by Hildebrand. According to one of the Swamp Scouts, Sgt. Thomas B. Hutchison:

> With my squad I joined Capt. Johns the next morning with his command and we proceeded on our homeward march by the way of Bloomfield—on our way we camped overnight at a school house in a thick wood near a little place called Scatterville—there was a little clearing of about 2 akers around the school house in which we lined up our horses and after feeding them and our selfs and placing pickets around

> the camp we laid down in front of our horses and tried to sleep. We had not unsaddled for we knew the country was full of Rebel bushwhackers and was liable to be attacked at any moment. At about midnight Capt. Johns mounted his big yellow horse and rode out the main road and just few feet past the pickets and that time we heard the rattle of a cowbell and immediately after a shot was fired—in a second every man was on his feet and ready to mount and in a few minutes Capt. Johns came into camp with a broken arm. After he had passed a few paces beyond the pickets and just as the cowbell rang out in the stillness of the night a man stepped out into the road and fired point blank at the Capt. with a double barrel shotgun. The Capt. seen him and aimed to wheel his horse as the fellow fired and the whole load of buckshot passed between his body and his left arm—one shot breaking his arm just above the elbow. The picket fired one shot at Rebel as he retreated to the brush and he was sure he hit him but could not find him the next morning. (T. B. Hutchison to Dr. C. A. Peterson, 2 Jan. 1905, Peterson Papers, box 4, folder 3)

See also *Portrait and Biographical Record of Marion, Ralls, and Pike Counties,* 744.

The cowbell that Sergeant Hutchison heard immediately prior to the shooting was a Hildebrand trademark—see chap. 35.

2. This second, July raid that Hildebrand wrongly mixes with the May raid was led by Lt. Col. John T. Burris, Tenth Kansas Infantry, who was in charge of a task force made up of hundreds of troopers from the Union First Missouri Cavalry, the Second MSM Cavalry, the Third MSM Cavalry, and the Sixth Missouri Cavalry. Their target was reported to be bands of Rebel irregulars gathering in Greene County, Ark., and the Bootheel region of Missouri under the command of the Bolins and "Colonel Cowen" (Hildebrand associate/McGee in-law Dick Cowan, who was now riding for Tim Reeves), as well as the Confederate Second (McCulloch's) Missouri Cavalry (which almost certainly refers to David Reed's reconstituted company of former members of Co. C/K of that unit, since the regiment itself was east of the Mississippi River and hundreds of miles away in the Department of Alabama, Mississippi, and East Louisiana).

With the Federal task force converging on Bloomfield in late July, it then moved south, attacking Scatterville (where Hildebrand's wife was residing) on the evening of 28 July. According to Lieutenant Colonel Burris: "There we routed a rebel recruiting party, under Colonel Clark, and had a skirmish with Bolin's guerrillas. We killed 1 rebel lieutenant, took Captain [William T.] Lineback [Co. B, Fourth Missouri Cavalry] prisoner, captured some arms and horses, and burned the houses, under cover of which the guerrillas had fired on my command" (*O.R.*, ser. 1, vol. 39, pt. 2, pp. 805, 809; ser. 1, vol. 41, pt. 1, pp. 77–79; ser. 1, vol. 41, pt. 2, pp. 240, 405–6; *St. Louis Republican*, 15 Aug. 1864).

3. At this point, Hildebrand's version of events diverges wildly from Lieutenant Colonel Burris's version. After leaving Scatterville, the Federal force spread out to the south and east, moving into the Missouri Bootheel and passing through Clarkton and Kennett on 30 July and Hornersville on 31 July. Capturing some "bushwhackers and thieves" on 1 Aug., the Federals then advanced on Osceola, Ark., and engaged in "quite a hard fight" there on 2 Aug. After a running skirmish in which the extreme, humid summer heat took a toll in and of itself, the Union troops reported that "the enemy's forces were scattered in every direction." Proceeding back into the Bootheel, the Federals met the Confederate irregulars at Elk Chute on 4 Aug. According to Burris:

> The rebels fled, and were pursued. . . . We pursued the enemy six miles across Dogskin Swamp, when we found him in line of battle in a dense forest. . . . I immediately formed my battalions in line and attacked him. Our first volley partially broke the rebel line, when I ordered a charge, which was made with spirit. The whole rebel force fell back in confusion. A running fight was kept up for two miles, through the swamp, among the trees, and over logs. The enemy several times succeeded in partially reforming their lines, but each time only to be driven back in greater confusion . . . the impetuosity of the charge of my battalions on their line, the deadly fire poured into their ranks, and the exultant shouts of my pursuing forces were more than they could stand. They again fled precipitately, many of them rushing, panic-stricken, into the stream. (*O.R.*, ser. 1, vol. 41, pt. 1, pp. 79–81)

During the course of the raid, Burris claimed killing 47 rebels, wounding 46, emancipating 20 slaves, and capturing 57 prisoners, 200 stand of arms, and 230 horses. One Federal was reported killed, with several more being wounded. See the *St. Louis Republican,* 15 Aug. 1864; "Co. D, 3rd M.S.M. Cav.," Peterson Papers, box 1, folder 29; John R. Allcom, Pension File, Third MSM Cavalry, National Archives.

4. Hildebrand did not kill Captain Johns. After Johns was shot by Hildebrand during the May raid (not the July raid in which Scatterville was burned), Sergeant Hutchison claimed: "The next morning we found a spring wagon and a feather bed in the village, and placed the Capt. in it and carried him to Bloomfield. . . . We reached Bloomfield that night, we found a comfortable place for the Capt. and we left the next morning for Patterson, our headquarters, leaving a man to wait on and nurse our wounded Capt., and it was 3 months before he could assume command of the company." Back on duty after the second raid, Johns served until the expiration of his term of service on 16 Mar. 1865, afterward returning to his home in Clarksville, Mo., and engaging in the saddlery and harness business. He died in Clarksville on 29 June 1891, at the age of sixty-five. See Hutchison to Peterson, 2 Jan. 1905; *Portrait and Bio-*

graphical Record of Marion, Ralls, and Pike Counties, 743–45; Abijah Johns, Record of Service Card, box 44, reel S837.

5. Regimental returns fail to confirm Hildebrand's claims of a slaughter, showing only one man killed in action. See the Muster Rolls, Third MSM Cavalry, Missouri State Archives.

6. This party of Federals that Hildebrand claimed attacked him "with a perfect fury" was led by Sgt. James C. Steakley, Co. K, Third MSM Cavalry, who had a long, documented history of aggressive behavior. Steakley provided an account of this action that generally agrees with Hildebrand's regarding the casualties inflicted on the Confederates but is greatly at odds regarding the result of the fighting. Confirming having chased down Hildebrand in the aftermath of the robbery, Steakley reflected upon his experience in 1903, stating that he and his squad

> were almost continually in the saddle or on the "go" and had numerous scraps with Hilderbrandt, [Pete] Smith and [David] Reed rebel bushwhackers. I never had over 15 men under my command at one time. About July 20, '64, 15 of us caught up with the Peet Smith gang, whipped them, 24 or 30 strong, killing one on the ground and captured 7 horses that were loaded with all manner of stuff that they had stolen; the man killed had on butternut suit, but underneath, a new Broad cloth suit, although so hot. In his pockets were 5 pocketbooks, each containing some money; this being proof of what the gang had been doing. We never knew how many of them were wounded. We lost one horse killed, and one man's arm injured by a grape vine jerking him off his horse in the charge. Sam Hildebrandt was with them. (James C. Steakley, "Brief Biographical Sketch of the Life of James C. Steakley," 14 July 1903, p. 14, Peterson Papers)

A Federal report filed in the aftermath of the skirmish also alleges a different outcome to the skirmish than Hildebrand's version, stating: "Fredericktown, Mo. July 31, 1864—[Steakley] met a squad of bushwhackers under one Smith, killed 2 of them, captured 7 horses and 2 revolvers. The sergeant had about an equal force with the rebels, but gave them a good whipping. He and his men deserve great credit for their conduct. The rebels were in the woods and fired on his command from behind trees and at a distance of less than forty yards, but he charged upon them and they fled" (Col. J. F. Tyler, First MSM Infantry, *O.R.*, ser. 1, vol. 41, pt. 2, p. 492).

7. Casualty returns for the Third MSM Cavalry provide no evidence that any troops were killed or wounded in action at this time. See the Muster Rolls, Third MSM Cavalry.

CHAPTER TWENTY-NINE

1. If, as is related in chap. 23, Hildebrand did stumble across the killers of McGee/Cato patriarch Thomas McGee just after McGee's murder, it would have been during this trip north. McGee's slave Rhody Holsell asserted: "De boss was also killed. . . . Dey killed de boss in August on Monday. De boss was going that day to Greenville to make his will." McGee's headstone verifies this timeframe and pinpoints the date as 10 Aug. 1864. See Holsell, interview, vol. 10, p. 200; Thomas McGee, gravestone, McGee Cemetery, McGee, Mo.

2. "Capt. Milks" was Capt. Henry B. Milks, Co. H, Third MSM Cavalry. Milks and his men had been stationed in St. Francois County at Farmington after Hildebrand's raid there on 25 Nov. 1863 (see chap. 22). They had more recently been ordered to garrison Ste. Genevieve, on 14 Apr. Hildebrand is confusing his timeline: most of the events of which he speaks transpired in Oct., not Aug. See *O.R.*, ser. 1, vol. 34, pt. 3, pp. 42, 43, 63, 81–82, 155; Record of Events, Third MSM Cavalry.

3. Actually, while there was a seizure of horses from Judge Charles Burks Sr.'s son, there seems to have been a combination of reasons for the assassination. Charles Jr., known as "a long disloyal character," was arrested on 21 July 1864 by Captain Milks for having served in the Confederate Army and not having surrendered himself to authorities upon his return to Ste. Genevieve County. Burks Jr. was released on 29 Aug. 1864, after taking the Oath of Allegiance and posting a two-thousand-dollar bond.

In the face of a major Confederate raid through the area a month later, on 28 Sept. Burks Jr. brought a herd of horses into the town of Ste. Genevieve with the stated intention of moving it on over into Illinois. The local provost marshal, suspecting that Burks's true intent was to take himself beyond the reach of Missouri authorities, subsequently reported that he "thought it prudent to retain said Burks [Jr.] and took possession of his horses which he willingly gave up and have since returned said horses to the said father of said Burks."

Soon afterward Burks Jr. was released and then "joined and connected himself with a band of murderous Bushwhackers and Guerrillas, outlaws and enemies of the United States government thus violating his oath of allegiance and terms of his bond." With the Federal powers-that-be taking measures to collect the two thousand dollars, "said collection was stopped by orders from the Prest. of the United States. Said Burks has never surrendered himself . . . since he joined the guerrillas and is still at large in the character of an outlaw and rebel enemy of the Government of the United States."

It is likely that Burks Sr. had secured the bond and consequently would have been the one to engage the use of influence to thwart the efforts to collect it. This was probably as much of an impetus for his murder as was the matter relating to the horses. In any event, according to his probate court file, Charles

Burks Sr. died sometime during the month of Oct. 1864. See Charles Burks, Provost Marshal File, Statements of Charles Burks Jr., 28 Sept. 1864, and Captain/Assistant Provost Marshal Gustavus St. Gem, 14 Oct. 1864 and 5 June 1865, File of Papers Relating to Individual Civilians, Bul–Burk; Charles Burks Probate File, Letters of Administration, 30 Apr. 1866, Ste. Genevieve County Probate Court, drawer 13, folder 353.

A regional history confirms that Charles Burks was county court judge for Ste. Genevieve County during the Rebellion and touches upon his death without providing any details, simply stating that "he was killed in this county during the war." See *Goodspeed's History of Southeast Missouri*, 315, 625.

4. Irvin M. Haile was killed on 10 Aug. 1864, the same day that Thomas McGee died in Wayne County. See Irvin M. Haile, gravestone, Herod Cemetery, Desloge, Mo.; Bettye Warner to Kirby Ross, 25 Oct. 2004 (Warner is a St. Francois County genealogist and historian).

While no primary-source documentation regarding Irvin Haile's death has been uncovered independent of Hildebrand's version of events, lore passing down through the family holds that Irvin and his father, Thomas, hid Confederate supplies and money on their property during the war and provided shelter and medical aid to Hildebrand. In addition, some Haile family descendents believe their ancestors were members of the Knights of the Golden Circle, a Confederate-supporting secret society. Irvin's brother Stephen Ferguson Hale (he spelled his last name differently) was married to a niece of Confederate major general Sterling Price and had been a colonel in the Confederate-supporting Fourth Infantry Regiment, Eighth Division, Missouri State Guard, in the first months of the war. Stephen was severely wounded in the Battle of Wilson's Creek in 1861, afterward taking up civilian life in St. Louis. See the obituary of Dr. Stephen Ferguson Hale, *Daily Enquirer* (Carlinville, Ill.), 28 Jan. 1901; Reverend Sean L. Haile to Kirby Ross, 25 Oct. 2004; Jack Hale Jr. to Kirby Ross, 25 Oct. 2004. (Sean Haile and Jack Hale are both direct descendants of Thomas Haile, Sean through the line of Irvin, and Jack through the line of Stephen.)

5. For decades after the end of the war Milks doubted Hildebrand's claim of killing two of his men, but in 1904 he took a closer look at the issue pursuant to the prompting of Dr. Cyrus A. Peterson, who shortly afterward became president of the Missouri Historical Society. Coming to a distressing conclusion after reviewing company records, and placing the likely occurrence of the event a few weeks after the timeframe stated by Hildebrand, Milks responded:

> The Co. was at Pacific [in Franklin County] several month in comd of Lieut. [James] Copp [Co. H, Third MSM Cavalry]—while there a Co. Record was made giving a short historical sketch—names of officers—Deaths &c. It gives the date of the desertion of Fry & Guittar. It may be that Hilderbrand told the truth about killing two of Co. H. I always

> thought he did lie—til now. The boys deserted or left the Co. at Rolla after the fight at P.K. [Pilot Knob, 26–27 Sept.] and probably intended to return after a short visit with home folks. I can't recall their residence—but am impressed that it was either St. Francis Co. or St. Genevieve. Yes, its rank injustice that the odiom of desertion should rest on them if Sam told the truth in his book. (H. B. Milks to Cyrus A. Peterson, 17 July 1904, Peterson Papers, box 4, folder 8)

But Milks was mistaken. Brothers-in-law Henry Fry and Gideon Guittar, who survived the war, were without a doubt the men to whom Captain Milks was referring: both were from Ste. Genevieve County, and both deserted from Rolla on 14 Oct. 1864. While Guittar failed to return to the Third MSM Cavalry, Fry did so on 7 Feb. 1865, afterward transferring to the Fourteenth Missouri Cavalry. Furthermore, both Gideon Guittar and Henry Fry appear as residing side by side in the 1870 census. Interestingly, they were neighbors of Charles Burks Sr., who was killed right after they deserted. See Gideon Guittar and Henry Fry, Military Files, State Historical Society of Missouri; 1860 Census for Union Township, Ste. Genevieve County, Mo., Dwellings 798, 802, 811; 1870 Census for Union Township, Ste. Genevieve County, Dwellings 236, 237; Ed Frye to Kirby Ross, 23 Aug. 2004 (Frye is Henry Fry's great-grandson).

6. Baron Hieronymus Karl Friedrich von Munchausen (1720–97) was a native German who in his youth served as an officer in the Russian army and participated with them in a war against the Turks. In later life he told stories of his life experiences that proved to be so fanciful that they soon found their way into print. As a series of writers built upon the works, they invented new yarns that became ever more exaggerated and in the process caused the name Munchausen to become synonymous with a teller of tall tales. See http://www.munchausen-museum.com/eng.

7. Captain Leeper had been discharged from the Third MSM Cavalry for incompetence in Apr. 1864 and was currently serving as a private in Co. F, Sixty-eighth EMM. No evidence of this skirmish has been found in the *Official Records* or in the regimental records of the Third MSM or the Sixty-eighth EMM.

Leeper, who is mentioned so prominently in Hildebrand's memoir, helped recruit Co. A, Forty-seventh Missouri Infantry Volunteers, in Aug. 1864. Despite being elected captain of that unit he was denied a commission by the governor. Within months he would undergo a drastic reversal of fortune after the Radical Unionists took control of the governorship and state legislature in the Nov. elections (during which Leeper ran unsuccessfully for the U.S. Congress). Private Leeper was thereafter considered for appointment as brigadier general before being given command of the Twenty-fourth Missouri Militia Regiment, headquartered in Iron County, at the rank of colonel. See William T. Leeper, Record of Service Cards, box 50, reels S804, S837; *Annual Report of the Adjutant General . . . 1865*, 463, 654; *Perryville Union*, 11 Nov. 1864; *Perryville Union*, 13 Jan. 1865; "Story of James Brown, Co. A 47th Regt. Mo. Inft. Vols.," 13 Oct. 1904, pp. 1–2, Peterson Papers, box 2, folder 12.

The Missouri Militia (MM) is not to be confused with the Enrolled Missouri Militia or the Missouri State Militia. It was created to assume the roll of the EMM, which was being disbanded. For a profile of the Missouri Militia, see *Organization and Status of Missouri Troops*, 90–96, 97; Ross, "Federal Militia in Missouri."

8. Sterling Price (1809–67), a hero of the Mexican War and former governor of Missouri, was appointed commanding general of the Missouri State Guard in 1861. Commissioned as a major general in the Confederate Army in 1862, he led an epic, ill-fated raid into Missouri in Sept. 1864. While Hildebrand was in fact a scout with the Seventeenth (Harrell's) Arkansas Cavalry Battalion in the advance of one of three Confederate columns in the initial stages of Price's Raid (see chap. 30), he was but one of twelve thousand Confederates who participated, and it is doubtful he was present at the personal invitation of General Price. Note that in this passage the supposed Major Hildebrand is asserting that he responded to an entreaty from the senior commanding general of the Missouri and Arkansas Theater by presenting that general with conditions.

For a biography of Price and a profile of his raid into Missouri, see Albert E. Castel, *General Sterling Price.*

CHAPTER THIRTY

1. On 19 Sept. 1864, Doniphan, the seat of Ripley County and home of many of the men belonging to the command of Tim Reeves, was put to the torch by elements of the Third MSM Cavalry and the Forty-seventh Missouri Infantry (very recently recruited from the Sixty-eighth EMM). While it had been threatened by troops of the Third MSM for some time, the burning of Doniphan was the immediate consequence of a townsman's mistreatment of politically connected Col. Greenville Mitchell, a paroled prisoner of war from the Fifty-fourth Illinois Infantry. See William Nevin to Dr. Cyrus A. Peterson, Oct. 1903, Thomas Ewing Family Papers, box 13, Manuscript Division, Library of Congress; Ross, "Burning of Doniphan," 79–80.

2. Hildebrand's presence in the Rebel advance and the misdeeds committed by him may be verified through the comments of a fellow Confederate. Pvt. George W. Rea of the Seventeenth (Harrell's) Arkansas Cavalry Battalion was with Hildebrand in the front ranks and spoke of witnessing actions undertaken by Hildebrand that "contributed much to the atrocity stories that came out of the raid." Of Private Rea's experiences, writer Ralph R. Rea stated: "Often grandfather told me of the terrible nightmare of this raid. The person I remember him

mentioning most often was Sam Hildebrand—Hildebrand, the most daring and most ruthless man he had ever seen in combat" (Rea, *Sterling Price,* 120–21). Also see Ross, "Burning of Doniphan," 82.

In chap. 14 Hildebrand claims he never was involved in the burning of any homes. His admission here is doubly ironic in that the house he burned was not the residence of a Federal officer, as he thought, but the home of the widow of Col. Aden Lowe, a secessionist hero killed in 1861 at the Battle of Fredericktown, Mo. Nevin to Peterson, Oct. 1903; Ross, "Burning of Doniphan," 81–82.

3. The Federals who burned Doniphan were overtaken on the Little Black River between Doniphan and Poplar Bluff. With a sharp skirmish ensuing, the bulk of Union troops escaped, aided by the confusion caused by a large number of Confederates in the melee being clothed in Federal uniforms. Hildebrand's claim of murdering sixteen prisoners at the Little Black is partially correct—around ten Federals died in actual combat while six more were taken prisoner, with two officers being shot almost immediately and four enlisted men being put to death two weeks later. Hildebrand's assertion of Confederate executions of seven Union prisoners at Patterson is true, occurring on 22 Sept. See Peterson, *Narrative of the Capture and Murder,* 8; Peterson and Hanson, *Pilot Knob,* 94–95; J. C. Steakley Memoir, 24 June 1903, p. 4, Ewing Family Papers, box 216; Nevin to Peterson, Oct. 1903; Ross, "Burning of Doniphan," 82.

On 3 Oct. another in a series of Confederate executions occurred in Franklin County, involving Maj. James Wilson and six of his men from the Third MSM Cavalry who were killed by Tim Reeves. In reprisal, six Confederate enlisted men held at Gratiot Prison in St. Louis were shot. (The scheduled execution of a Confederate major was halted through the intervention of President Lincoln.) Notably, in a final chapter of the McGee/Cato saga, one of the executed Rebels included Asa Ladd, a member of the McGee/Cato clan. Out of the hundreds of captives confined at the prison, Ladd's inclusion as one of six victims of a retaliatory execution seems to have been more than coincidental. See Ross, "Burning of Doniphan," 83; Cato, Palmer, and Cato, "Research on the Name Cato."

4. Tim Reeves's regiment was continuing its participation in Price's Raid, which took it out of the area, and Hildebrand was now closely associating himself with elements of the regiment of Confederate Willis Ponder. Colonel Ponder, Lt. Col. (not captain) Benjamin Holmes, and Maj. Richard Berryman (a prewar neighbor of Hildebrand) were the three senior leaders of the Twelfth Missouri Infantry (CSA), which was a sister regiment of sorts to Timothy Reeves's Fifteenth Missouri Cavalry: both had large numbers of recruits from Ripley County, Mo.; Colonel Ponder, like Colonel Reeves, was also from Ripley County; and finally, like Hildebrand and Ponder's troops, Reeves was executing prisoners without benefit of trial at this time. See Gen. Joseph Shelby to Maj. C. C. Rainwater, 1 Jan. 1888, Ewing Family Papers, box 213; Stanton, Berquist,

and Bowers, *Jeff Thompson*, 294; Peterson, *Narrative of the Capture and Murder*, 8; Peterson and Mills, *Pilot Knob*, 94–95; Steakley Memoir, p. 4; Nevin to Peterson, Oct. 2003; Ross, "Burning of Doniphan," 82.

After the war, Hildebrand allies Tim Reeves, David Reed, Daniel McGee, and Dick Berryman were named as codefendants in a one-hundred-thousand-dollar civil lawsuit filed "for certain property alleged by plaintiffs to have been unlawfully taken by defendants and converted to their own use and to the use of an unlawful conspiracy." See *James Lindsay et al. vs. Sterling Price et al.*, Iron County Circuit Court, 23 Jan. 1866, book A, p. 500.

5. According to a local newspaper account:

> Potosi, Mo. September 18, 1864—Raid by Dick Berryman and His Forty Thieves. . . .—After the robbing of Esquire Patterson, they then visited the residence of M. A. Todd, our old-time Sheriff and loyal citizen, and robbed him of a fine English double-barreled shot gun, worth seventy-five dollars, and one Colt's revolver, (navy) worth twenty-five dollars. Thence to Wm. Nicholson, on Little Fourche-a-Renault Creek, and ordered the women to prepare them something to eat. During that time they went to the stable, and robbed it of a fine stallion, belonging to Captain George Towl, of this place. After Dick's murderous raid on the soldiers and citizens of Caledonia, they made another raid on the town of Iron Mountain. (*St. Louis Republican*, 21 Sept. 1864)

Also see the *St. Louis Union*, 23 Sept. 1864.

Note should be made of the fact that Hildebrand's compatriot Bob Highley (see chap. 24) was also reported to be operating with Berryman around this time:

> Affairs in the Southeast—Colonel Fletcher Again—Four Guerrillas Killed. The camp of Dick Berryman, Bob Highley and Bob Grady—the worst desperate and notorious bushwhackers infesting the Southeast, and long a terror to the whole of that region—were surprised on last Sunday night, in St. Francois county and four of these desperadoes were killed.
>
> Lieut. [Christian] Hilber, a gallant officer belonging to the St. Francois county company of Colonel Fletcher's regiment [Co. F, Forty-seventh Missouri Infantry], was wounded in the arm in the fight, which was the only injury suffered by our force. The killing of these men was undoubtedly done, as "we are informed by reliable Union men, with the connivance of Tom Fletcher." (*St. Louis Democrat*, 1 Sept. 1864)

In addition, according to a sworn statement, the names of Bob Grady and Bob Highley again were tied to Hildebrand's when it was alleged that they were "pressing" St. Francois County civilians into Confederate service. One of these reluctant would-be warriors, Peter Carron, claimed he was forced to join their "gang of Bushwhackers" on 28 Sept. and was with Hildebrand while Hildebrand was stealing horses and robbing property over the next few days. Then on 1 Oct. the squad met with a number of other conscripts from the area in order to form a company. In the vote for officers Grady was defeated in his attempt to become captain. According to Carron, "After the election Hildebrand, Grady & Bob Highly went another way and we remained." Criminal charges were later filed against Grady for a burglary alleged to have been committed three days later.

Failing to join the main Confederate Army passing through the area, the conscripts instead disbanded and went home. Carron turned himself in to authorities and was released on a five-hundred-dollar bond after taking the Oath of Allegiance on 15 Oct. See the Peter Jas. Carron File, Testimony of Peter Jas. Carron, 8 Nov. 1864, File of Papers Relating to Individual Civilians, Carn–Cars; *State of Missouri vs. Robert Grady*, St. Francois County Circuit Court, 22 Mar. 1865, St. Francois County Circuit Court Records, reel C15693.

6. Francis W. Fite, Thomas Haile, and George W. Vandiver Sr. all died on 7 Oct. 1864, in the midst of a Federal counteroffensive mounted in response to the Hildebrand/Berryman/Grady/Highley raiding. Little else is known regarding Fite and Vandiver, but "Judge Haile" was seventy-three-year-old Thomas Haile, who had been a St. Francois County court judge from 1831 to 1838 and was probably a cousin or uncle of Hildebrand's close ally Devilish Tom Haile. (Judge Haile's son Stephen had served in the same company with Devilish Tom during the Mexican War.) Haile family lore holds that the judge and his son Irvin rendered aid and shelter to Hildebrand during the Civil War. Census records indicate that Judge Haile lived near Hildebrand prior to the conflict, while a postwar regional history confirms "he was shot during the late war, while on his farm." The perpetrators of the act are not named in this account. See *Goodspeed's History of Southeast Missouri,* 349, 352, 622; 1850 Census for Liberty Township, St. Francois County, Dwellings 343, 355; Francis W. Fite, gravestone, Fite Cemetery, Bonne Terre, Mo.; George W. Vandiver Sr., gravestone, Germania Cemetery, Bonne Terre, Mo.; Thomas Haile, gravestone, Herod Cemetery, Desloge, Mo.; Haile to Ross, 25 Oct. 2004; Warner to Ross, 25 Oct. 2004, 4 Nov. 2004; Stephen F. Hale and Thomas J. Hale, Record of Service Cards, box 35, reel S911, Mexican War, 1846–47.

With their father and brother having been killed, Samuel G. Haile and Stephen Ferguson Hale fled to Illinois. Up until the deaths of his family members, ex-Rebel Stephen F. Hale was residing in St. Louis. Afterward he moved to Bunker Hill, Ill., remaining there for the remainder of his life. Up to this time Samuel G. Haile lived in St. Francois County (see chap. 25) but, according to a regional history, "removed from Missouri to Perry County, Ill. After the close of hostilities during the war he returned to his native county" (*Goodspeed's History of Southeast Missouri*, 638). Also see the obituary of Dr. Stephen Ferguson Hale, *Daily Enquirer*, 28 Jan. 1901; Haile to Ross, 25 Oct. 2004; Hale to Ross, 25 Oct. 2004.

Another brother, Thomas H. Haile (also not to be confused with Devilish Tom Haile), seems to have managed to stay out of harm's way by serving in Co. B, Sixty-eighth EMM (the same company to which Ross Jelkyll and George Hart had once belonged). See the Muster Roll, Co. B, Sixty-eighth Enrolled Missouri Militia, box 16, folder 90, Missouri State Archives; Thomas H. Haile, Record of Service Card, box 35, reel S804.

7. "In Field, October 9, 1864—A scout under Major Montgomery returned last evening to De Soto from a scout in Saint Francois County, broke up a rebel camp of 300 under the guerrilla chiefs Dick Berryman and Sam ——, and killing 21, capturing 1" (Brig. Gen. Madison Miller, EMM). Also see the following account:

> De Soto, Mo. October 8, 1864—I have the honor to report that I left camp at this place at 5 P.M. on the 6th instant, with 200 men, for Potosi. After proceeding about ten miles learned there was a party of rebels between Lawson and Cadet Stations. I changed my course and marched for Cadet Station, which had not been burned as reported to me, but the stores were robbed and Mr. Marr carried off a conscript. I took their trail from that place and followed them to Tyler's Mills, on Big River, where I found a camp of 300 under Dick Berryman and the notorious Sam Hilderbrand. Attacked their camp, scattering them in confusion in all directions, killing 21. . . . A portion of the party were the same that were driven from Richwoods on the morning of the 4th instant by [1st Lt. Roderick D.] Russell [Co. A, Sixth Missouri Cavalry]. They had with them eleven who were wounded at that place. There was a large number of the citizens of that neighborhood present who were on very intimate and friendly terms with the rebels, still they were loud in their professions of loyalty upon our arrival. (Maj. Samuel Montgomery, Sixth Missouri Cavalry, *O.R.*, ser. 1, vol. 41, pt. 1, p. 456)

See also the *St. Louis Republican*, 10 Oct. 1864; *O.R.*, ser. 1, vol. 41, pt. 1, p. 883.

Three of those citizens were Haile, Fite, and Vandiver, whose headstones indicate they died on this same day. Independent notations in the regimental books for the Sixth Missouri Cavalry confirm that Cos. A, D, and E converged from St. Louis and De Soto, routing a force of Rebels at Richwoods on 4 Oct., reportedly killing twelve Confederate recruits. On 7 Oct. this same Union force then attacked a large contingent of Rebels at Tyler's Mill, reportedly killing twenty-one. Co. L of the Sixth Missouri Cavalry also engaged in skirmishing that same day at Big River Mills. (Hildebrand's old home was at Big River Mills, and his mother was currently residing at Tyler's Mill.) See the Record of Events, Co. A, Co. D, Co. E, Co. L, Sixth Missouri Cavalry, State Historical Society of Missouri.

CHAPTER THIRTY-ONE

1. Robert J. Manning, age twenty-two in 1860, a prominent merchant living in Punjaub in Ste. Genevieve County, was a second lieutenant of Co. H, Seventy-eighth EMM. See the 1860 Census for Jackson Township, Ste. Genevieve County, Dwelling 654; Robert Manning, Record of Service Card, box 53, reel S811.

2. A local Union commander who seems to have wanted nothing to do with Hildebrand and his men reported Hildebrand's presence in the area and suggested he could not deal with him personally due to a more pressing matter: "Pilot Knob, Mo. October 15, 1864—Dick Berryman, Hildebrand, and other leaders are on Saint Francis River with a variously estimated force, I think 300, but increasing in strength by recruiting parties coming in. I intended to finish the telegraph line to Fredericktown to-day, but can't do it and look after the rebels too. What are the troops doing at Cape Girardeau . . . ?" (Maj. H. H. Williams, Tenth Kansas Infantry, *O.R.,* ser. 1, vol. 41, pt. 3, p. 887).

3. This was the second Hildebrand slaying in ten months that had ties to North (see chap. 22).

CHAPTER THIRTY-THREE

1. There were reports around this time that Hildebrand had moved his headquarters from Scatterville into the marshland around ten miles to the northwest: "March 3, 1865—I have the honor to inform you that official notice has been given to me by the provost-marshal of the Third District of the existence of a band of guerrillas two miles below Poplar Bluff, in Butler County, under Jennings; also that Cache Swamp is the chief resort of guerrillas under Hilderbrand and Neighbors. These bands rob and murder the people, scouring the country in small squads, and have even attacked the pickets at Ironton, and unless they are checked or driven off it is feared this coming summer may bring new raids, murders, &c." (Col. E. B. Alexander, Tenth U.S. Infantry/Acting Provost Marshal General, *O.R.,* ser. 1, vol. 48, pt. 1, pp. 1069–70). Note the continuing Hildebrand/Neighbors association dating from at least Mar. 1863 (see chap. 16).

2. "Bloomfield, Mo. March 9, 1865—I will send a force to watch for Hilderbrand at the Indian Ford. . . . [My men] came upon Bolin's gang Tuesday and killed two and wounded several" (Col. H. M. Hiller, Second MSM Cavalry, *O.R.*, ser. 1, vol. 48, pt. 1, p. 129).

3. "Pilot Knob, Mo., March 14, 1865— . . . I have had several parties after the guerrillas, Hilderbrand and his gang, about Farmington. As yet no success" (Col. John L. Beveridge, Seventeenth Illinois Cavalry/Commanding Third Sub-district of St. Louis, *O.R.*, ser. 1, vol. 48, pt. 1, p. 1171). (Beveridge and the Seventeenth Illinois Cavalry had arrived at Pilot Knob in Jan. and would move on to Cape Girardeau in Apr.)

4. "St. Louis, March 14, 1865—See if you can't devise some plan to catch Hilderbrand and his Confederates on Big River. The force you stationed at Farmington better be placed at Tyler's Mills. Hildebrand's family [mother] lives there. . . . By sending men in citizens' clothes to watch for him he could be caught" (Maj. H. Hannahs, Fiftieth Missouri Infantry/Acting Assistant Adjutant General, *O.R.*, ser. 1, vol. 48, pt. 1, pp. 1170–71).

CHAPTER THIRTY-FOUR

1. "Pilot Knob, Mo. April 4, 1865— . . . Yesterday, 3 P.M., Hilderbrand, with fifty men appeared at Doe Run, about four miles south[west] of Farmington, robbing teams, &c. I have 115 men after him, and have sent instructions to outposts to endeavor to head him off" (Lt. Col. D. J. Hynes, Seventeenth Illinois Cavalry, *O.R.*, ser. 1, vol. 48, pt. 2, p. 28). Simms Mountain is a few miles northwest of Doe Run.

2. See the following account:

> Farmington, Mo. April 4, 1865—Yesterday about 9 o'clock a report was brought to me by citizens that Hilderbrand and his gang, numbering eight men in all, were at Hered's [Joseph Herod's] place, near Big River Mills, at daylight and took breakfast. On receiving this report I immediately sent out two details, one under Sergeant [John H.] Hood, the other under Sergeant [Benjamin C.] Cable, to intercept them. Sergeant Hood proceeded on the Potosi road about four miles, when he struck their trail on the Iron road. They were evidently making their way toward Dent's Station, Iron Mountain Railroad, but hearing of my men being in pursuit changed their course and struck south. Sergeant Hood followed the trail as best he could, now and then getting off the track as they traveled on plain roads, but took through thick woods and by-paths. They had about fourteen led horses, according to citizens' reports. (Capt. John Noyes, Seventh Kansas Cavalry, *O.R.*, ser. 1, vol. 48, pt. 1, p. 178)

3. Robert Hill's residence was near to those of Orville McIlvaine and Hildebrand's relatives John and Allen Roan. See the 1860 Census for Liberty Township, St. Francois County, Dwelling 5.

4. Crunkleton resided a few houses from sworn Hildebrand enemy Joe

McGahan. See the 1860 Census for Liberty Township, St. Francois County, Dwelling 149.

5. "Farmington, Mo. April 4, 1865— . . . About two miles from this place they ran in and took out an old black man, and killed him about seven miles from town" (Capt. John Noyes, Seventh Kansas Cavalry, *O.R.*, ser. 1, vol. 48, pt. 1, p. 178).

The Third MSM Cavalry was in the final stages of its existence and was disbanding due to the expiration of the enlistments of its troops. Filling the void left by its absence in southeast Missouri were the Seventeenth Illinois Cavalry and the Seventh Kansas Cavalry, which assumed the Third MSM's role of being Sam Hildebrand's primary adversary. See the *Annual Report of the Adjutant General . . . 1865,* 467; William A. Lyman, "Diary of Union Soldier of Company G, 7th Regiment, Kansas Volunteer Cavalry, Served in Missouri," 24–25, Western Historical Manuscript Collection, University of Missouri, Columbia; Fox, "The Story of the Seventh Kansas," 45; Carpenter, "History of the 17th Cavalry Volunteers," chaps. 34–35; Dyer, *A Compendium of the War of the Rebellion*, 1032, 1183, 1304–5.

6. "Farmington, Mo. April 4, 1865— . . . They crossed the Pilot Knob plank road about five miles from here, and took six horses from teams on the road. My two details united about noon and followed the trail as far as Burnham's Mills, on the Blairsville road. The horses being so fatigued, having traveled some forty miles, Sergeant Hood thought it advisable not to pursue farther. I afterward learned that they passed on the west side of the Saint Francis River and probably about seven miles east of Pilot Knob, so on through what is called Flat Woods" (Capt. John Noyes, Seventh Kansas Cavalry, *O.R.*, ser. 1, vol. 48, pt. 1, p. 178).

Also see the following: "Patterson, Mo. April 7, 1865—The force I sent to Indian Ford has returned. They could not find Hilderbrand or hear anything of him" (Capt. James Smith, Seventh Kansas Cavalry, *O.R.*, ser. 1, vol. 48, pt. 2, p. 45).

7. Hildebrand kept Jim's son as a slave for several years after the war was over; see chap. 34.

8. Hildebrand appears to have his date off by a few days: "De Soto, Mo. April 26, 1865—Hilderbrand was day before yesterday again four miles east of Big River Mills with some men. It is new moon again, and he is getting ready for another raid. For pity's sake do detail ten men to Cadet" (F. Kellerman, *O.R.*, ser. 1, vol. 48, pt. 2, p. 207). Note that Hildebrand claimed he had also robbed Kellerman's store in Cadet in late 1864—see chap. 30.

9. The six paragraphs preceding the callout for this note were originally at the beginning of chap. 35, where they were chronologically out of order.

10. Abram W. Keith, an editor of the 1870 version of this memoir, was a neighbor of George Hart, the man tortured and killed by Hildebrand in chap. 26. See the 1860 Census for Liberty Township, St. Francois County, Dwellings 782, 787.

11. Nesbit Orton, who had had a horse stolen by Hildebrand a short time earlier, lived just two houses away from Herod. In addition, intelligence reaching Federal forces asserted that Hildebrand had been received in the Herod home on the morning of 3 Apr. and had taken his breakfast with Herod (right around the time Orton had his horse taken). Coupled with the irate exhortations of Robert Hill, Herod's fate thus seems to have been sealed. See *O.R.*, ser. 1, vol. 48, pt. 1, p. 178; 1860 Census for Liberty Township, St. Francois County, Dwelling 81.

12. This is 1st Lt. John W. Brown of the Perry County Missouri Militia. Lieutenant Brown had just mustered into the service on 13 Apr. See the *Annual Report of the Adjutant General of Missouri . . . 1865*, 695.

13. The logic that Hildebrand's robberies should be ignored during this raid because one of his victims had a personality conflict with a third person in the neighborhood seems to have been lost on the Federal authorities and civilians who were caught in the maelstrom: "Cape Girardeau, Mo. May 18, 1865—Major [Levi H.] Utt [Seventh Kansas Cavalry] telegraphs from the Knob that Hilderbrand's gang were in Saint Francois County yesterday, robbing citizens. One company from the Seventh Kansas are in pursuit"(2nd Lt. William L. Stafford, Seventeenth Illinois Cavalry, *O.R.*, ser. 1, vol. 48, pt. 2, p. 496). A newspaper account follows:

> Potosi, Mo. May 18, 1865—Our situation is desperate; I shall proceed to give you some facts showing how terribly we are suffering:
>
> First, Friday a store was robbed at De Soto Station, on the Iron Mountain railroad. Last Monday night at 12 o'clock, six men came to Mr. Hunter, in Belleview, took his horse, money, papers and all the clothing of the women and children. No man in our part of Free Missouri pretends to have more clothing than he wears; so they have to take now the clothing of women and little children. The same night a fine horse was taken from John Huff. The life of old Mr. Hunter was only saved because they could not find a rope to hang him, and because his family begged so much for him; but their main object was to get hold of the old man's son, a brave soldier who was just mustered out and expected home that evening; providentially he was detained at Potosi that night [Capt. William T. Hunter, Third MSM Cavalry]. The next day, Mr. Shelton, of Iron County, was robbed of all he had. Yesterday the stage between Fredericktown and Pilot Knob was attacked and the driver shot through his leg. By a hasty retreat towards Fredericktown the mail was saved. The attacking party being encumbered by too many stolen horses they could not pursue fast enough. Last night another band was again in the neighborhood of Mr. Hunter's house. The horses of several teams were taken from private wagons returning from St. Genevieve.

> The people are harassed to death. Hunger stares them in the face. They were robbed by Price's raid of all they had, and now perhaps a few men are trying to plant a little corn, while others stand watch with rifles and revolvers. In the night they sleep in the woods, and the first thing they know some scoundrels come and take their last horse which they had perhaps bought on credit, and steal the little clothing of their women and children. If we say anything the reply is "Ah, we have now civil law. You must protect yourselves. Our courts will punish the bushwhackers."
>
> I would like to see that declaration of Governor Fletcher carried out which he made last winter, namely: "If there is but one loyal citizen in a county, he shall be protected." (*St. Louis Democrat*, 19 May 1865)

For insight into why Captain Hunter, mustered out on 9 May, may have been targeted for death, see chap. 36, footnote 17.

Apparently these depredations were the final straw for local Unionists who believed Joseph Herod to be a member of secret Confederate societies and a man who offered aid to Sam Hildebrand. Another member of the Herod family, Samuel Herod, married to the sister of Devilish Tom Haile, sheltered Hildebrand as he was being sought by law-enforcement authorities after the war (see chap. 36).

CHAPTER THIRTY-FIVE

1. Two Federal accounts and a newspaper account follow. For additional information, see the *Annual Report of the Adjutant General . . . 1865*, 695.

> De Soto, Mo. May 22, 1865—This morning at 7.30 o'clock Sam Hilderbrand and four men were attacked at Valley Mines, while robbing a store, by the U.S. troops stationed at Big River Mills, and one man killed by our troops, a large, black-haired man, said to live when at home south of Farmington; also Hilderbrand is supposed to be wounded in the leg, as he had great difficulty in getting on this horse. They are supposed to have started south. (Capt. H. Bailey, Fifty-first Wisconsin Infantry, *O.R.*, ser. 1, vol. 48, pt. 1, pp. 287–88)

> Cape Girardeau, Mo. May 29, 1865—Captain [Hiram] Minor [Perry County Missouri Militia] reports from Perryville that on the 22d his company had a fight with Hilderbrand's gang near Big River Mills. Killed one man and wounded two others. It is supposed that Hilderbrand is dead, as he was one of the wounded. (Lt. Col. F. M. Malone, Seventh Kansas Cavalry, *O.R.*, ser. 1, vol. 48, pt. 2, p. 666)

> June 2, 1865—A Fight With Guerrillas—Captain Minor has shown us the report of the fight between a squad of his men, under the command of Lieutenant Brown, and Helterbrand's guerrillas. Lieut. Brown came upon them at Stony Point in St. Francois county, on the 22nd of May, when a fight took place. After a few rounds the guerrillas fled to the woods. One of Helterbrand's men was killed and two others wounded. They captured two splendid horses and saddles and equipments, also two United States revolvers, four United States blankets, and about six hundred dollars worth of dry goods, which the guerrillas had just taken out of Mr. Taylor's store. They also captured several hundred dollars of confederate script. It is believed that Helterbrand was wounded in the fight. The last accounts from Lieut. Brown stated that he and his squad of Perry county men were in pursuit of the guerrilla thieves. (*Perryville Union*, 2 June 1865)

2. Note that the men of Co. A, Third MSM Cavalry, heard a cowbell rattle right before they were attacked by Hildebrand in May 1864 (see chap. 28, n. 1).

3. Actually the claims were rejected because Brown's company and the rest of the Missouri Militia had had its funding cut off and was disbanding. On 21 June orders were promulgated that "no further issuances" were to be made to these units. This was the direct "consequence of the refusal of the United States Government to issue subsistence to the companies of volunteer militia . . . and the inability, for want of appropriations, of the State to subsist them" (*Annual Report of the Adjutant General of Missouri . . . 1865*, 701–2).

4. The two paragraphs preceding the callout for this note were originally at the end of chap. 34, where they were chronologically out of order.

5. Like his claim of being granted a major's commission, Hildebrand's claim of receiving his parole at Jacksonport is problematic. Certainly if he did receive one it was not on 26 May, or even 5 June, which was the actual date of the Jacksonport surrender. Hildebrand was reported to be in St. Francois County through late May. Not only would Hildebrand have had to travel the two hundred miles across rivers, through swamps, and over mountains on horseback from St. Francois County to Jacksonport in just a matter of days, but by his own account he would also have had to schedule the bushwhacking of Miller and the beheading of Johnson into that time period, along with his "leisurely" return trek to Greene County (his own description of his pace), as well as his *weeklong* sojourn in Greene County, during which he was considering whether he was going to apply for the parole.

Neither has any independent primary-source documentation been located indicating that Hildebrand received a parole.

CHAPTER THIRTY-SIX

1. Major Surge is believed to have been James Surridge, a native Englishman and veteran of the Third Missouri Cavalry (CSA). See *Goodspeed's History of Southeast Missouri*, 509: James Surridge, Index to Compiled Service Records of Confederate Soldiers, M380 roll 14.

2. Hildebrand's mother apparently passed away within weeks of their return. See n. 4 below.

3. One published account of the era discusses Hildebrand and his victims, stating:

> His [Hildebrand's] wounds were dressed by a woman who afterwards married a man who squandered all her means. He [the married man] then left his wife and lived with her negro servant in Arkansas. Hilderbrand, stung with resentment at the way in which the woman who attended to him while sick was treated, went with a few men, and, tying the man and negress together, flung them into the river. For this act Hilderbrand was tried and sentenced to be hung. Before the time of execution, two hundred men, clothed in Federal uniform, went to the jailor and demanded that the prisoner be given to them. The jailor supposed the object was to lynch him, instead of which they put him on a horse and he made his escape. Hilderbrand is described as of tall, slender form, sharp features, grey eyes and red hair. He has a feminine voice, steps as lightly as an Indian, and can clear a seven rail fence with the agility of a deer. (*St. Louis Republican*, 15 June 1869)

4. Hildebrand's capture in Arkansas and his looming date with the hangman were apparently the final blow for his mother, who "died of grief after the massacre of her family," according to one report. Hildebrand's first order of business upon his return was to begin having her property probated, the file of the procedure indicating that Sam lived in Jefferson County on 17 Sept. 1868. Hildebrand was said to have opened the estate because he had "returned to St. Francois county . . . in poor circumstances. He gave out that he wanted to settle up his mother's estate, from which he expected some $300 or $400." See Rebecca Hildebrand, Probate File, Letters of Administration Granted 18 Sept. 1868, St. Francois Probate Court Records, reel C8797, Missouri State Archives; James F. Hildebrand, Probate File, Letters of Administration Granted 8 Mar. 1865, St. Francois Probate Court Records, reel C8796 (this file shows the last known independently documented date that Hildebrand's mother was alive, 8 Mar. 1865); *St. Louis Republican*, 15 June 1869.

5. "Poverty drove him to engage in hard work. He chopped cord wood for a time at Rush Tower Bend, some thirty miles below St. Louis" (*St. Louis Republican*, 15 June 1869).

6. "Hilderbrand is charged with many atrocities committed during the war. Since then he has been suspected of being connected with a gang of horse thieves and counterfeiters, whose operations extend through the lower tier of counties of Missouri and Illinois" (*Jefferson Democrat* [Hillsboro, Mo.], 17 June 1869).

Samuel Herod was the brother-in-law of Devilish Tom Haile (Bettye Warner to Jack Hale, 15 Nov. 2004).

7. "It was understood between the State and county authorities that Hildebrand would be allowed to return home and live in peace, if he would only do so. He did return home but it was not long afterwards until he was at his old tricks again, stealing and threatening to kill his enemies. The State authorities, under the administration of Governor Joseph W. McClurg, determined to have him arrested and answer for some of the many crimes which he was accused of" (*Farmington News*, 23 Jan. 1914).

8. See the following newspaper account:

> All attempts to capture Hilderbrand proved abortive and early this spring efforts were renewed by organized parties to take him dead or alive. The Police Commissioners of St. Louis, we are informed, at the request of the Governor, took the matter in hand, and on the 21st of April last, Col. Wm. D. Bowen, Sergeant of Police, with Officer McQueen and Mr. James McLane, went in quest of the murderer. They took with them a boiled ham, a sack of crackers and coffee, and walked during the night from Irondale, twenty-three miles, to the home of Hilderbrand, between the Big River Mills and Farmington, but nearer the former than the latter place. There they concealed themselves in the brush, in sight of Hilderbrand's house for two days and nights. Hilderbrand's family were seen walking about, and also a brother-in-law of the former, named Harris, who was, during the war, a soldier in the Federal army—the 10th Missouri. Getting destitute of provisions, and coming to the conclusion that the party for whom they were lying in wait was absent from home, Bowen and his party abandoned the search, and returned to St. Louis. (*St. Louis Republican*, 14 June 1869)

Note that the name of James McLane was spelled a number of ways. Assuming the census enumerator to have made a direct inquiry as to the proper spelling, unless it is contained in a direct quote, his version will be used.

9. "These alleged murders have inspired terror in the people residing in St. Francois county, and soon after the murder of McIlvane the Governor offered a reward of $300 for his capture. Rewards were also offered of $4,000 by St. Francois county; and the father of McIlvane, who has since removed to St. Louis, also offered a reward" (*St. Louis Republican*, 14 June 1869).

Also see the following account: "A number of Hilderbrand's partisans united in offering the reward, to save themselves from being distrusted by the Union men. But he evaded capture. He boasted that, with twenty feet the start in the bush, he would bid defiance to a regiment of men in pursuit" (*St. Louis Republican*, 15 June 1869).

10. "It is alleged [Hildebrand] was famous during the war as a daring bushwhacker, and his name became as notorious as those of Quantrel and Bill Anderson. . . . His enemies allege that he has killed in all 78 (?) men, since and during the war, and that he keeps a tally of every man killed notched with a file on his gun barrel. He wears a steel breast-plate, carries two revolvers, and has besides two trusty rifles. He is about 40 years of age, of powerful build, and fearless" (*St. Louis Republican*, 14 June 1869).

11. "Finding Hilderbrand standing out in the yard, he fired at him, and wounded him severely in the thigh. Hilderbrand then retreated into the house, and there being three or four other men there at the time, and finding it impossible to capture him without assistance . . . was obliged to return for reinforcements during which time Hildebrand escaped from the house" (*St. Louis Republican*, 14 June 1869).

The following account, reprinted from the *Ironton Register*, was dictated by a participant in the upcoming gun battle at Williams's farm: "About daylight Sam came out of the house and Peterson took deliberate aim with a ballard rifle and fired, but he must have lost his nerve, for instead of shooting him in the heart, he shot him in the flesh part of the thigh. Sam then ran into the house and closed the door and Peterson made no further attempt to get him, but struck out for tall timber. He arrived at Fredericktown and at once wired the governor of what he had done. The governor wired Sheriff Breckenridge, of Potosi what Peterson had done, and told him to take a posse and go get Hildebrand, which the Sheriff proceeded to do" (*Farmington News*, 23 Jan. 1914).

12. Worth noting is the fact that census records indicate William Highley had sons named John and Robert (see chaps. 24 and 30). See the 1860 Census for Liberty Township, St. Francois County, Dwelling 91.

13. Cyrus A. Peterson was twenty-one years old at the time he ambushed Hildebrand and three and a half decades later became president of the Missouri Historical Society. In explaining his actions, something quite different than the prospect of reward was raised as his motivation for shooting Hildebrand:

> I was born and raised in North Carolina and came to Missouri just at the outbreaking of the civil war. I was then only 13 years old. My father's family settled down 20 miles south of Fredericktown and 40 miles from Pilot Knob where we lived through the war in one of the worst rebel sections of the State of Mo. My father and only brother (18 yrs. old) being intense unionists, in spite of the fact that we were from

> the South, were both driven into the Union army early in the war. I lived and worked on a farm until the spring of 1863 when at the age of 15 years I took a gun and joined the Union forces in driving Gen. Marmaduke from the state when he was in on one of his horse stealing and pillaging raids. After that, for the next two years, I slept in the brush or in caves or out houses and worked on the farm while my younger sisters stood sentinel for me to warn me of approaching bushwhackers. My only brother was sacrificed for the Union cause and my father came out of the Union army a broken down man in 1865. For 10 years I had to go armed against the rebel and bushwhacking hosts in S.E. Mo. and in 1869 shot (and almost killed) and drove from our State their leader an arch fiend in that section, the notorious murderer Sam. Hillabrand. I still hate them and their so-called "cause" with a hatred so intense that it keeps me awake of nights. (C. A. Peterson to Hugo Hoffbauer, 9 Jan. 1903, Ewing Family Papers, box 216)

Also see Robert Jefferson Bartholomew Jr., Pedigree Chart and Cyrus A. Peterson Notes, 20 Sept. 2001. (Bartholomew is a direct descendant of Peterson.)

Cyrus Peterson's father, Daniel (born 1823), enlisted on 4 Apr. 1862 in Capt. William T. Hunter's Co. H, Twelfth MSM Cavalry (later redesignated Co. M, Third MSM Cavalry), and rose to the rank of sergeant. In 1861 Cyrus's brother Sidney joined Pinkney Powers's Wayne County Cavalry, Six Month Militia (a.k.a. the Haw Eater Scouts), and on 26 Mar. 1862 enlisted in Co. F, Twelfth MSM Cavalry. He died at age nineteen in Jackson, Mo., in Nov. of that year. See Wilkinson, "Biographical Sketch"; "Roster of Haw Eaters—Wayne County Cavalry," Peterson Papers, box 1, folder 22; C. A. Peterson to H. C Wilkinson, 28 Oct. 1902, Peterson Papers, box 7, folder 1, ; *Annual Report of the Adjutant General . . . 1863*, 168; Military Files of Sidney Peterson, Twelfth MSM Cavalry, Daniel Peterson, Twelfth MSM Cavalry, and Daniel Peterson, Third MSM Cavalry, all at the State Historical Society of Missouri.

Regarding the alleged participation of Walter Evans in the ambush of Hildebrand, it might be relevant that several members of the Evans family were targeted for assassination during the war. See the *St. Louis Union*, 23 Sept. 1864.

14. See the following newspaper account:

> Breckinridge, with the posse, arrived at the house where Sam was shot, late in the afternoon, but the bird had flown. Hildebrand had a neighbor who lived a short distance from his house. The sheriff went there to inquire of this man if he knew anything of him. The man told him that when he went to his corn-crib early in the morning and opened the door of the crib Sam was in there and pulled a gun on him and told him to hitch up his team and take him away; and if he didn't he would kill him. The man told the sheriff that he had hauled him to Buck

> Highley's, about five miles from there. The sheriff took the man along with him and went to Highley's. Highley told the sheriff that this man brought Hildebrand to his house and that Hildebrand had compelled him, Highley, to haul him to John Williams. (*Farmington News*, 23 Jan. 1914)

15. "On Thursday, the 10th inst., Mr. Breckenridge, the Sheriff of Washington county, received information that Hilderbrand was concealed in the house of his uncle, an old man named Williams, about 12 miles south-east of Irondale, in St. Francois county. On Friday morning last, Breckenridge went to the place indicated, with a posse of four or five men, and found Hilderbrand on the premises. He informed him that he had a warrant for his arrest, and demanded his surrender. Hilderbrand made no reply, but pushing his hand out the door shot at the Sheriff with a pistol, wounding him severely in the groin, and also wounding another person slightly" (*St. Louis Republican*, 14 June 1869).

16. See the following newspaper account:

> The posse stopped at the barn and waited for Williams to come out to feed. Williams soon made his appearance at the barn to feed his stock. The sheriff then arrested Williams and turned Highley loose. Williams told the sheriff that Hildebrand was in the house. They took Williams and all proceeded to the house. The sheriff told Williams to call Hildebrand and tell him that the sheriff was there with a warrant for his arrest and for him to come out and surrender. Williams told the sheriff there would be something doing that; that Sam would not surrender, but kill him (Williams) the first man. But Williams knocked on the door & told Hildebrand what the sheriff had told him. In a second or two the door opened a small crack and the battle was on. The first shot from Sam's big Remington revolver took off Williams' finger. The next shot struck the sheriff in the groin, and the next shot took out a bunch of whiskers from Andy Bean's chin. The battle became general. The posse found what shelter it could and kept up the battle, but Sam held the fort. The sheriff was badly hurt and had to be taken where he could receive medical attention. Part of the posse was left to guard and keep Sam in the house, while the others took the sheriff away, and called for reinforcement.
>
> Sam was kept in the fort by the guards until reinforcement came. They shifted their positions and fired from different places to make him think there were several men guarding the house. Williams' wife and a little girl were in the house all through the battle. After the fire slackened somewhat Sam told Mrs. Williams to take the bucket and the little girl and go to the spring and bring him a bucket of water, but Mrs. Williams was not allowed to return to the house. Sam, not getting any

> water, was very thirsty, and quenched his thirst during the day by sucking raw eggs. (*Farmington News*, 23 Jan. 1914)

17. Capt. "Todd" Hunter was William T. Hunter, former captain of Co. M, Third MSM Cavalry, who had narrowly avoided assassination in May 1865 (see chap. 34). Hunter was a long-time resident of Washington County and was its postwar county clerk in Potosi. Early in the war he had served as ordnance sergeant in Capt. Thomas Castleman's company of the Washington County Six Month Militia when that unit became one of the first to array itself against the Hildebrand faction in 1861 (see chap. 4). Hunter subsequently recruited Co. H, Twelfth MSM Cavalry (redesignated Co. M, Third MSM), which was directly involved in the destruction of Hildebrand's allies in the McGee/Cato Gang on 4 Feb. 1863 (see chap. 15) and the rout of Reeves's command at Pulliam's Farm on 25 Dec. of that same year (see chap. 23). See *History of Franklin, Jefferson, Washington, Crawford and Gasconade Counties*, 998–99; *O.R.*, ser. 1, vol. 22, pt. 1, pp. 225–27; William T. Hunter, Record of Service Cards, box 42, reels S837, S844.

18. See the following newspaper account:

> About nine or ten o'clock in the morning a few of the reinforcements that had been sent for began to arrive. They asked us if Sam was still in the house and why we did not go in and bring him out. But they were not there long until they were fully convinced of the reason why. For Sam took a pop at every thing that moved, and he was generally pretty close to the mark. The firing was kept up all day between us of the posse and Hildebrand until about a half hour before sundown, when deputy sheriff John T. Clarke with about fifteen men arrived on the scene. He took in the situation and decided to burn the house. He placed his men around the place and at once made preparations to set the house afire. He secured some coal oil and candle wick. The candle wick was rolled into a ball and saturated with coal oil and Jim McLain volunteered to climb onto another house which adjoined the one Sam was in. (*Farmington News*, 23 Jan. 1914)

19. "After several efforts had failed, he finally lodged one of the balls between the comb of the house and the stick chimney. When the house got to burning pretty good McLain came down and took his gun and attempted to go back in the back door of this vacant house. This building stood only a few feet from the one Sam was in. The back door stood open and a chink had been knocked out [in the front of that house] leaving an open range [straight through the house] from the building Sam was in to the door. When McLain entered the door, Sam shot him" (*Farmington News*, 23 Jan. 1914).

20. Captain Hunter afterward provided a sworn statement regarding his participation in this gunfight:

> Had been acquainted with dec'd: James McLean. Met him at Farmington—again at Williams farm in Ste. Francois Co. yesterday, Friday. I was deputized by the sheriff of Washington Co. Mo. to assist in arresting one Samuel Hildebrand. The dec'd and Wm. Schultz and John Clark, dept. Sheriff of Washington County and I went to the house adjoined the one in which Hildebrand was concealed. The dec'd had been up on the roof of the house & called to Hildebrand, two or three times, to come out and surrender himself to the sheriff & that he would not be injured. Deceased then came down from the house, & was going into the door of the house adjoining the one in which Hildebrand was—was in a stooping position. I was standing at the door but outside—about six feet from the deceased. Just as deceased stepped in, Hildebrand fired at him & deceased fell back. I caught him & he exclaimed, "I'm shot." I led him off about thirty or forty feet when he dropped & lay groaning about five minutes—when he stopped. The next I saw of him he was dead. (Coroner's Inquest, James McLean, testimony of William T. Hunter, 12 June 1869, St. Francois County Office of the Coroner, Inquests 1850–1932, reel C31546)

McLane's unrelenting pursuit of Hildebrand and Hildebrand's assumption that McLane was the one to ambush and wound him a few days earlier may have been rooted in a wartime incident that was reported in the press immediately after McLane's death: "St. Louis July 15, 1869—James McLean was one of the first volunteer soldiers in Bowen's battalion in 1861. After the consolidation of Bowen's battalion with the Tenth Missouri cavalry, he served three years as an honorable and faithful soldier. . . . While in the service, defending gallantly the flag of his country, the bushwhacker and outlaw, Sam. Hildebrand, cruelly and wantonly outraged his (McLean's) wife, and within the same hour held her hands to allow Bob Hiley to accomplish the same diabolical purpose. These facts are vouched for by the most respectable Democrats of St. Francois county" (W. D. Bowen, Late Lt. Col., Tenth Mo. Cavalry, *St. Louis Democrat*, 16 July 1869). The Democratic Party was the primary mainstay of political support for ex-Confederates against the ruling Radical Republicans.

A separate account concurs with the above: "In 1863 Hilderbrand made a raid on McLean's farm, and besides assaulting his wife, took away his stock, valued at between $5,000 and $6,000" (*St. Louis Republican*, 14 June 1869).

With his regiment in Mississippi at the time, note that James McLane, perhaps tending to his wife, went home on sick leave in Nov. 1863 and did not return to duty until Jan. See James McLaine, Military File, Tenth Missouri Cavalry, State Historical Society.

21. See the following newspaper accounts:

> The time had now arrived when Sam thought he could make his get-away. He pried up a board on the floor, which stood off the ground about two feet, and crawled under and to the steps of the door. These he pushed aside and crawled out, and made his way about twenty feet to a rail fence which surrounded the yard, took out the bottom rail and crawled through. Two men were on each side of the panel of the fence that he went out, but did not hear him until he started to run. Then they fired a regular fusillade, but Sam got away. The light from the burning roof made it dark immediately around the building, and the weeds in the yard were about ten feet high, which all favored Sam in his get-away. He left his rifle in the weeds in the yard, which was now useless as he had gotten a bullet choked into it during the day. He took his two revolvers with him.
>
> In the battle in the morning Mrs. Williams and the little girl that were in the house with Hildebrand were both shot, but not seriously hurt. After Hildebrand escaped the fire was put out and the posse entered the house, and there they could view his preparations for battle. He had piled all the furniture and things in the house and fenced off one corner of the house with them, making a fort within a fort, and had the posse rushed the doors he no doubt would have killed half of them before they got to it. He had an old table in this corner which he used for his guns, ammunition and other weapons—among them was an old corn knife made from a scythe, which would have been a bad weapon in close quarters. This weapon and old Kill-Devil (his rifle) and his hat, which was shot full of holes, were taken to the rogue's gallery in St. Louis. . . .
>
> After his escape from the house, he went about two miles and laid in ambush near the road, and waited for someone to come along. About midnight, a Mr. Aubuchon came along on horseback, and Sam stopped him and compelled him to let him get up behind him, and take him to where a sister of his lived, about ten miles from there. Such was the fear of this man that Aubuchon did not tell of this until after he [Sam] was killed. (*Farmington News*, 23 Jan. 1914)

> An attempt was made on Friday by Sheriff Breckinridge, of Washington county, assisted by a posse of men, to capture the noted desperado, Sam Hilderbrand, of St. Francois county, which resulted in the killing of one of the attacking party, James McLean, and the escape of Hilderbrand. . . .
>
> Word was then sent to Irondale, De Soto and Potosi, for reinforcements, and a telegraphic dispatch was also sent to St. Louis for the police. Sergeant Bowen and officers McQueen and Voris, were detailed

for that purpose, and left here on the 4 o'clock freight train Friday afternoon. . . .

The St. Louis policemen arrived at Irondale at 2 o'clock Saturday morning, and walked twelve miles to the scene of action, arriving there at daylight. They found the building occupied by Hilderbrand nearly burned down, and still smoking. Hilderbrand's rifle and hat were left as trophies. They got on Hilderbrand's trail and followed it for some distance, and scouted the woods for four miles around, but with no success. (*St. Louis Republican*, 14 June 1869)

This last escapade and its accompanying tragedy seems to have aroused the country, and the greatest excitement has existed for some weeks in regard to the capture of the man considered so dangerous to the community. (*St. Louis Republican*, 16 July 1869)

After this, the whole country was aroused. A company of militia was organized in St. Francois county, and Colonel W. D. Bowen, a captain of St. Louis police and five other policemen, were sent into the field to run him down. They stayed in the field about three months. (*Farmington News*, 23 Jan. 1914)

CHAPTER THIRTY-SEVEN

1. Hildebrand's narrative in the first few paragraphs of chap. 37 closely follows an article that had appeared a year earlier in the *St. Louis Republican*, which is quoted in detail below, beginning at n. 2.

This foray, described by both Hildebrand and in the *Republican,* occurred in the immediate wake of reports of a very large reward being offered for Hildebrand:

SAM HILDEBRAND—The Outlaw of the Southeast.—A Reward of $10,000 Offered for His Head.—Description of the Boldest Desperado of Modern Times. The good people of Washington and St. Francois have for several years been kept in awe by the bold and bloody acts of the notorious Sam Hildebrand. This man, it is said, has murdered at least eighty persons in those counties and in Arkansas. When the rebellion broke out he espoused the cause of the rebels and became a daring and ruthless bushwhacker. It has been asserted that he suffered injury at the hands of a Union officer—having his house burned down and his family driven forth homeless and shelterless. Whatever of truth or falsehood may be in these stories, it is certain that Hildebrand became a desperate and unscrupulous man. He wreaked a terrible vengeance upon those who had been his enemies, shooting men down in their fields and by the wayside, burning houses and outraging women.

All attempts to kill or capture this man have proved abortive. He has been hunted by companies of determined men, tracked by detectives from the city, but has always eluded pursuit and successfully resisted attack. A few days ago we gave an account of an attempt to capture Hilderbrand by the Sheriff of Washington county and a squad of fifteen or sixteen men, which resulted in the wounding of the Sheriff, the killing of one of his men, and the escape of the outlaw.

Since the renewed efforts have been made to arrest the desperado, and in order to effect the object, a reward of $10,000 has been offered for him. The following is the

PROCLAMATION

Whereas, Governor J. W. McClurg of Missouri, has authorized and empowered us to organize a special armed force to search for and arrest Samuel Hildebrand, of St. Francois county, charged with murder and other crimes, and, if necessary, in capturing said Hildebrand to kill him; and, whereas, we have been specially deputized and by John C. Breckenridge, Sheriff of Washington county, Missouri, to execute a warrant issued by William Carter, a Judge of the Circuit Court of said State, authorizing and commanding this arrest of said Hildebrand, charged with the crime of murder. This is to notify all persons who have knowledge or information of the whereabouts, or recent whereabouts of said Samuel Hildebrand, that they are commanded to communicate such knowledge or information to us or some of the men in our command forthwith, and all persons are hereby forbidden to aid, harbor or conceal the said Hildebrand, under penalty of being deemed accessory to his crimes and escape, if he should escape, and that they will be arrested and dealt with accordingly. All information voluntarily given will be deemed confidential.

By order of John C. Breckenridge, Sheriff Washington County, Missouri. John T. Clark, Deputy. Col. W. D. Bowen, Chief of Armed Posse. Potosi, Mo., June 17, 1869.

It is probable that this large amount will induce men of nerve and shrewdness to undertake his capture; but it is generally believed that Hildebrand will never be taken alive. He knows that he will receive no mercy at the hands of the law, and that his capture will result in ignominious death. (*St. Louis Democrat*, 30 June 1869)

2. The following account appeared in the *Republican*::

ADVENTURES OF THE PARTY IN SEARCH OF HILDEBRAND—Col. Bowen left St. Louis on the last expedition on the 17th of June, and arrived at Potosi on the 19th. He stopped at Irondale waiting for the Sheriff's posse, when twenty men reported. Sheriff Breckinridge, of Washington county, could not get a man to volunteer.

On the 20th Col. Bowen started with ten of the Irondale men, and officers McQueen, Schulster and Watson, of the St. Louis police force, in quest of Hilderbrand.

At 10 o'clock that night they arrived at the house of one Hill, a loyal man, and said to have suffered from Hilderbrand in various ways, and here they rested until 3 o'clock A.M. of the 21st. (*St. Louis Republican*, 16 July 1869)

3. The *Republican*'s account continues:

A CALL ON HILDEBRAND'S SISTER—They marched before daylight to the house of Hildebrand's sister, having received information that the outlaw was stopping there. Soon after daylight they learned that Hilderbrand had left the premises in the night some two hours before their arrival. They obtained their information in this way: The family at first obstinately refusing, as was natural, to inform against their relative they threatened to hang up two of the youngest boys, when the smallest—a lad eight years old—divulged the secret.

The boy said his uncle had been there two days, and that his wounds were dressed by his mother. He left the house, as stated, just in time to elude capture.

After obtaining this important information, the posse did not arrest the woman, or treat her with any disrespect, it being considered that she had only performed a sister's part towards a brother, in harboring him, though an outlaw, contrary to the recent proclamation. It would have been against the promptings of human nature to have done otherwise. (*St. Louis Republican*, 16 July 1869)

4. The *Republican*'s account continues:

ARREST OF HILDERBRAND'S BROTHER-IN-LAW—On the evening of the 22nd the party arrested Wm. Harris, the brother-in-law of Hilderbrand. This Harris formerly served under Col. Bowen, his present captor, in the 10th Missouri Cavalry. They also arrested a man named Cash, and another named Dunham.

These men were believed to be in the habit of conveying messages from Hilderbrand to various parties in that section, threatening them with harm if they did not immediately comply with his demands. This black-mailing system, it is stated, has been carried on by Hilderbrand among loyal citizens ever since the close of the war.

MORE HANGING FOR INFORMATION—After promising bribes, threats were resorted to, and finally the hanging process was tried, in order to extort information from the prisoners. After hanging awhile, the truth was choked out of them, and they informed Col. Bowen that Hilderbrand lived in a cave on Big river, on Squire Wesley Murphy's place, about half a mile from the old resident recently occupied by the outlaw.

Dunham said that he had done the bidding of Hilderbrand through fear that he would kill him if he refused. Harris informed his captors that two days before he had taken a side of bacon and some corn bread to Hilderbrand's cave, and that the provisions had to be lowered from the top of the cliff down to the mouth of the cavern with a rope. (*St. Louis Republican*, 16 July 1869)

5. The *Republican*'s account continues:

MARCH TO THE CAVE—The prisoners [Harris, Dunham, and Cash] were still kept under arrest, and employed as guides. On the morning of the 23d Col. Bowen having made a disposition of the force under his command, went in search of the cave where it was believed the outlaw was concealed. They started at 2 o'clock in the morning. Two of the men were ordered to proceed along the top of the bluff to a point where they were told the mouth of the cave could be seen. The balance of the command marched along the bottom between the river and the bluffs, with a view of scaling them from below. The bottom land was heavily timbered, and a silent gloom pervaded the deep recesses of this wild and broken region. At length they arrived at the vicinity of the cavern. The overhanging cliffs towered up 300 feet above the river. The mouth of the cavern was found to be 200 feet above the foot of the bluffs, and about 100 feet below the top of the cliff. In this almost inaccessible place there was discerned a narrow ledge jutting out about ten feet from the face of the cliff, and below and on a level with the mouth of the cavern. This narrow ledge afforded a platform for standing room, but how to reach it was the next question which engaged the attention of the attacking party. Several attempts were made to scale the bluffs at this point. Some of the more daring would get up forty or fifty feet, and, finding a little niche in the rocks, sufficient to maintain their position, saw nothing but a perpendicular wall of stone rising above them for perhaps twenty feet, with no chance to obtain a foothold, and they had to descend. The attempt to reach the cave at this place was abandoned. They went back a quarter of a mile and found a place where they succeeded, with great difficulty, in climbing to the top of the ledge. The man ahead would grasp hold of the bushes, and assist the next behind with one hand, in pulling him along.

Large rocks would become detached and roll down into the chasm below with a thundering crash. These loosened stones opened up the hiding places of several rattlesnakes. Three snakes were killed, and the rattles brought away as trophies.

ENTERING THE CAVE—After gaining the top of the bluffs with the whole force, they descended amid considerable peril to the jutting ledge which led to the cavern, by letting each other down. It was about an hour after daylight. Two entrances were found to the cavern. About twenty feet from the mouths the passages united, forming a long, dark chamber about two hundred feet in depth and fifteen feet in height. A walking-stick, which had been previously described to the party as belonging to Hilderbrand, was found at one of the entrances to the cavern. Ashes from a recently built fire were also seen outside the entrance. Two men were posted at each of the entrances, and the siege was commenced. The men thought they had the refugee almost within their grasp. Col. Bowen believing it to be altogether too perilous to risk his men in the outlaw's den, determined to starve or smoke him out. The latter could be effected whenever the wind blew in the right direction, so as to drive the smoke into the recesses of the cavern.

A quantity of dry wood was lowered down from the heights above, eight rifles were kept cocked and aimed so as to cross-fire on the occupant within should he attempt to make an exit from his place of concealment. Thus they remained all day. After dark a fire was kindled, which illuminated the wilderness below to a great distance. The place was a perfect lookout for the whole country, and the fire was visible at a great distance. The point is half way between Valle's Mines and Skintown or Big River Mills, about eight miles distant from each.

THE BIRD FLOWN—Next morning a report was brought to the besiegers that there was another outlet to the cavern, the mouth of which was half a mile distant on the other side of the hill. Fearing that this might be the case, it was determined to search the interior of the cavern at all hazards. Four men volunteered for the enterprise, two taking one entrance, and Col. Bowen and two men the other.

They proceeded cautiously to the farthest extent of the cavern, and found—nobody there. A bed of leaves, from appearances recently occupied, cap boxes, bullets, some powder in tin cans, fishing tackle, empty bottles and other relics denoting recent occupancy, were discovered.

Much disappointment was felt. It was subsequently ascertained that Hilderbrand left the cavern on the night previous to the arrival of his pursuers. (*St. Louis Republican*, 16 July 1869)

6. The *Republican*'s account continues:

WHERE HE WENT—The fact was learned from one Nash, who was arrested half a mile from the cave. Nash said that Hilderbrand came to his house on the night of the 23d, arriving about midnight. He stopped

> till morning and went away carrying off Nash's rifle. As he left he told Nash he would kill him if he gave any information. It is proper to mention that Nash was strung up by a rope and hung till he turned black in the face before imparting the above information.
>
> Nash's son, a boy twelve years of age, on the evening of the 25th told Bowen that he had agreed to take to Hilderbrand, by consent of his father, a quart of whiskey, for which Hilderbrand had furnished him the money. The boy was to procure the whiskey at Mathew's store, on "Vinegar Hill," five miles distant, and to bring it to Hilderbrand at 12 o'clock that night on a path leading from the road passing Nash's house to old Mrs. Adams' house, and that he would find him (Hilderbrand) on that path, where there were two large rocks on either side. (*St. Louis Republican*, 16 July 1869)

7. The *Republican*'s account continues:

> ANOTHER PLAN OF CAPTURE—Col. Bowen immediately formed a plan to capture Hilderbrand and his quart of whiskey. He moved his force away from that neighborhood, some eight miles distant, in order not to excite the suspicion of Hilderbrand's friends as to his intention. During the remaining hour of light the ground in the vicinity was reconnoitered.
>
> A NIGHT MARCH—At dark the command was countermarched, and pickets were posted along the path leading to the two rocks from both directions. At midnight the entire force moved on the rocks, where they expected to find the outlaw. It was dark, and the rain poured down in torrents. The men could not distinguish each other. They stumbled over rocks and ran against trees, and at last surrounded the rocks, but Hilderbrand was not there. The next morning they discovered signs of his having been in the vicinity, such as bacon rind, some venison, and the ashes of a recent fire. A deerskin was found hanging on the limb of a tree. (*St. Louis Republican*, 16 July 1869)

8. "SCOUTING OPERATIONS—After this the scouting force was divided in squads of three or four, and scattered over the country—some fifteen miles in extent. They were picketed on the by-paths, in the woods and the approaches to the caverns. Col. Bowen, as stated by a correspondent, took up his headquarters at Wesley Murphy's, where he and his men fared well, waiting for information from his different scouting parties" (*St. Louis Republican,* 16 July 1869).

9. Hildebrand's magnanimity likely had much to do with entreaties from friends imploring him to maintain a low profile since their own self-preservation and economic well-being were at stake: "We warn the citizens of St. Francois county, that unless they secure the arrest of the desperado now in their midst,

the Governor may see fit to station a company in the county for the protection of the citizens, and this company have orders to subsist upon those who are friendly to the desperado. Let the people of St. Francois county be up and doing if they would avoid military interference in this matter" (*St. Louis Democrat*, 10 July 1869, quoting an article from the *Ironton Enterprise*).

10. The *Republican* account quoted earlier continues as follows:

> NEWS FROM SKINTOWN—In a few days information was received from Mr. Turley, living one mile from Skintown, that Hilderbrand had been into his wheat field. He did not see him till he came plump upon him. Hilderbrand was barefooted, and, holding up one foot, he said he wanted a pair of shoes. Turley, getting alarmed, told his visitor to leave immediately, as the woods were full of soldiers. This he reported to headquarters, the ruling motive being attributed to fear in both cases. The men were again freshly posted in sight of every house and cave where there was reason to believe the fugitive might take shelter, and Col. Bowen returned to St. Louis. (*St. Louis Republican*, 16 July 1869)

11. Camden County Radical Republican Joseph W. McClurg (1818–1900) was no favorite of ex-Confederates, and Hildebrand's biographer may have been attempting to curry favor with the incumbent chief executive when these words were published in 1870. McClurg was a colonel of Federal troops during the war, and his service overlapped his three terms as a U.S. Congressman, from 1862 until 1868. Elected governor in 1868, he was once described by an opposition newspaper, fairly or unfairly, as being "the embodiment of all that is narrow, bigoted, revengeful, and ignorant in the Radical party." See Parrish, *Missouri under Radical Rule,* 247, 257; Conard, *Encyclopedia of the History of Missouri,* vol. 4, p. 242.

McClurg's son-in-law and personal secretary, Charley Draper, was a member of a prominent Radical family from Pike County and had been orderly to Maj. James Wilson when the Third MSM Cavalry decimated the command of Hildebrand ally Timothy Reeves at Pulliam's Farm in Ripley County on Christmas Day, 1863 (see chap. 23, footnote 4). Draper personally captured three Confederate prisoners in that skirmish. See the *Louisiana Journal*, 9 Jan. 1864; Art Draper to Kirby Ross, 27 Mar. 2000. (Art Draper is the great-grandson of Charley Draper and the great-great-grandson of Governor McClurg.)

12. "Sheriff Murphy" was Franklin Murphy, who has been mentioned throughout this book. He served as the chief law-enforcement officer of St. Francois County from 1866 until 1870. See *Goodspeed's History of Southeast Missouri*, 351.

Until he was ordered to call out the militia, Murphy, who had officiated at Hildebrand's wedding before the war, seems to have been content in maintaining his personal truce with Hildebrand and allowing the lead role in the manhunt in his own county to fall by default to John Breckinridge, sheriff of neighboring Washington County—so much so that Hildebrand was reported in 1870 as having "determined not to return to this vicinity till after Sheriff Breckenridge's term of office has expired." See the *Washington County Journal*, 12 May 1870, reprinting an article from the *Sioux City Times*.

13. "Hilderbrand is roaming about in Ste. Francis county, unmolested. We learn that a force of detectives have been attempting his arrest, but thus far have not succeeded in doing so, and there is no knowing when they will. We certainly trust that he may be captured and punished to the full extent of the law, for if any man ever did deserve it, he does. It is stated that he has so many friends to aid him in his escape, that he is enabled to elude his pursuers. No one should aid such a desperado, on the contrary, it is the duty of all good law abiding citizens to use their utmost influence to have him arrested and punished" (*Perryville Union*, 16 July 1869).

14. The following account appeared in the *St. Louis Republican:*

> The Governor After Hilderbrand—Gov. McClurg, accompanied by Col. W. D. Bowen and one or two officials of St. Francois county, went down on the Iron Mountain road to Potosi yesterday, where an escort will be provided to accompany the party to Big River Mills, the scene of Hilderbrand operations. It is the purpose of the Governor, we understand, to confer with the authorities of St. Francois county with a view of securing a more prompt, willing and efficient enforcement of all processes issued by any court in the region of country. The Sheriff must be obeyed, and all citizens when summoned as a posse must be required to respond to the call and not be let off on frivolous excuses. Differences of opinion have arisen in regard to the jurisdiction of the respective Sheriffs, growing out of the transfer of a posse, raised in one county to an adjoining county—as to whose direction such a posse should come under—which have produced a want of concert and no little ill-felling.
>
> The sentiment prevailing, and other particulars bearing on the matter, will be looked into by the Governor, who, as the chief executive, is required to see that the laws of the State are inforced and carried out. We understand that it is not the purpose of the Governor to call out a military force, although that course has been recommended, until all other legal measures have been exhausted. All law-abiding citizens will approve of the latter course, rather than hazard a recurrence—by a resort to a military force—of the outrages that were enacted in Lafayette county. (*St. Louis Republican*, 17 July 1869)

15. The following account appeared in the *Republican:*

> Arrival of Gov. McClurg.—Gov. McClurg returned yesterday afternoon from the scene of Hilderbrand's operations in St. Francois county. He left Irondale on Friday evening for Big River Mills, fifteen miles distant, and remained there over Saturday and Sunday. He heard various statements in regard to Hilderbrand, some conflicting, others confirmatory. On Monday he rode over to Farmington, fifteen miles distant, where a meeting of the citizens had been called by Sheriff Murphy. The courthouse was filled. The Governor, in response to an invitation, made a speech, giving his reasons why the people should take it upon themselves to see that laws are executed, and support the authorities in arresting all outlaws and disturbers of the public peace. He advised them to avoid the necessity that might require the declaration of martial law. A large committee was appointed on resolutions. The committee made a report, which was unanimously adopted. The purport of the resolutions were that a hearty co-operation should be given by all good citizens for the arrest of Hilderbrand and other outlaws, and that an earnest endeavor would be made to secure the enforcement of the laws. The Governor was called to state whether the resolutions were satisfactory, and he assured the meeting they were in wording and spirit. The Governor authorizes us to say that it is his belief they will be carried out, and that the necessity of martial law will be obviated.
>
> The Governor requests us to correct an error to the effect that the citizens of Washington county had not responded to the call of a posse for the pursuit of Hilderbrand. This, he says, is a mistake. The Sheriff, Deputy Sheriff and citizens generally have made a ready and willing response. He could hardly find words sufficiently complimentary to the energy of Sheriff Breckenridge and others who have risked their lives in the effort to capture the outlaw. The Governor informs us that the people of St. Francois county have authorized the County Court to give additional pay to the deputy sheriffs that the Executive may appoint under the act of March 1866 for that county, to be called into service by the deputy sheriffs, if needed. The proceedings of the meeting are entirely satisfactory, and the Governor believes the people will act in good faith. The Governor deputized Col. Wm. D. Bowen to act as special deputy under the law of March 14, 1866, giving him the power to appoint ten deputies. The Governor leaves to-day for Jefferson City. (*St. Louis Republican*, 21 July 1869)

16. "Hildebrand is still roaming at large. It seems he continues to elude the vigilance of those who are in pursuit of him. Many are of the opinion that he still inhabits St. Francois County" (*Perryville Union*, 27 Aug. 1869).

17. "McLean's corpse was put in a wagon and brought to Irondale, where it was put in a coffin and sent down to his family, who reside eight miles from Farmington. . . . In 1863 Hilderbrand made a raid on McLean's farm, and besides assaulting his wife, took away his stock, valued at between $5,000 and $6,000. . . . The tragedy is one which has thrown a gloom over the community in the neighborhood where it occurred, and much sympathy is felt for McLean's family. He leaves a wife and nine children" (*Jefferson Democrat*, 17 June 1869).

18. Hildebrand and/or his biographer's emphasis on Mrs. McLane's failure to know what he looked like may have been an attempt on their part to draw doubt to the widely circulated reports that he had "outraged" her during the war. See the *St. Louis Democrat*, 16 July 1869; *St. Louis Republican*, 14 June 1869.

Furthermore, if Margaret Hildebrand did in fact take such pains to present herself to Louise McLane, it was probably in an effort to draw the manhunt away from Sam Hildebrand and to help stop the havoc the posse's methods were wreaking locally on his friends and relatives:

> It is conjectured that Hildebrand is making his way toward the Mississippi. Those who formerly harbored and assisted him have become alarmed, and are now anxious that he should be brought to justice. It is hoped that the people of the river towns will be on the lookout for him. (*St. Louis Democrat*, 30 June 1869)

> Hildebrand is six feet one inch in height; sandy complexion; beard rather thin, and mostly on chin; keen blue eyes; on each side of his face he has a florid or blood-vein colored spot the size of a half a dollar; hawk nose; small mouth; feminine voice; light, thin hair; aged about thirty-five years; weight about 170 pounds; walks very erect; carries his head back. Had on, when last seen, a brown butternut coat, a very old pair of shoes, black slouch hat. Had a scar on one of his legs, caused by a shot passing through the calf and coming out below the knee. (*St. Louis Democrat*, 30 June 1869)

19. Reports that Hildebrand was lurking about occasionally swept through skittish local populaces, including one that had him taking refuge in northern Missouri: "The *Randolph Citizen* says a man with three revolvers strapped around him, and exactly answering the description of the noted Sam. Hildebrand, passed through Huntsville a few days since. He said he was going to Shelbina, and the editor let him go. He did not try to arrest Hildebrand, he says, because he was 'not fond of that sort of fun; besides, $10,000 was too insignificant a sum to induce an editor to neglect his business'" (*St. Louis Republican*, 13 July 1869).

Another rumor resulted in promises to do violence to Hildebrand's supporters should there be any new trouble:

> Sam Hildebrand Heard From—We have heard various reports at Irondale and Bismarck, on Monday, of Sam Hildebrand at Big River Mills. Although doubts are expressed as to the correctness of the rumor, yet many incidents of recent occurrence are cited in support of it. Messages have been received by parties residing at Irondale and vicinity in this county, as well as in St. Francois county, threatening various punishments on those who have incurred Hildebrand's enmity, aiding in the several attempts to capture him in the past, and other acts of which he did not cordially approve. A gentleman who is the subject of one of these hostile messages seems inclined to give partial credit to its authenticity, and returned word that while he could be readily found at any time, yet nothing but the most covertly managed plot of assassination could harm him, and even should such a vengeance succeed, neither Hildebrand nor certain parties who are known to shield his presence in this country, could by any possibility escape a fearful retaliation. On the whole, we are not inclined to credit the rumor of such foolhardiness on the part of one whose capture has become the object of so great solicitude to the authorities of the State. (*Washington County Journal*, 3 Mar. 1870)

20. As it has passed down the "corridors of time," the legend of Hildebrand continues into the twenty-first century in southeast Missouri:

> Cape Girardeau, Mo. June 23, 2002—BUSHWHACKER HILDEBRAND STILL BUGS ME—. . . The name Sam Hildebrand jumped out at me from the printed page, a shiver passed over my body. I'm still afraid of Sam. . . .
>
> Sam was dead long before I was born, but Mama, Dad, Grandma and Grandpa continued to use his name as a tool to control the wanderings of my sisters and me. "Be sure you are home and in the house before dark or Sam Hildebrand will get you. He's a bushwhacker," was a constant admonition. I had no notion what a bushwhacker was, but when told about some of the mean things he had done, I was glad to be home after dark. . . .
>
> Here's a footnote that might be suitable to mention regarding my relationship to Sam Hildebrand: I was christened in the Elvins, Mo., Methodist Church South. To the rear of this church is a cemetery. Midway in it is where Sam is buried.
>
> REJOICE! (Jean Bell Mosly, *Southeast Missourian*, 23 June 2002)

21. Hildebrand was unable to keep his boast: two years later he was arrested ninety-one days after the death of his wife and was then killed in a fight with a law-enforcement officer while being escorted to jail following a court appearance:

DIED—At the residence of her husband, of erysipelas on December 21st, Margaret Hilderbrand, wife of Samuel S. Hilderbrand, of whom so much was heard a few years ago. The subject of the above notice was born and reared in St. Francois county, where she leaves a large circle of relatives and friends to mourn her untimely death. She left six small children. (*Jefferson City People's Tribune*, 31 Jan. 1872)

SMITH OR HILDEBRAND?—A Distinguished "Bushwhacker" Again Killed—Pinckneyville, Ills., the Last Place Honored with His Presence—A Man with Many Lives and Knives—Pinckneyville, Ills. March 22—Hilderbrand has at last ceased to exist, and has met a most desperate death. It would seem that he had located with his family, consisting of six children, (the mother having died about three months since), in a tenant house in town until he could rent a farm. He came here on Tuesday last, remaining about town going by the assumed names of Smith and Thompson. He went about the streets visiting saloons during Wednesday and Thursday and little attention was given him until on Thursday evening when the fracas took place which eventually resulted in his instant death.

At 5 o'clock Thursday evening he, in company with one Sullivan, was in the saloon of Joseph Bishop, drinking and talking, in an indifferent manner, without creating any particular attention from the bystanders. Sullivan, however, remarked to several persons pointing to Hildebrand that he was a peculiar man, that men did not know how to take him, that they did not know what to make of him. Hildebrand requested several men to sit down and talk with him, and he being to some extent under the influence of liquor, talked at random, and in such a way as to render men cautious if not afraid of him, though he made no unusual demonstrations toward them. At about fifteen minutes after five a man stepped up to the bar and called for liquor for the crowd, and here the fracas commenced. Sullivan got into a dispute with the saloon-keeper, and gave him the lie, whereupon the saloon-keeper Bishop, replied, "that if I am a liar you are a liar." Hildebrand, or the man reported to be Hildebrand, interposed, and took up the quarrel without a word. He stepped up to the counter, immediately in front of Bishop, with a heavy dirk in his right hand, about fifteen inches in length, and made a thrust at his throat. Bishop retreated from the infuriated man, and the point of the knife only struck his chin, inflicting a slight gash. Still bent on his work of blood, however, he was not to be thus thwarted, and he immediately drew a revolver with his left hand, and was in the act of using it, when Mr. Bishop's wife grasped his hand, and other persons pushed him out of the door. He attempted to get back into the saloon through another door, but failed. At this juncture the town constable, Wm. G. Gordon appeared, to take him in custody.

Hildebrand seeing that the officer proposed his arrest, was about to draw his revolver when Gordon grasped him. Being a man of great muscular power Hildebrand soon disentangled himself, and was procuring his revolver when the officer knocked him down, inflicting a gash over his right eye. The man was then taken in company with Sullivan, before Squire Hamilton for trial on a charge of having violated the town ordinance. The charge being against both, the trial was so conducted. E. H. Lemen and Thomas Boyd were retained by the defendants as counsel. The evidence not sustaining the charge against Sullivan, he was dismissed from custody. Hildebrand was found guilty and fined. He paid part or the whole of the fine. At the close of the trial on the part of the town authorities, for a violation of the town ordinances, he was taken in charge by officers who were about to convey him before Esquire John B. Davis to be held to bail, for an assault with a deadly weapon upon Bishop, at suit of the state. It was now about nine o'clock at night, when he was attempted to be conveyed from the offices of Justice Hamilton to the offices of J. B. Davis, and it was during this transfer that his murderous resistance to the officers cost him his life. Three officers assisted in taking him, Matthew Rule, John L. Ragland and Wm. G. Gordon. The office of Esquire Davis was about forty rods distant from that of J. D. Hamilton. At the distance of some ten rods from the office of the latter, notwithstanding he was in charge of three strong, energetic and cautious officers, he managed to get a knife in his hand. This was knocked out of his hand promptly, and when at a distance of perhaps five rods he displayed another knife, it being the third one. He was knocked down, and this too was taken from him, the officers thinking it certainly must be the last. They were surprised, however. Almost instantly recovering from the effect of the officer's club, he was soon on his feet, being dragged and pulled in the direction of Squire Davis's office, not apparently the least overawed. They had gone but a few paces when the report of a pistol was heard in the midst of the crowd; the shot, however, was harmless. A few paces further and Hildebrand displayed his fourth knife and with it wounded Constable Ragland in the left thigh, the gash laying his thigh open from the knee to the hip, when the constable drew his revolver and shot him, the ball entering his neck from the right side and entered the base of the brain, producing almost instant death. In person he was tall athletic and muscular, measuring upwards of six feet in height. After his death an inquest was held by Justice Davis, and upon a hearing of the evidence the following verdict was given—

"We, the jury, impanelled and sworn to inquire into the cause of the death of a man whose name is supposed to be John Smith, said to be late of Farmington, Mo., find from the evidence that said deceased came to his death by a pistol shot fired by John L. Ragland in self-

> defence, and while in the discharge of his official duties as a constable of said county." (*St. Louis Republican*, 23 Mar. 1872)

Note that Pinckneyville, Ill., is in Perry County, which was where Samuel G. Haile had sought refuge in 1865 (see chap. 30). Hildebrand's identical choice for a place of sanctuary may have involved assistance from a local network of supporters.

Given Hildebrand's many escapes over the years from what seemed to be certain death or capture, every effort was made to determine whether the dead man was truly Hildebrand:

> SAM HILDEBRAND'S CAREER & DEATH— . . . Now as to the end of the career of this desperate man. . . . An inquest was held and he was buried as an unknown man the next day. A full account of which was in the *St. Louis Republican* the next morning. The writer of this article was then on the St. Louis police force. Reading the article in the paper, he showed it to another policeman by the name of Dennis O'Leary, who had grown up from boyhood with Hildebrand. We at once agreed that it must be Sam Hildebrand. We took the paper and at once went to our chief and told him what we thought. He sent us to Pinckneyville to identify him, advising the authorities at Pinckneyville by wire who he thought it was, and that two officers were on the road then to identify him. When we arrived there they had dug him up and had the body in the coffin up stairs in the circuit court room. With the head of the coffin leaning against the judge's stand, the foot resting on the floor, and the lid off, so that any one coming into the court room could distinguish his features plainly. We at once recognized him, but for further identification had him stripped and found the wound in his thigh where Peterson had shot him and also the wound in the left ankle where he had been shot in the war. The wound across the forehead where he was shot at the battle at Williams' house was still very plain. We then went to the house where the children were, who knew both of us very well, but we had hard work making them own it up. Hildebrand's body was shipped to Farmington, and was hauled from there to a graveyard near John Williams' and buried. And the children were distributed around among relatives. (*Farmington News*, 23 Jan. 1914)

In a postscript to this affair, the specter of Hildebrand's wartime alliance with the McGee/Cato clan was raised one final time in local authorities' efforts to definitively identify the body. Rhody Holsell, the former slave of family patriarch Thomas McGee, was called upon to assist in this effort: "When Sam was killed in Southern Illinois dey tried to get me to go up to Farmington to identify him. But I would not do it" (Holsell, interview, vol. 10, p. 201). Also see the following newspaper accounts:

> Sam Hildebrand's Death Confirmed—Sam Hildebrand, the outlaw of Missouri, has been reported dead about as many times as Dr. Livingston, the African explorer, has been reported alive and still traveling. Hildebrand, however, persists in living down these reports of his demise to such an extent that nobody paid any more attention to the stories concerning him. The consequence was that the report of his death at the hands of constable Ragland, in Pinckneyville, Ill., on the 21st of last month, was very generally discredited. Since that date several newspapers in localities where Hildebrand was well known have asserted that he was still alive. The identification of Hildebrand and the dead man of Pinckneyville has, however, been established beyond a doubt.
>
> On the third day after death, the body was taken up and photographed by an artist residing at Pinckneyville. A copy of the picture was sent to the Sheriff of Washington county, Mo., as that officer had taken active part in the effort to arrest Hildebrand two years ago. The Sheriff [Breckenridge], from the general outlines, declared it to be Sam's face. The photograph was shown to others who knew Hildebrand well. He is identified without a doubt by William Hildebrand, his brother; Joab Ringer, a schoolmate; J. W. S. Boye, a citizen of Irondale; and M. Adams and Frank Simms, neighbors of Hildebrand. On the presentation of the photograph to Wm. Hildebrand he was very much affected, and exclaimed, "That's Sam." When told that some one who knew Sam had failed to recognize the picture, he said that any one who had ever seen Sam lying down was bound to recognize it. He manifested great anxiety to obtain a copy of the picture for preservation. The others named above, some of whom had known Hildebrand almost from infancy, have without the least hesitation made the most positive identification, as the features are perfect as at the moment of death. A serious wound, which he had received at the time of a former attempt to capture him, presented a very conspicuous scar, which rendered the identification complete. —[Quoting the] *Missouri Republican.*
>
> The above facts remove the last lingering doubt, in regard to the identity of the man who was killed by Constable Ragland. That it was Sam Hildebrand, is, we think, fully established.
>
> Our readers are familiar with the facts concerning the manner of his death, as they were at the time furnished by our correspondent, at Pinckneyville.
>
> Mr. Ragland who received such a fearful knife wound from the hands of Hildebrand, is slowly recovering from the same, but it will be

many months before he will be able to do any work; besides the citizens of Pinckneyville have been put to no small expense and trouble, resulting in the killing and identification of the body of this notorious outlaw. In view of these facts, and in asmuch as the Governor of Missouri, and citizens of that State offered rewards for Hildebrand's capture, dead or alive, we hope these pledges will be fulfilled, as a just recognition of the services of Messrs. Ragland, Gordon and others by whose instrumentality Hildebrand's career has been closed. (*DuQuoin Tribune*, 25 Apr. 1872)

Ragland collected about $1500.00 of the reward. At one time there was a reward of about $10,000.00 for Hildebrand's capture or death, but at the time of his killing could not be collected. John Ragland is now dead, but he was never able to go without crutches after Hildebrand cut him. And thus ends the story. (*Farmington News*, 23 Jan. 1914)

22. "Sam Hildebrant, the noted desperado and guerrillo, is buried near Flat river, his grave green and not far from the places where he murdered McLane, McElvane and others" (*Jefferson City Tribune*, 20 June 1894). See also the *Perry County Star*, 1 June 1894.

Bibliography

MILITARY HISTORIES/ADJUTANT GENERAL REPORTS

Adjutant General's Report of Missouri State Militia for the Year 1861. St. Louis: George Knapp and Co., 1862.

Annual Report of the Adjutant General of the State of Missouri for 1863. St. Louis: Adjutant General's Office, 1864.

Annual Report of the Adjutant General of Missouri for 1864. Jefferson City: W. A. Curry, Public Printer, 1865.

Annual Report of the Adjutant General of Missouri for the Year Ending December 31, 1865. Jefferson City: Emory S. Foster, Public Printer, 1866.

Carpenter, F. A. "History of the 17th Cavalry Volunteers." Illinois State Historical Society. Springfield, Ill., ca. 1886.

Dyer, Frederick H. *A Compendium of the War of the Rebellion.* Des Moines: Dyer Publishing Company, 1908.

Eddy, T. M. *The Patriotism of Illinois.* Vol. 2. Chicago: Clarke and Co., 1866.

Field, Charles D. *Three Years in the Saddle.* Goldfield, Ia.: 1898.

Fox, Simeon M. "The Story of the Seventh Kansas." In *Transactions of the Kansas State Historical Society 1903–1904,* vol. 8. Topeka: Geo. A. Clark, State Printer, 1904.

Frost, M. O. *Regimental History of the Tenth Missouri Volunteer Infantry.* Topeka: M. O. Frost Printing Co., 1892.

Hewett, Janet B., ed. *Supplement to the Official Records of the Union and Confederate Armies.* 100 vols. Wilmington, N.C.: Broadfoot Publishing Company, 1994–2001.

Moore, Frank, ed. *The Rebellion Record.* Vol. 6. New York: G. P. Putnam, 1863.

Official Army Register of the Volunteer Force of the United States Army. Vol. 7. Washington, D.C.: Adjutant General's Office, 1867.

Organization and Status of Missouri Troops in Service during the Civil War. Washington, D.C.: Government Printing Office, 1902.

Report of the Committee of the House of Representatives of the Twenty-second General Assembly of the State of Missouri Appointed to Investigate the Conduct and Management of the Militia. Jefferson City: W. A. Curry, Public Printer, 1864.

Scott, John, ed. *Story of the Thirty-Second Iowa Infantry Volunteers.* Nevada, Ia.: John Scott, 1896.

Stanton, Donal J., Goodwin F. Berquist, and Paul C. Bowers, eds. *The Civil War Reminiscences of General M. Jeff Thompson.* Dayton, Oh.: Morningside House, 1988.

The Union Army: A History of Military Affairs in the Loyal States 1861–1865. Vol. 8. Madison, Wisc.: Federal Publishing Company, 1908.

The War of the Rebellion: A Compilation of the Official Records of the Union and Confederate Armies. 128 vols. Washington, D.C.: Government Printing Office, 1880–1901.

REGIONAL/COUNTY HISTORIES

Douglass, Robert Sidney, ed. *History of Southeast Missouri.* Chicago: Lewis Publishing Co., 1912.

Goodspeed's History of Southeast Missouri. Chicago: Goodspeed Publishing Company, 1888.

Hahn, Mary Louisa Hopkins. *Bollinger County 1851–1976.* Marceline, Mo.: Walsworth Publishing Company, 1977.

History of Franklin, Jefferson, Washington, Crawford and Gasconade Counties, Missouri. Chicago: Goodspeed Publishing Company, 1888.

Ponder, Jerry. *History of Ripley County.* Doniphan, Mo.: Jerry Ponder, 1987.

Portrait and Biographical Record of Marion, Ralls, and Pike Counties, Missouri. Chicago: C. O. Owen and Co., 1895.

Webb, Robert T. *History and Traditions of Clay County.* Little Rock: Parke-Harper Co., 1933.

OTHER BOOKS

Castel, Albert E. *General Sterling Price and the Civil War in the West.* Baton Rouge: Louisiana State University Press, 1968.

———. *William Clarke Quantrill: His Life and Times.* New York: Frederick Fell, 1962.

Conard, Howard L., ed. *Encyclopedia of the History of Missouri.* Vol. 4. New York: Southern History Company, 1901.

Fellman, Michael. *Citizen Sherman: A Life of William Tecumseh Sherman.* New York: Random House, 1995.

———. *Inside War: The Guerrilla Conflict in Missouri during the American Civil War.* New York: Oxford University Press, 1989.

Garraty, John A., and Mark C. Carnes, eds. *American National Biography.* Vol. 20. New York: Oxford University Press, 1999.

Gerteis, Louis S. *Civil War St. Louis.* Lawrence: University Press of Kansas, 2001.

Ingenthron, Elmo. *Borderland Rebellion.* Branson: Ozarks Mountaineer, 1980.

Journal of the Missouri State Convention, July 1861. St. Louis: George Knapp and Co., Printers and Binders, 1861.

Leslie, Edward E. *The Devil Knows How to Ride: The True Story of William Clarke Quantrill and His Confederate Raiders.* New York: Random House, 1996.

McGhee, James E. *Campaigning with Marmaduke: Narrative and Roster of the Eighth Missouri Cavalry Regiment CSA.* Independence, Mo.: Two Trails Publishing, 2002.

Murdock, Gene P. *Sam Hildebrand's Footprints.* Bonne Terre, Mo.: Murdock's Historical Publications, 2000.

Nichols, Bruce. *Guerrilla Warfare in Civil War Missouri, 1862.* Jefferson, N.C.: McFarland and Co., 2004.

Parrish, William E. *A History of Missouri, 1860 to 1875.* Columbia: University of Missouri Press, 1973.

———. *Missouri under Radical Rule 1865–1870.* Columbia:University of Missouri Press, 1965.

Peterson, Cyrus A. *Narrative of the Capture and Murder of Major James Wilson: Read Before the Pike County Historical Society, January 26, 1906.* St. Louis: A. R. Fleming Printing Co., 1906.

Peterson, Cyrus A., and Joseph Mills Hanson. *Pilot Knob: The Thermopylae of the West.* New York: Neale Publishing Co., 1914.

Proceedings of the Missouri State Convention Held at Jefferson City, July 1861. St. Louis: George Knapp and Co., 1861.

Rader, Perry S. *The Civil Government of the United States and the State of Missouri.* Columbia, Mo.: E. W. Stephens, Publisher, 1898.

Rea, Ralph R. *Sterling Price: The Lee of the West.* Little Rock: Pioneer Press, 1959.

Rombauer, Robert J. *The Union Cause in St. Louis in 1861.* St. Louis: Press of Nixon-Jones Printing Company, 1909.

MISCELLANEOUS SOURCES

Bartholomew, Robert Jefferson, Jr. "Pedigree Chart and Cyrus A. Peterson Notes." N.p., 2001.

Cato, Shirley Whitley, Bonnie Baker Palmer, and Adruain Cato. "Research on the Name Cato." N.p., 2000.

Murdoch, Lindsay. "Narrative of the Service of Lindsay W. Murdoch in the War of the Rebellion." *Echo* 1 (October 1979): 130–54.

Ponder, Jean. "Doniphan during the Civil War." In *Doniphan and Ripley County History*. Doniphan, Mo.: N.p., n.d.

Ross, Kirby. "The Burning of Doniphan." *North and South Magazine* 6, no. 7 (2003): 76–84.

———. "Federal Militia in Missouri." 16 January 2004. Civil War St. Louis. http://www.civilwarstlouis.com/militia/federalmilitia.htm.

———. "The Fight at Jackson Fairground." 16 May 2004. Civil War St. Louis. http://www.civilwarstlouis.com/JacksonFairgrounds/index.htm.

———. "James O. Broadhead: Ardent Unionist, Unrepentant Slaveholder." 6 December 2002. Civil War St. Louis. http://www.civilwarstlouis.com/History2/broadheadprofile.htm.

ARCHIVAL SOURCES

Adjutant General Papers. Missouri State Archives, Jefferson City.

Court-martial Records. National Archives, Washington, D.C.

Cyrus A. Peterson Papers. Missouri Historical Society, St. Louis.

Federal Writer's Project. Manuscript Division, Library of Congress, Washington, D.C.

File of Papers Relating to Individual Civilians. Provost Marshal Papers. Missouri State Archives, Jefferson City.

Index to Compiled Service Records of Confederate Soldiers Who Served in Organizations from the State of Missouri. National Archives, Washington, D.C.

Military Files. State Historical Society of Missouri, Columbia.

Pension Records. National Archives, Washington, D.C.

Record of Service Cards. Office of Missouri Adjutant General. Missouri State Archives, Jefferson City.

Regimental Records of Events. State Historical Society of Missouri, Columbia.

Register of Confederate Soldiers, Alton, Illinois. Register of Confederate Soldiers Who Died in Federal Prisons or Military Hospitals in the North, 1861–1865. National Archives, Washington, D.C.

St. Francois County Office of the Coroner, Inquests 1850–1932. Missouri State Archives.

Thomas Ewing Family Papers. Manuscript Division, Library of Congress, Washington, D.C.

Western Historical Manuscript Collection. University of Missouri, Columbia.

William L. Skaggs Collection. Arkansas History Commission, Little Rock.

COUNTY RECORDS

Probate Files. St. Francois County Probate Court. 1865, 1868.

Probate Files. Ste. Genevieve County Probate Court. 1866.

St. Francois County Marriages, 1818–1903. St. Francis County Clerk.

Records. Iron County Circuit Court. 1866.

Records. Lincoln County Circuit Court. 1863.

Records. St. Francois County Circuit Court. 1863, 1865.

Records. Stoddard County Circuit Court. 1865, 1866.

CENSUS RECORDS

Slave Census—Missouri. St. Francois and Stoddard Counties, 1850. Wayne County, 1860.

Population Census—Missouri. St. Francois County, 1850. Cape Girardeau, Madison, Ste. Genevieve, St. Francois, Stoddard, and Wayne Counties, 1860. Ste. Genevieve County, 1870.

Index

ABOUT THE EDITOR

Journalist and author/historian Kirby Ross is the recipient of a Kansas Governor's Proclamation for his first book, *The True Life Wild West Memoir of a Bush-popping Cow Waddy*. Ross is a staff writer for a major Kansas newspaper chain and has been a feature story contributor for *North & South* magazine as well as the online magazine CivilWarStLouis.com. He resides in north central Kansas.